The Book
of The Laurel

The Book
of The Laurel

John Skelton

Edited by
F. W. Brownlow

DELAWARE

Newark: University of Delaware Press
London and Toronto: Associated University Presses

Associated University Presses
440 Forsgate Drive
Cranbury, NJ 08512

Associated University Presses
25 Sicilian Avenue
London WC1A 2QH, England

Associated University Presses
P.O. Box 39, Clarkson Pstl. Stn.
Mississauga, Ontario
Canada L5J 3X9

The paper used in this publication meets the requirements
of the American National Standard for Permanence of Paper
for Printed Library Materials Z39.48–1984.

Library of Congress Cataloging-in-Publication Data

Skelton, John, 1460?–1529.
 The book of the Laurel / John Skelton ; edited by F. W. Brownlow.
  p. cm.
 Includes bibliographical references.
 ISBN 0–87413–372–6 (alk. paper)
 I. Brownlow, F. W. (Frank Walsh), 1934– . II. Title.
PR2347.B66 1990
821'.2—dc20
                                                                88–40580
                                                                CIP

PRINTED IN THE UNITED STATES OF AMERICA

Contents

Illustrations

A Note upon the Title

Like other medieval poems, *The Laurel* has acquired a nineteenth-century title. At the head of his text (1843), Alexander Dyce printed the title page of the 1523 quarto. Although Skelton certainly wrote this title page, it is not a title to the poem but, like other title pages of the period, an advertisement of the book's contents to a prospective buyer. For a running title Dyce condensed a phrase from this title page: *The Garlande of Laurell*, and this has been the accepted title ever since. It has a pretty, Victorian ring, but in modern use "garland" suggests something made of flowers or leaves, or a floral decoration, not an elaborately worked hat.

In 1927, E. P. Hammond used no title, although for a running title she adopted Dyce's. In 1983, John Scattergood, following the quarto, printed its title page at the head of his text. For running title and table of contents he restored the phrase Dyce had condensed, *Garlande or Chapelet of Laurell*, an awkward if understandable choice that had the virtue of explaining "garland."

In 1568 John Stow called the poem *The Crown of Lawrel*, a phrase perhaps based on "A cronelle of laurel" (776). On the other hand, Stow used a MS version of the poem besides the quarto. This was a good text, perhaps MS *A* on which the present edition is based, and so Stow's title may be authorial. Unfortunately MS *A* now lacks its title.

In the text, at 1497 and 1609a, Skelton calls his poem *The Laurel*. Because this title is simple, begs no questions, and is undoubtedly authoritative, I have restored it. To judge from his practice elsewhere, in the "bibliography" of *The Laurel* for instance, Skelton would probably have expanded this to *The Book of The Laurel*.

9

Preface

The Laurel or, as Skelton would probably have called it, *The Book of The Laurel*, is the most elaborately conceived and finished as well as one of the longest of Skelton's surviving poems, a dream-allegory about its author's life as a poet, his vicissitudes, his joys and hopes.

This edition began as preparatory work for a critical study of the poem. When I began work on Skelton about twenty years ago, I discovered that there was almost everything to be learned, almost nothing to be taken for granted, and that the best way to proceed was to begin by editing the text. In the case of *The Laurel*, which presented a complex set of problems, editing produced so many interlinked, mutually corroborative findings about the text, date, form, and meaning of the poem that an edition seemed the only adequate form through which to communicate them. The edition thus displaced the essay, and absorbed it.

I have tried to produce a text that represents the poem sympathetically and accurately. The first part of the introduction concerns the surviving texts and the poem's date, matters in many ways external to the poem itself, but essential preliminaries to an accurate description of any aspect of it. The second part of the introduction is about the poem, especially its structure, form, and allegory. The textual notes, commentary, appendixes, and glossary are meant to supply a complete apparatus for text and introduction alike.

Skelton evidently intended *The Laurel* to enact his poetic career in microcosm. This is why it is so compendious a work, despite its comparative brevity, and why it poses so many problems for the interpreter and commentator. Nonetheless, every sympathetic reader would agree, I think, that for all its variety *The Laurel* is mainly about the survival of poetry in an antipoetic world, and that one of the poem's strongest implications is that poetry is a hardier essence than it appears to be. Skelton's own survival seems to prove his point, for it is one of the more astonishing facts of the recent development of English poetic tradition, a vindication of Skelton's faith in the power of poetry. For Skelton has outlived a three-hundred-year fashion in denigration, having maintained his place in Fame's palace—as *The Laurel* seems to prophesy—with little help from the official keepers of Fame's literary canon.

11

It is uncannily fitting that, according to *The Laurel*, one of the mysteries of poetry should be its capacity for self-regeneration and renewal.

More than once the death of Skelton's poetry has been announced, and even as the undertakers were at their work the supposedly dead body has risen up and begun talking as wisely and amusingly as ever to a new generation of readers. In 1589 Puttenham called Skelton "a rude railing rhymer," and at virtually the same time Edmund Spenser took for himself the name Colin Clout, thus paying a graceful compliment, and acknowledging a considerable debt, to his predecessor. Warton had not long announced that "Skelton could not avoid acting as a buffoon in any language or any character," when Wordsworth and Coleridge rediscovered him, and found him as Wordsworth later wrote, "a demon in point of genius." In 1927 E. P. Hammond spoke for orthodoxy once again when she abused Skelton for "pothouse vulgarities," apparently not knowing that Robert Graves, having come upon Skelton in the middle of the First World War, was introducing him to a whole generation as a model of poetic integrity, a guide for poets in difficult times. And so the prophecies of *The Laurel* have in a way come true. As Graves claims to have quoted in the ruins of a French village in 1915, "When Parrot is ded she doth not putrefy." Skelton has lasted, as he said he would.

I hope very much that this edition will add to knowledge of Skelton, and encourage the appreciative reading of this great and fascinating poet's work.

At every stage of this project I have found myself indebted to my fellow Skelton scholars, and especially to Robert Kinsman, whose many articles and *Canon and Census* are indispensable; to Melvin J. Tucker, whose articles have made the most important contribution to knowledge of Skelton's life in recent years; and to Nan Cooke Carpenter, whose work on Skelton's knowledge of music is so important to understanding him as man and poet. I am also grateful to my colleagues Tom Dennis, Marilyn Dunn, Anthony Farnham, Eugene Hill, Louise Litterick, and Donald Weber, for their help and encouragement. I owe a special debt to George and Philippa Goold for help with Skelton's Latin, and to Owen Gingerich, who very kindly sent me computations of planetary positions from the Alfonsine Tables. David Hiley, Laura Youens, and John Stevens sent generous replies to my inquiries about numerical form in English fifteenth-century music. I am also grateful, for the use of their collections and the unfailing helpfulness of their staffs, to the Beinecke Library, Yale University; the British Library; the Chapin Library, Williams College; Mount Holyoke College Library; Smith College Library, and the New York Public Library.

I would also like to thank the students of the course in sixteenth-century English literature at Mount Holyoke, spring 1987, in particular Erin Davies and Alice Stuckey, whose questions and suggestions proved very helpful.

Finally, I must also salute Arthur Kinney, good friend of many years, and publisher of two of my previous Skelton studies, who has caught the Skeltonic enthusiasm and written his own book, and who has insisted with his customary genial firmness that I finish this work.

Woodcuts of planets and signs of the zodiac are reproduced by kind permission of the Chapin Library, Williams College, Williamstown, Massachusetts, from Albumasar, *De magnis coniunctionibus*, Augsburg, E. Ratdolt, 1489, and *Introductorium in astronomiam*, also published by E. Ratdolt, Augsburg, 1489. Nancy Leavitt drew the astrological charts.

Abbreviations Used in
the Introduction and Commentary

Aubrey	John Aubrey, *Remaines of Gentilisme and Judaisme*, ed. John Buchanan Brown, 1972.
Butler	*Butler's Lives of the Saints*, ed. Herbert Thurston and Donald Attwater, 1956.
Child	*The English and Scottish Popular Ballads*, ed. F. J. Child, 1884–98.
DCM	Boccaccio, *De claris mulieribus*, trans. Guido A. Guarino, New Brunswick, N.J., 1963.
DNB	*The Dictionary of National Biography*.
Dyce	*The Poetical Works of John Skelton*, ed. Alexander Dyce, London, 1843.
Edwards	H. L. R. Edwards, *Skelton: The Life and Times of a Tudor Poet*, London, 1949.
ELN	*English Language Notes*.
ELR	*English Literary Renaissance*.
Fish	S. E. Fish, *John Skelton's Poetry*, New Haven, 1965.
Hammond	E. P. Hammond, ed., *English Verse between Chaucer and Surrey*, Durham, N.C., 1927.
HLQ	*Huntington Library Quarterly*.
Hodnet	Edward Hodnet, *English Woodcuts, 1480–1535*, London, 1935.
Leland	*The Itinerary of John Leland*, ed. Lucy Toulmin Smith, London, 1907.
MED	*Middle English Dictionary*.
Migne, *PL*	J. P. Migne, ed., *Patrologiae Cursus Completus: Series Latina*, Paris, 1844–1904.
MLN	*Modern Language Notes*.
N&Q	*Notes and Queries*.
NCE	*New Catholic Encyclopedia*.
Nelson	William Nelson, *John Skelton, Laureate*, New York, 1939.
OED	*Oxford English Dictionary*.

PMLA	*Publications of the Modern Language Association.*
Pollet	Maurice Pollet, *John Skelton*, Lewisburg, Pa. 1971.
PQ	*Philological Quarterly.*
RQ	*Renaissance Quarterly.*
Scattergood	*John Skelton: The Complete English Poems*, ed. John Scattergood, London and New Haven, 1983.
SP	*Studies in Philology.*
Tilley	M. P. Tilley, *A Dictionary of Proverbs in the Sixteenth and Seventeenth Centuries*, Ann Arbor, Mich. 1950.
VCH	*Victoria History of the Counties of England.*
Whiting	B. J. Whiting, *Proverbs, Sentences, and Proverbial Phrases*, Cambridge, Mass., 1968.

Note. Biblical references are to the Vulgate. English translations are from the Authorized Version, with the exception of that on p. 49, translated directly from the Latin.

Introduction 1

The Text

Three witnesses to the text of Skelton's *The Book of The Laurel* survive, two contemporary with the poet, none complete.

1. *British Library MS. Cotton Vitellius E.X, ff. 208–225v (A)*. This manuscript is an historical and poetic miscellany, severely damaged in the Ashburnham House fire of 1731, now consisting of 272 separately mounted leaves. Skelton's poem, fortunately, was written by a scribe who left large margins, and so it is one of the less damaged items. Even so, a good many words are lost where the fire, having consumed the spine, destroyed the inner margins. The signature of John Stow appears on f. 2v. It is not clear whether this indicates ownership of the whole codex (which in that case would have formed an entity in his day), or of the first item only, which begins on f. 3. The former seems more likely. Stow collected Skelton's works in manuscript and in print, and edited the first complete edition of his poems.[1]

In the original table of contents Skelton's poem appears as *Rithmi aliquot Anglici & heroinas aliquot Anglice* ⟨. . .⟩; it is preceded by [*The Bible o*]*f Englyshe Pollicye* and followed by [*Instituta*] *et Statuta Collegii de Rotherham*. The original foliation of *The Laurel* does not survive in the mutilated table of contents, but the *Bible* [*sic*] began on f. 206, ending on f. 221v, and the *Statuta* began on f. 242. With an interleaf separating the items, the poem would have occupied ff. 223–40, the same number of leaves as now; this original foliation in fact survives in a modern hand at the foot of the repaired leaves. The soiled and rubbed condition of the outer pages tells us that it was handled as an unbound fragment for many years before it was bound into the present volume. (The outer pages of quires D and E are also soiled, but less so.)

What survives of this text, then, is eighteen leaves forming three quires of a paper folio in sixes. The quires are signed, in small letters and Roman numerals, A1–3, [D1]–3, E1–3, and one catchword remains, *poeta* at the foot of Sig. A6v. (Other markings record the later

17

vicissitudes of the MS, the signatures FF, GG, HH in an 18C. hand, and 19C. editorial marks, for instance.)

Quire A contains lines 1–245 of the poem as it appears in the printed texts. Quires D and E contain lines 721–1135. In Quire A there are about twenty lines per page, and so by a simple calculation one can deduce that lines 246–720 would fit exactly into the missing quires B and C. Similarly, the last part of the poem would have occupied one or two quires, depending upon whether this MS represented the poem in its revised or unrevised form.[2] In either case, it appears that the MS was once complete. It was a folio volume of six or seven quires, which very probably included two or more unsigned leaves devoted by Skelton, in characteristic fashion, to prefatory matter. The present surviving fragment preserves two-fifths of this original, a little more than 40 percent of the text.

The manuscript was written in a handsome cursive script by a trained writer who understood the form and the details of his text very well. In one striking way this text differs from that of the two printed witnesses; it has been divided into sections called *capitula*, each with its own heading. Three of these headings survive, the first, eighth, and ninth. The first, *Capitulum Primum*, is written in the outer margin of f. 209 opposite stanza eight. *Capitulum Octavum* is squeezed into rather narrow space on f. 215 between stanzas 107 and 108. *Capitulum Nonum* appears in the wide upper margin of f. 217, over stanza 117, where the scribe originally wrote it; it was later crossed out, then rewritten in a second hand. From these positions one infers that there was some indecisiveness over whether to include the headings in this MS; yet the divisions are original, because in writing the first stanza of each of his *capitula* the scribe had indicated a new section by leaving space for a decorated capital. These spaces with their guide letters, as well as the expansive, often fantastic initial flourishes found on every page, are the marks of a book that, though unfinished, was meant to be fairly handsome.

There are very few mistakes, none of them significant. They are of two kinds. Two examples will illustrate the first:

~~Buth~~ Bot sithe he hathe tastid   (73)

That bannysshid ~~his~~ was he by his   (132)

These slight errors, made and corrected *currente calamo*, reveal a copyist holding in memory a line at a time, and sometimes anticipating, sometimes forgetting a word. Errors of the latter kind emerge from

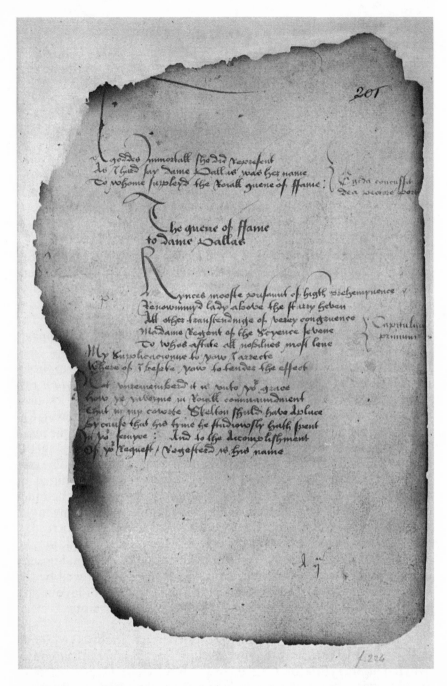

MS Cotton Vitellius E.X., f. 209, showing the fragmentary gloss to 47–49, the guide letter, signature, and *capitulum*-heading. By permission of the British Library.

collation with the other texts, although sometimes context alone suggests that something is missing:

> Or why is had in mynde
> Plato: bot for [that] he left wryting behynde

(126)

or:

> Of vertew [and] konyng the wel and parfight grownd

(866)

Nowhere has the scribe misunderstood his text, whether in Latin or English. His spelling, which is consistent (according to his own conventions), represents the language in transition from late Middle English to early Modern English. He uses several northernisms.

There are some additions and corrections in a second hand. The letter-forms are identical with the copyist's; such difference in appearance as there is might be caused by a different pen and time of writing rather than by a different writer. On f. 209 this hand supplies a *marginalium* in Skeltonic style, as well as the heading, *Capitulum Primum*. It makes minor corrections on ff. 216, 217, and 211. Its most interesting appearance is on f. 214v. At this point Skelton inserts a Latin satire against an adversary whose name he conceals in a simple number code.[3] Here the copyist made a small mistake, reversing the numbers 19 and 8 (the letters *t* and *h* in the victim's surname). The corrector crossed out this version, began a new one to the right of it, crossed that out, and wrote out the whole code correctly in the inner margin. He, or someone with a similar hand, also wrote roughly in the margin opposite the Latin "Ryght truly theys versis." The corrector, then, knew the code as well as the person whom it concealed, and he approved of Skelton's attitude to him. If he was not Skelton himself, then he knew him well, and copyist and corrector might well be the same person. This text, which follows Skelton's habits of layout and embellishment, and is very accurate, is an authoritative one.[4]

2. *STC* 22610 (hereinafter referred to as *B*).
Title Page] ❡ A ryght delectable tra | tyſe vpon a goodly Gar| lande or Chapelet of Laurell by mayſter Skelton Poete | laureat ſtudyouſly dyuyſed at Sheryfhotton Caſtell. In | yᵉ foreſte of galtres / where in ar cōpryſyde many & dyuers | folacyons & ryght pregnant allectyues of ſyngular plea- | ſure / as more at large it doth apere in yᵉ‚pces folowynge. | [Within two vertical rows of type ornaments (*Plomer* 11), a woodcut (*Hodnett* 2056)]|

Colophon, F4v] ⦅ Here endith a ryght delectable tratyſe upon a goodly | garlonde or chapelet of laurell dyuyſed by mayſter Skel | ton Poete laureat. | Inpryntyd by me Rycharde faukes dwellydg in durā | rent or els in Powlis chyrche yarde at the ſygne of the | A.B.C. The yere of our lorde god .M.CCCCC. | xxiij. The .iij. day of Octobre. | [Within a frame of type ornaments (*Plomer* 12), a device (*McKerrow* 31b) inscribed "Richard Fakes"] |

Collation] 4°, A⁶B–F⁴, signed A, A³, B, C, D, E, F = 26 leaves.

Contents] A1 title, A1v woodcut (*Hodnett* 2058), A2–F2v text, with two woodcuts (*Hodnett* 2052, 2053) on A2v; F2v "Skeltonts alloquiū Librum ſuum.", F3 "Lenuoy.", F3v "Admonet Skeltonis: omnes arbores dare locū viridi lauro Iuxta genus ſuum.", F4 "En parlament A Paris.", F4v colophon.

Copy] British Library 82.d.25.

This handsome little black-letter quarto survives in a unique copy once owned by King George III, now in the British Library.[5] With its four woodcuts, ornamental initials, and elaborate marginalia, it imitates closely the appearance of Skelton's manuscript copy. The printing, however, is careless. Stanzas 49 and 59 (337–43, 407–13) and line 662 are missing. The compositor has turned five lines into nonsense, and he has made many small errors, some of them undoubtedly not now detectable. He is especially given to inversions, of letters and words:

> the were they (68)
> banssihed (93)
> uiro [i.e., riuo] (1462)
> numera [i.e., munera] (1622)

It is likely, therefore, that when variants caused by inverted word order occur between *A* and *B*, *A*'s scribe is correct, not *B*'s compositor:

B	*A*	
that he his tyme	that his tyme he	(60)
a grete parte yet	yit a grete parte	(171)
ye shall	shalle ye	(197)
wolde to me	to me wold	(1113)

Difficulties in reading copy have caused other errors. In early sixteenth-century cursive hands certain letters are easily mistaken for others. An *a* can look like *o*, and *B*'s compositor has mistaken the letter several times, producing *paroblis* for *parablis* (101), *engolerid* for *engalarid* (460), and *come* for *came* (511). A similar mistake substitutes *e* for *o*;

examples are *surmewntynge* for *surmountynge* (901) and *meledyously* for *melodyously* (272). There are many mistaken readings of minims, among them *elycoms* for *elyconis* (74), *conuecture* for *coniecture* (107), *Icononucar* for *Iconomicar* (328), and *conucar* for *comicar* (353). Other errors include *k* misread as *t*, producing *hastardis* for *haskardis* (607), and *sc* misread as *st* (combined with a minim error) producing *stormis* for *scorn[n]is* (1376).

Since these letters are sometimes quite indistinguishable, these errors reveal a negligent rather than an incompetent compositor. Accurate reading of any handwriting depends upon attention to context, and *B*'s compositor's attention often wandered. The result is a text that reproduces the appearance of the copy fairly accurately, but often garbles its meaning. It does tell us, however, that the copy was in a cursive hand very like *A*'s, its *o*'s, *a*'s, and *e*'s often identical.

3. *STC* 22608 (hereinafter referred to as *C*).
Title Page] ❰ Pithy plea- | faunt and profita- | ble workes of mai- | fter Skelton, Poete Lau- | reate. | Nowe collected and | newly pub- lifhed. | *ANNO* | 1568. | [rule] [four leaves lozenge-wise] ❧ *Imprinted at London in Fletefítreate,* | *neare vnto faint Dunfítones* | *churche by Thomas* | *Marfhe.* |
Note. "Skelton, Poete Lau-reate" is in roman type.
Collation] 8°, [   ]⁴A–Z⁸2A⁴.

Under the title "The crowne of lawrel" *The Laurel* occupies Sigs. A1–D6v of this volume "*newly collected by I.S.*" ([   ]4v), who was undoubtedly John Stow. This text lacks *B*'s title, *explicit*, and marginalia, and Stow has removed Skelton's Latin poem on the laurel (*B*, Sig. F3v) and "En Parlament A Paris" (*B*, Sig. F4) to a later part of his book (Sigs. Y5, X8). He supplies *B*'s missing lines and a second envoy addressing the poem to the king and to Cardinal Wolsey.

It was *B*, however, that provided Stow with his copytext, as the numerous errors they have in common prove.[6] That being so, Stow's text has no independent authority except for the fifteen lines for which it is the only witness, and for certain corrected readings. Some of these, e.g., *rokky wall* for *wall* (473), must come, like the missing lines, from another source. Others could easily have been supplied by common sense. As is usually the case in sixteenth-century printing, although this text corrects many of *B*'s errors (among them all the errors of copyreading listed above), it also introduces many of its own. The most obvious change in the text is in its appearance. *C* modernizes the spelling, a process already begun by *B*, and regularizes the Latin according to midsixteenth-century usage. Also, by presenting the poem without illustration, decoration, or flourish, this text translates it completely into the medium of the printed, rather than the written, book. *The Laurel* thus acquires a subtly different character from the work that Skelton first composed, a change no doubt unintentional that the modern editor should recognize.

The existence of these three texts raises two basic questions: what relationship is there, if any, between *A* and *B*, and what materials, other than *B*, did Stow use to prepare the text found in *C*?

There seems to be no immediate connection between *A* and *B*; there are no common errors, and the variants (of which there are many, some important) reveal texts representing different "states" of the poem:

96. *A* ffor y^t he enveiyd: yit wrate he none Ille
     B For certayne enuectyfys: yet wrote he none ill
755. *A* How daungerows it is to stop vp his sight
     B How daungerous it were to stande in his lyght

Such variants do not tell one which text came first, but one otherwise unimportant variant suggests that *A* was the earlier:

739. *A* To vnderstande who dwellythe In yonder pyle
         And what blunderar is yonder that plaiyth diddil diddil[le]
     B To vnderstande who dwellyth in yone pile
         And what blunderar is yonder y^t playe[t]h didil diddil

A's repeated *yonder* is the kind of repetition an author makes in a first text; *yone* is an effective, simple revision.[7] *A*'s reading, of course, could be a simple mistake, an anticipation of the word in the next line; but some other variants also suggest that *A* was the earlier text:

863a. *A* To my Lady Elisabethe
      B To my lady elisabeth howarde
877a. *A* To my Lady Myrryel
      B To my lady mirriell howarde
891a. *A* To my Lady dakers
      B To my lady anne dakers of the sowth

A's shorter headings address the poems to the ladies themselves, whereas *B*'s more formal headings are really titles or captions. The difference is subtle, but real, and it is likely that *A*'s headings are the earlier. Skelton addressed his poems to their recipients before he published them for a larger audience.

Although *A* and the manuscript underlying *B* differed in details of layout and text, in some ways they were similar, especially in language

and spelling. *B*'s compositor altered the spelling of his copy to con-
form more closely to the orthography of standard London English in
his time. He did this fairly consistently, so that the manuscript spellings that survive stand out clearly. The spelling thus revealed is like *A*'s.
To take the most obvious examples, *A*'s suffix for the third person
preterit of verbs ending in -*er*, is -*erd*[*e*]; he spells syllabic *l* (as in *noble*) -*il*[*le*], and represents the gutturals -*ough* and -*igh* with -*owthe* and
-*igthe*. *B*'s forms for these sounds are, respectively, -[*e*]*red*, -*le*, -*ough*,
and -*igh*. When other forms appear in *B*, they are like *A*'s. Toward
the end of the poem, preterits in *A*'s style appear: *encouerde* (1158),
sufferd (1372), and *Recouerd* (1401). Position as a rhyme word preserves *bybille* (209), but not its rhyme, which appears as *ydle* rather
than *ydille*. Stanzas 111–13, perhaps because they were either difficult
or unusually interesting, caught the compositor's attention, and he preserved many manuscript spellings: *nedill* (804), *rowthe* (803), and *purpill* (800). Other characteristics of *B*'s MS copy, also found in *A*, are
w for *u* in *browght* (792) and *bownte* (806), and the doubling of final
consonants before suffixes: *tappettis* and *carpettis* (787).[8]

This latter characteristic of the manuscript explains some peculiar
errors in *B*: *murmyng* (295, 1371), *phillistimis* (1345), and *stormis*
(1376). In these cases the compositor may have misread a double *n* as
m. *A*'s scribe regularly uses these doubled consonants: his first page
has *sygnnys, ascenddinge, stormmy, drownnyd*, and *fryththy*.

B's copy and *A*, therefore, though not identically spelled (something
one would not expect even if they were both written by Skelton), used
the same orthographical principles. Since these spellings appear in the
better Skelton texts (e.g., *Ware the Hauke, The Bowge of Courte*), they
are evidently Skelton's own. *A*, therefore, is considerably closer to
Skelton's original than is *B*, and this enables us to detect a few more
survivals of Skeltonic practice in *B*.

A's text, besides being in general more old-fashioned than *B*, also
uses several northern forms, e.g. *beseke* (56, 215, 835), *slawthfulle*
(120), *enbrawder* (794), *lawly* (837), *mageran* (906). *B* regularizes most
of these, but *beseke* remains at 835, and *enbrawderyd* occurs twice in
the poem to Margery Wentworth. This suggests that *B*'s *byrnston* (631)
is another northernism. Even *B*'s *hus* for *us* (1115) may be original.
Skelton was very well educated, and spent most of his life among gentle
speakers in the south, but he came from the north, perhaps the far
north,[9] and one would expect some northern habits to persist in his
speech. He was, indeed, one in that influx of educated northerners into
the south that distinguished the early modern period, and marked the
end of a distinctive literary and intellectual culture in the north.

Inevitably, as one considers the features of *A*, the question arises: is this Skelton's own work, or the work of a scribe who faithfully copied his original? One undoubted holograph of a Skelton poem survives, "A Lawde and Prayse Made for Our Sovereigne Lord the Kyng," written on two leaves of MS. PRO E 36/228, one of the records of the treasury. It is a short sample, written rapidly, though with some elaboration and care. The date is 1509. If we compare this text with *A*'s, then the spelling (allowing for a degree of variation typical of all early hands) is similar. The following words are either identically spelled or use the same orthographical pattern: *acorde, browght, com, flowris, gaddir (gadder, A), hight (pp.), hunderd, kowde, mo, moost, pepil (pepille, A), souereine, starry, streight, thorow, wele, wrowght, yowthe.* In so short a text, this is a high degree of concordance. *Noble,* however, used twice, always appears in *A* as *nobille* or *nobil,* where Skelton's *white* also appears as *whight;* the more standard spellings of the PRO MS, nonetheless, are unusual for Skelton. *Ware the Hauke,* approximately contemporary with "A Lawde and Prayse" and printed carefully from holograph copy, has *nobyll. White,* too, seems untypical. Skelton seldom uses the word, almost never in a rhyme;[10] but we know that he favoured the spelling *wright,* or its variants, for *write.*

In comparing the hands themselves one must remember that the samples might be separated by ten years or more in either direction, and that Skelton undoubtedly wrote in more than one kind of hand with different degrees of care at different times. Everyone knows how a hand can change over a decade; but it can vary in a single day with changes of mood, place, pen, and ink. With those cautions in mind, the first thing to say about these two hands is that both are forms of the same early Tudor cursive. Closer comparison shows striking similarities of letter-form and penmanship; letters are similarly shaped with similar movements of the pen. This is especially noticeable in flourishes and capitals. Both Skelton and *A* like to extend their capitals well above the line, and form their flourishes with freely drawn lines that have a life quite separate from the letter they form. Skelton's initial *T* is a good example, and it is identical with the capital *T* used repeatedly by *A*. *A*'s fondness for verticals leads him to draw many—though not all—of his *t*'s very tall; Skelton, writing with a thicker pen, makes fewer of these high *t*'s, but when he does, they are the same as *A*'s. Another feature of *A*'s hand is the pointed *b*; Skelton, too, points his *b*'s. In fact, there is only one sharp dissimilarity: *A* makes a *w* with a single movement, the letter made of two minims, sometimes with a strong upstroke, the second minim drawn forward into the letter's final reverse curve. Skelton uses two movements, two minims, the second

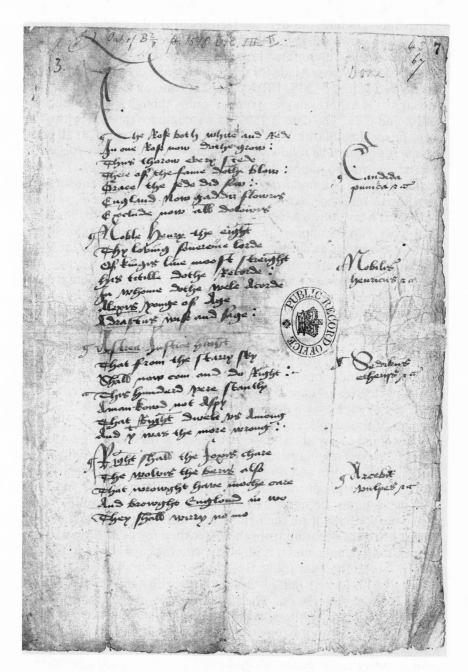

The first page of "A Lawde and Prayse Made for Our Sovereigne Lord the Kyng," MS PRO E 36/228, f. 67. By permission of the Public Record Office.

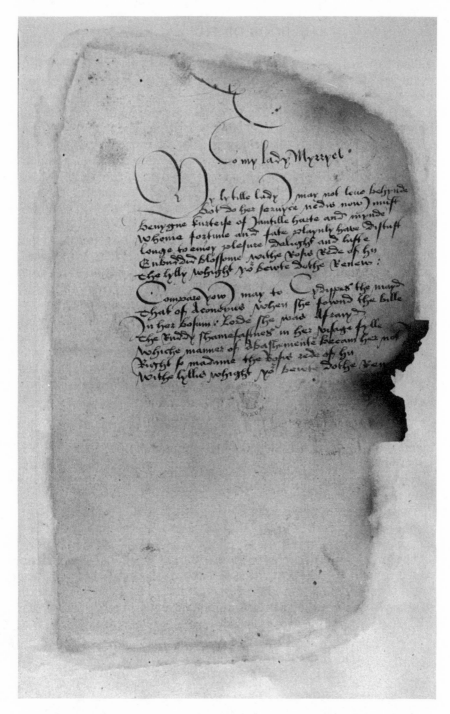

MS Cotton Vitellius E.X., f. 218v, "To my Lady Myrryel." By permission of the British Library.

pulled forward, after a pause, into the reverse curve. Of thirty-four examples of the letter, thirty-one are as described, and three are more like *A*'s.

On the whole, then, although a good case can be made that *A* is a holograph, it is not an entirely convincing one. The manuscript preserves Skelton's habits of spelling and speech, and comparison with the one known holograph poem shows close similarities of penmanship. On the other hand, the writing is freer than the holograph's, less cramped, with less slope; the *w* is different, and the scribe writes *whight* instead of Skelton's *white, noble* for his *nobille*. *A*, too, has a professional look.

These objections are not unanswerable. Skelton was a professional author who, born about 1460, grew up among written, not printed, books. Material in his hand, and texts printed from holograph copy show him to have been an able writer, trained in a variety of hands, who took pleasure in writing. He could probably have earned his living as a scrivener. The similarities between *A* and the holograph are more striking than the differences, which can all be explained by the passage of more than a decade. The spellings of *noble* and *white* may be quite insignificant; rather than providing evidence that Skelton did not write *A*, they would suggest, were there not a strong probability in its favor, that he did not write the holograph!

Certainty in such cases is impossible, but my own verdict is that *A* is holograph, a decision further supported by evidence from the treatment of the *capitula* headings, described in detail in appendix 1. *A* is an authorial fair copy, one of the few really good Skelton texts that survive. A manuscript in a similar hand and spelling, representing a later revision, underlies *B*.

The additions to text *C* remain to be considered. This corrected reprint of *B* replaces the missing stanzas 49 and 59, and line 662. It also corrects many readings, and supplies the text of the Second Envoy.

The most obvious source for these materials would have been a corrected copy of *B* with the omitted passages tipped in on slips of paper; but this can be ruled out almost immediately. In the couplet-refrain of stanza 49, *C* has the unusual but more exactly rhyming noun *flotes* ("floats") instead of *dropes*, which would be the reading from *B*.

> Of clusters engrosed with his ruddy flotes
> These orators & Poetes refreshed their throtes
>
> (Sig. A7)

C also has *flotes* in stanza 48, where one would also expect *B*'s *droppes*, which provides *C*'s reading for the other six versions of the refrain.

Evidently the compositor, with his copy on hand for stanza 49, allowed it to influence his version of the refrain in stanza 48. Once he had set up the missing stanza, he put the copy for the replacements by and returned to *B*, his regular copy. The maneuver must have confused him.[11] A similar "overflowing" of the replacement-copy into the reprint from *B* also occurs in the neighbourhood of stanza 59, the second stanza that the compositor had to insert from another source. In *C*, stanza 60 has for heading "Maister Chaucher Lawreat poete to Skelton." (Sig. A8) instead of *B*'s "Mayster Chaucer To Skelton." It seems likely that *C*'s variant heading must also be from the replacement copy, and its presence, like the variant *flotes* in stanza 48, implies that *C*'s compositor was not following a corrected copy of *B* at these places, but a full page of copy in another version, as well as *B*.

Whatever this version was, we can only speculate about it and about the way the compositor used it. Since *C* is a corrected reprint of *B*, it is likely that most of *C*'s numerous corrections were indicated in the compositor's copy of *B*, most unlikely that he made continual reference to his second source. We have seen how that process confused him. Yet several of his variants suggest consultation of another source, e.g., *a lacke* (70) for *B*'s *grete lake*, and *rokky wal* (473) for *wal*. A few variant spellings also suggest the influence of MS copy: *sloughtfull* (120) for *B*'s *slowthfull* (cf. *A*'s *slawthfulle*); *sklaundred* (140) for *slaundred* (*sclaunderde*, *A*), and *yolowe* (289) for *yalowe*. Two faint signs of MS copy also show through *C*'s version of the missing stanzas, the spellings *yow* and *laudabyle* (Sig. A8).

It is just possible that this MS version was *A* itself—in which case one could speculate that its present state is due to its printing house adventures. A MS as good as *A*, however, is not likely to have spelled *Chaucer* as *Chaucher*, and it is doubtful whether it would call Chaucer a "lawreat" poet after Skelton had said a few lines earlier of all three English poets, Gower, Chaucer, and Lydgate, that "Thei wantid no thynge bot the laurelle" (397). This opinion goes back to Dyce, who said in his note to line 413a that *C*'s reading "contradicts what our author has just told us." Yet this may be too literal a reading. Skelton calls all the poets in his procession "poetis laureat" (324); the compliment to Chaucer in *C* is far more likely to be Skelton's own way of singling out Chaucer than to be a scribe's, editor's, or compositor's absentminded way of improving his copy. The curious spelling of *Chaucer* need be no more than a misprint. The likelihood that *C*'s heading is Skelton's own not only improves the authority of *C*'s manuscript source, and with it *C*'s own text; it increases the possibility that the manuscript was *A* itself, always the most economical hypothesis. After all, Stow owned it.

Whatever *C*'s MS was, the compositor did not use it enough to allow a confident description of it now. That it was used at all, however, confers a degree of authority on *C* that it does not have considered simply as a modernizing reprint of *B*.

There is also the Second Envoy to be considered. It must have been attached to some version of the poem in Stow's possession, otherwise he would have had no reason to associate it with *The Laurel*. It can be dated independently of *The Laurel* to about 1523.[12] Editors have naturally associated it with *B*, published 3 October 1523, even though the unique copy does not contain it and, as the collation shows, was planned with no thought of including it. Yet it must have been the revised text of the poem printed in *B*, playing down the anti-Wolsey poems, that Skelton presented to king and cardinal. He will have given each a copy with the Envoy attached, and to own the Envoy Stow must have owned a presentation copy. Since the Envoy expressed more than a private gesture, there will have been several in existence.

At the time of printing *C*, then, Stow owned at least two copies of the poem: *B* and a MS version, one of which may have been a presentation copy with the Second Envoy attached. His MS may have been the now-fragmentary *A*. If it was, then *A* was complete when it was used in the printing house. Stow reprinted *B* because it was the more recent version of the poem, and because compositors naturally preferred printed to MS copy. Whether *C*'s MS was *A* or not, *C*'s additions to *B* stem from a MS textual tradition similar to that represented by *A*. This explains why *C*'s heading to stanza 59 ("Poeta Skelton to Maister Gower") follows *A*'s form rather than *B*'s ("Poeta Skelton answeryth.") and it allows one to infer that *C*'s interesting variant *flotes* (335) is an earlier MS reading of which *B*'s *droppes* is the later, pallid revision.

These inferences are necessarily tentative, based upon fragmentary evidence. *A* and *B* are each unique representatives of their respective classes. There will have been other MSS, perhaps even other editions, now lost. Of the three surviving witnesses, each has its own specific authority.

The Date

The one firm piece of evidence is Fakes's colophon to *B*:

Inpryntyd by me Rycharde faukes . . . The yere of our lorde god .M. CCCCC.xxiij. The .iij. day of Octobre.

This tells us that the text was finished at the latest sometime in the autumn of 1523. Internal evidence supports that date. Skelton's "bibliography" includes, besides *The Laurel* itself, *Colyn Cloute* (1522), *Speke, Parrot* (1519-21), and *Magnyfycence* (usually dated 1515-16). It was natural that students of Skelton's poetry, beginning with Dyce, should identify the countess of Surrey whom Skelton addresses in the poem as Elizabeth, née Stafford, the wife of Thomas Howard II, earl of Surrey, son of the victor of Flodden, Thomas Howard I, duke of Norfolk since 1514. Since the title page of the 1523 text also says that Skelton wrote the poem at Sheriff Hutton castle, it was an easy step to join the date, place, and people mentioned into a chapter of Skeltonic biography.[13]

Skelton's astrological description of time in the first stanza apparently corroborated this dating. Helen Stearns Sale was the first to attempt the necessary calculations.[14] With help from the Yale department of astronomy, she learned that Mars retrogrades once in approximately two years, and that the planet was "retrogradant" in the spring of 1523, just as it is in Skelton's opening stanza. William Nelson and H. L. R. Edwards followed her; calculations made independently for them confirmed her results. There was some minor skirmishing in the attempt to fix a more precise date, with the result that Edwards announced in 1949 that "The action of the poem, then, must be imagined as taking place on New Year's Eve—the last day of 1522."[15]

This astronomical dating had a very scientific look to it, yet it was based on vague criteria. The appearance of scientific precision was illusory, the result only corroborative of a date arrived at by other means. Edwards's confidence, especially, was extravagant: "For anyone who cared to work it out [the first stanza] gave the time within a matter of minutes." At the time this was not so, because as Sale, Nelson, and Edwards used it, the first stanza only gave a date accurate to a month or so *provided one first knew the approximate date to within two years*—the period within which Mars's retrograde motion occurs. Besides, the larger argument rested upon very literal readings of the poem's prologue. Sale thought it was written in spring because Skelton seems to fall asleep in the woods. Nelson preferred an autumn date because the stags of the forest were in rut. Edwards thought the poem was written during Skelton's Christmas holidays because the action ends on New Year's Eve.

Textual evidence, as already explained, suggests that the poem existed in some earlier, slightly different state. Melvin J. Tucker, approaching the question as a historian of the Howard family, found that Dyce had been wrong to say that Henry VII had given Thomas Howard I a grant of Sheriff Hutton castle for life. He could not find that either Thomas I (the duke) or his son Thomas II (earl of Surrey after 1514) was resident at the castle in 1522-23. Thomas I, however, as earl of Surrey and Lieutenant of the North, had lived there for ten years a generation earlier, from 1489–99. This seemed to Tucker the only period when Skelton could have written a poem at Sheriff Hutton celebrating a countess of Surrey. The countess addressed, therefore, must be Elizabeth née Tylney, the first wife of Thomas I, and not Elizabeth née Stafford, the wife of Thomas II.[16]

Tucker then turned to the ladies of the countess's household to whom Skelton also addressed poems, and found that they too belonged to the decade 1489–99.[17] Genealogical research is a slippery subject, but Tucker seems to have made five definite identifications: the ladies Elizabeth and Muriel Howard; Lady Anne Dacre of the South; Margery Wentworth and Margaret Tylney. The first two were the young daughters of Thomas Howard I by his first wife Elizabeth. Both, according to Tucker, married circa 1500. Lady Anne was the countess's daughter by her first marriage; she married Lord Dacre in about 1492. Margery Wentworth was daughter to Sir Henry Wentworth and a niece of the countess. She married John Seymour, was mother to Queen Jane Seymour, and grandmother to Edward VI. Tucker gives 22 October 1494 as the date of her wedding, but in a footnote (p. 336) says only that "It seems a reasonable surmise that she married Seymour in 1494." Margaret Tylney was wife to Sir Philip Tylney, auditor to the earl, and steward of his manor of Framlingham. His sister married the earl as his second countess in 1497.

If the commendatory poems are a group composed at approximately the same time (a conclusion implied by "What thowthe my pen wax faynte?" in the poem to Jane Hasset), these identifications provide a *terminus ad quem* of 1497, when the Countess died, and a *terminus a quo* of 1492 when Anne Bourchier became Lady Dacre. If Margery Wentworth married on 22 October 1494, then the *terminus ad quem* is correspondingly earlier.

Tucker also used the poetic horoscope of stanza 1. With help from Owen Gingerich (of the Smithsonian Astrophysical Observatory) he describes a horoscope distinguished by Mars retrograde, the moon full, both in conjunction at Scorpio 18°, with Mars also "lord of the year," i.e., the planet strongest in relation to the other planets at the vernal equinox (the start of the astronomical year). This striking and unusual pattern of celestial events occurred on 8 May 1495.[18]

Unlike the earlier attempt at astronomical dating, Tucker's requires a prior approximate date accurate not to two years, but to about a generation—such is the infrequency of the configuration stanza 1 describes once it is properly understood. That being so, Tucker's astronomical date and his historical date are independent of each other, and so mutually corroborative. Yet Tucker is not convinced that he has dated the poem.

He tentatively identifies Margaret Hussey of the famous "myrry Margarete" poem as the wife of John Hussey, sheriff of Lincolnshire in 1493-94. This lady died, he thinks, in 1492: "If the lines to Margaret Hussey were written before 1492, doubt may be cast on the usually accepted hypothesis that Skelton is recording an actual event taking place at Sheriff Hutton in which all the ladies physically participated" (*RQ* 22: 339). Although he is certain that the concatenation of persons and events datable to the 1490s forces a date approximately a generation earlier than the previously accepted one, he does not advance a more precise date, because Skelton's garland is "a figment of his imagination" (343). Obviously, we have to distinguish between what is historical and literal and what is figurative in *The Laurel*. Moreover, Tucker's evidence for the *termini a quo* and *ad quem* is so strong that his hypothesis itself becomes evidential, i.e., the fact that Margaret Hussey's poem is in *The Laurel* is evidence that she—whoever she was —was alive in 1492-97.

There are limits to imagination. Lady Anne's poem had to be written after her marriage to Lord Dacre, ca. 1492. There are also limits imposed by decorum. It is not likely that Skelton would have addressed Margarey Wentworth by her maiden name after she married, nor that he would have addressed the countess as if she were alive after her death in 1497. So with the horoscope. In an age fairly well-versed in astrology it would make no sense to describe a horoscope that bore no close relationship to the poem's date of composition. The two events must have been reasonably close together. Were *The Laurel* a novel, this would not be so; but it is an allegory with a basis of literal, historical significance. Moreover, one does not invent a horoscope, which is a description of time in the form of a diagram of celestial events synchronous with an earthly event; one finds it out, once one knows the date of the earthly event, by consulting tables. Skelton may have chosen that particular day for his poetic vision because its celestial events were unusually beautiful, dramatic, and significant; but it is hard to believe that he did not begin by knowing the year and season, if not the exact day, of his poem's events.

It is even possible that the horoscope was the spur to the whole celebration that the poem records. Tucker observes almost in passing that the nearest previous conjunction of Mars and Luna in Scorpio, Mars retrograde, to that of 8 May 1495, occured on 2 May 1463. We do not know when Skelton was born, only (from events later in his career) that it must have been about 1460. Tucker thinks it "an unlikely twist" that this conjunction is in any way part of Skelton's own nativity;[19] yet to anyone familiar with the thought processes of medieval and Renaissance poets, nothing is more likely than that this horoscope is connected with Skelton's own life, and that its recurrence in what would therefore have been his thirty-third year would have been an event of great significance to him.

Whatever the truth of this suggestion (more fully discussed below, in connection with the poem's structure), there is no escaping the conclusion that the weaving of the garland and its presentation was an historical event recorded not only by Skelton but also, he tells us (stanza 119), by Master Newton, an artist maintained in the earl's household. The commendatory lyrics continually refer to the weaving of the chaplet or garland. The countess is compared to two other artistic ladies, Pamphila and Thamar; Margery Wentworth wears her girlhood like an embroidered mantle; Jane Hasset "Smale flowris helpt to set / In my goodely chapelet"; Gertrude Statham helped to plan the gift, and Isbel Knyght helped "to warke my laureel grene / Withe silke and golde." This is very circumstantial, and as Leigh Winser has argued in an interesting article, the poem may be the record of a pageant-drama in which Skelton's "goodely garlande" was presented to him at Sheriff Hutton.[20] This event occurred ca. 1495, if not actually on 8 May of that year, then fairly close to it.

If the poem as originally conceived was written at about the same time, then there is no reason to believe that the version published in 1523 differed much from the original. The only major changes needed would be in the list of Skelton's works that ends the poem. This "bibliography" is not in chronological order, but it is noticeable that with one exception earlier and later work is not mixed up in the same stanza. Beginning at stanza 133, which mentions *Magnyfycence*, there follows a set of nine stanzas listing works of which none is datable before 1495, and of which those that are datable belong to 1497–1522. The last of these stanzas, 141, mentions *Phyllyp Sparowe*; then after quoting his long "adicyon" to that poem, Skelton's list reverts to earlier works, ending the whole with his *Diodorus*, followed by *The Laurel* itself.

Since *The Laurel* had to be the climactic work of the list, by definition his most recent, Skelton could not add later works to the end of his list. He would therefore have interpolated the nine stanzas of later works into the original list, and this must have been done after the writing of *Colyn Cloute*, ca. 1521–22.[21]

The exception mentioned above is stanza 132 in which Skelton mentions five works: a comedy, *Achademios*; his translation of Cicero's *Familiar Letters*; a treatise called *Goode Avysemente*; "*The Recule Ageyne Gagwyne*," and a poem called *The Popingay*:

> that hathe in commendacioun
> Ladis and jantylwomen, soche as deservid:
> And soche as be counterfettis, they be reservid.

Three of these, the comedy, the translation, and the "recule" are datable to 1488–89.[22] It is generally assumed that *The Popingay* is the poem now called *Speke, Parrot*, written 1519–21.[23] Here, then, are pre- and post-1495 works in one stanza.

The description of *The Popingay*, though, does not fit *Speke, Parrot* at all. Dyce thought that "Skelton must allude here to some portion, now lost, of that composition."[24] Nelson and Edwards (dating *The Laurel* in 1523, after the attacks on Wolsey) thought Skelton was intentionally misrepresenting an anti-Wolsey poem. This is not likely. To describe *Colyn Cloute*, a twelve-hundred-line satire on Wolsey, as a "trifel" of "honest myrthe" is a funny irony, and like many of Skelton's jokes, the funnier the more one thinks about it; but the description of *The Popingay* does not apply ironically to *Speke, Parrot*. It describes a quite different poem.

Was there an earlier poem centering upon a parrot? That there was one, also written for the countess, is certainly implied by her apparent reference to it at 784–86 in words similar to Skelton's description of *The Popingay*:

> For yit of women he never sayd shame
> Bot if they wer counterfettis that women them calle,
> That liste of ther lewdenes withe hym for to bralle.

As we have seen, the evidence for dating *The Laurel* in 1495 is very strong. In addition, the poem proves to have a numerological structure (as explained below, pp. 62–70) which corroborates the argument that an original work written ca. 1495 had nine stanzas added to it later. Since *The Popingay* is not in those stanzas, what is it?

As it happens, Skelton's marginal gloss to *The Popingay* (non mihi sit modulo rustica papilio: "Let not a rustic butterfly serve me as a model") underlies a stanza of *Speke, Parrot*, which is an amplification of it:

> For Parot is no churlish chowgh, nor no flekyd pye,
> Parrot is no pendugum, that men call a carlyng,
> Parrot is no woodecocke, nor no butterfly,
> Parrot is no stameryng stare, that men call a starlyng. . . .
>
> (204–7)

Since stanza 132 of *The Laurel* must date from ca. 1495, and since this gloss upon *The Popingay* connects with a stanza in *Speke, Parrot*, only one conclusion is possible: *Speke, Parrot*, dating as we know it from 1519–21, originated a generation earlier, like *The Laurel*. One cannot identify with certainty the portions of the original that survive in the present text, although it seems very probable that they include all the stanzas delineating the "myth" of Parrot. They may include everything in the poem not specifically related to persons and events of 1519-21, for Skelton may have been led to rework the poem by the same sense of a parallelism in events that led him to revive *The Laurel* itself. The prophetic authority of the popingay called Parrot is based on the idea that he, or the inspired poetic voice that speaks through him, can see the patterns of history, its recurrent configurations. Since literary criticism itself is a fantasia upon an historical groundbass, the likelihood that *Speke, Parrot*, like *The Laurel*, originated about thirty years earlier than has been thought, entails a considerable revision of the standard version of Skelton's career, especially of our ideas of the originality and development of his poetry.

To return to the dating of *The Laurel*. The appearance of *The Popingay* in stanza 132 of *The Laurel* by no means disproves Tucker's dating. On the contrary, it proves that Dyce was right to think that *The Popingay* was not the same as *Speke, Parrot*. Nonetheless, extreme skepticism might still argue that Tucker has dated, not *The Laurel*, but the event it celebrates, and that Skelton, like Dante, wrote his poem some years after the experiences upon which it centers. This is an attractive argument, but an untenable one. The horoscope of the first stanza, the ladies and their poems, existed ca. 1495 in relation to each other and to a larger whole that contained them, which must have been substantially the same poem as the *Laurel* text of 1523. The nine stanzas interpolated into the "bibliography" of this text mention fourteen works. The earliest of them, "Tryumphis of the Rede Rose," the fifth work listed, belongs to 1497-98, the latest, *Colyn Cloute*, eighth in the list, to 1522. The interpolation, therefore, occurred between the writing of *Colyn Cloute* and the publication of *The Laurel* in late 1523; but the work into which these stanzas were interpolated must have existed before 1497-98—a date already arrived at on other grounds. Moreover, the 1523 title page says that Skelton "studyously dyvysed" the poem in all its fantastic intricacy of structure at Sheriff Hutton castle, and it is the whole premise of Tucker's argument that Skelton could only have been at Sheriff Hutton with the Howards some time in the 1490s.

All the evidence converges to prove that *The Laurel* was first written ca. 1495, and published with minor revisions and the addition of nine stanzas in 1523.

This Edition

Skelton presents editorial difficulties not found in the case of other major authors. He was born and had his education in a world of written books, and lived his creative life in one increasingly dominated by the printed book. The learned intricacy of his early work, his sense that a poem was a space to be filled, ornamented, expanded, and added to, are signs of a mind that delighted in making manuscript books. Yet the boast of *Why Come Ye Nat to Courte?* (*Hec vates ille / De quo loquuntur mille*: "On these matters, the poet a thousand are talking about" [29–30]) and the form of the later satires tell us that Skelton understood, as well as the new medium's power of communication, its potential effect upon the form and content of the things communicated.

Although Skelton began as a writer for manuscript, few survive, no doubt because he wrote in the last days of the medium. There is no manuscript tradition enabling one to trace the transmission of a Skeltonic work. On the other hand, because he also wrote in the infancy of print, early editions are equally rare. The complete canon of his work represents a mixed tradition of MS and print extending over eighty years, from the earliest MSS, ca. 1490, to Stow's collected edition of 1568, a complex mixture of orthography and format, of scribes', redactors', editors', and compositors' modifications. The formidable task of analyzing the relationship of these texts to each other and to the Skeltonic originals has hardly begun.[25]

Skelton also wrote in a time of intense linguistic change. The *Middle English Dictionary* ends its collections ca. 1475, and it is conventional to consider ca. 1500 as the beginning of Early Modern English. Skelton thus straddles the boundary between the two forms of the language. Pronunciation and spelling were unstable, a situation rendered more complex in his case by his northern origins combining with a southern education. Nor has there been any detailed philological study of his language. Yet it is apparent from his texts that Skelton was remarkably learned in the forms and grammar of English, and conscious of its changes.

Finally, there is the notorious indeterminacy of fifteenth-century metrics to be considered, a phenomenon obviously related to the linguistic situation. It used to be fashionable to abuse fifteenth-century poets for incompetence. More recently, encouraged by the example of modern verse, readers have understood that fifteenth-century poets' competence has to be judged in relation to the language they were working in. In Latin, and in short measures disciplined by musical forms, these poets can be as correct as their sixteenth-century successors. In the long line, however, where regularity depends upon linguistic and cultural stability, fifteenth-century practice allows wide variations. Skelton's own long lines range from ten-syllable lines in alternating stress to a kind of fourteener. They can divide in half, in the old English manner, with stress indicated by alliteration. Sometimes, in the rhyme-royal stanza, he will cadence the half-lines in elaborate patterns according to the structure of the stanza. Often the indeterminacy of his metrical form leads to the elusively haunting rhythm that so appealed to W. H. Auden:

> A plesanter place than Ashrige is / hard were to fynde
>
> (*The Laurel*, 1459)

Fascinating and beautiful as the sounds of Skelton's verses are, however, they provide an editor little or no control over linguistic detail.

In these circumstances, it is important that as far as the materials permit, an editor should try to produce a text as faithful to Skelton's habits of orthography and format as possible, preserving in the process the openness of the text to the reader so typical of Skelton. In the case of *The Laurel*, this requires a text that reveals its origins as a manuscript book, lightly punctuated, idiosyncratically but learnedly spelled. It will not obscure the signs of variation in rhythm and meter, and it will respect the poet's profound knowledge of his language. It will preserve his playful editorializing, in the form of marginal notes, headings, and interpolated comment. Inevitably, in the present state of knowledge, many of the decisions the editor makes toward these ends will be tentative. Yet if Skelton and his readers are to be served, they have to be made, for, as I have said elsewhere in connection with the text of *Speke, Parrot*, critical theories about Skelton's poetry are often really theories about the nature and relationships of his surviving texts.[26]

As we have seen, *The Laurel* survives in a now-fragmentary but once complete manuscript (*A*) of very good quality, probably representing the first version of the poem; in a printed text (*B*) based on a different manuscript of similar orthography representing the revised version; and in a reprint of the latter (*C*). Text *B* was almost certainly published in consultation with Skelton himself. Unfortunately, as its omissions and many errors show, Skelton's role did not extend to proofreading, although he probably specified the general design of the book. Text *C* supplies *B*'s omissions and corrects many of its errors. It also contributes some of its own, and because seventy years of change in the sounds and orthography of the language separate it from the original, it is the least authentic textually. It also omits Skelton's marginalia. *A*, the best text, contains less than half of the poem. None of these texts is complete, and any edition must draw to some extent upon all of them.

There have been three significant editions in modern times: Dyce (1843), Hammond (1927), and Scattergood (1983).[27] Each approaches the problem differently. Dyce followed *B*, emending freely from *A* and *C*. He modernized the punctuation and, in the case of the Latin, the spelling. The result is a version of the poem that, despite its antique appearance, Skelton would have found peculiar in detail. Yet Dyce was an accurate as well as a sensitive and very learned editor, and the poor quality of *B* justifies the freedoms he took with it whenever *A* or *C* seemed preferable.

Eleanor Prescott Hammond printed a transcript of *A*, drawing upon *B* and *C* for the missing parts, and emending very little. This looks like a reasonable attempt to make the best of the available texts, yet to an attentive eye the result is a pair of fragments joined together, their separate styles of spelling and general presentation jostling each other with no attempt made to harmonize them. The transcripts, too, are wildly inaccurate. There are upwards of eighty errors in Hammond's text.

John Scattergood takes a more conventional approach. Following Dyce very closely,[28] he takes *B* as his copy because it is "the earliest and best," and emends very sparingly, thus producing a corrected reprint of *B*. Yet *B* is apparently later than *A*; and although it is more complete than *A*, it is less complete than *C*, and textually inferior to both *A* and *C*. In the case of these texts, completeness is not the same as textual quality, a point we can prove with Scattergood's text.

Like most editors, Scattergood emends rhyme words more readily than others, a reasonable proceeding because rhyme often reveals corruptions that would otherwise escape detection, and guides an editor in correcting them. Rhyme words, in effect, form a separate group, and if one assumes that they are at least as accurate as the rest of the text (they are probably more accurate), then their treatment implies a judgment of the accuracy of the rest of the text.

Applying this principle to Scattergood's old-spelling text of *The Laurel*, based on *B*, one finds that excluding the envoys and words repeated in refrains, there are 1,428 rhyme words, of which Scattergood emends 18, or 1.26 percent. In the remainder of the text there are approximately 8,830 words. These numbers are just large enough to allow statistical extrapolation, and if we apply Scattergood's judgment, that some 1.26 percent of the rhyme words are incorrect, to the rest of the text, we should expect to find about 110 to 115 errors in it. Scattergood, though, emends only about 70 readings. This leaves approximately 45 errors undetected, by the editor's own standard of judgment; and if we add to them the 30 or so errors he has himself introduced into the text, half of them substantial, we find that we have a text that still harbors upwards of 75 errors.

These figures, of course, are not to be taken too literally. To begin with, they are based on an attempt to distinguish between trivial emendations (of which the *B* text requires many), editorial error, and significant changes requiring judgment. This is not easy. If an editor preserves *dwte* for "duty" (212), are his changes of *wit* (358, 680, 1302) and *wiht* (455, 733) to "with" trivial corrections, considered decisions, or unintentional imitations of Dyce? If he keeps *fole/stol* (207–8), why in the pair *medytacyons/contemplacyouns* (1413–15) does he alter the second suffix to *-yons*? Decision or inadvertence? Easier though it would be to count all changes made to the original, the difficulty of separating mistakes from emendations would remain, and the result would be an inflated estimate of error in the original.

Yet this test is useful because it provides a fair estimate of the amount of error one should expect to find, and is a guide to the quality of an original as well as a check on editorial method.[29] Contemporary editorial practice is based on reverence for the copy-text, and yet there are few less rewarding occupations than the laborious reproduction of a poor original.[30]

A is better than *B* and so, fragmentary or not, must be used, and *B* and *C* must supply the remainder of the poem. So far Hammond was right. The difficulty is to make a single entity out of these differing sources. There is a common form of spelling, punctuation, and format to be settled upon, and the inferior texts must defer to the superior, for, as Dogberry says, "And two men ride of a horse, one must ride behind." Consequently *A*, the earlier and superior text, must be the copy-text for those portions it preserves, and the control-text for the treatment of its companions. Although it would be an exaggeration to claim that the result is a restoration of *A*, it is nonetheless a text very similar to *A*. The major difference is that this text includes the nine stanzas added in 1523 (133–41), and the "addicyon" to *Phyllyp Sparowe*, presumably inserted into the poem at the same time. Both would have been absent from the earlier *A* version.

SPELLING. The easiest way to reconcile differently spelled texts is to modernize them, but Skelton is not a suitable subject for modernization, which would tend to obscure the original sound, sense, and effect of his language. A line like "Hard to make owght of that is nakid nowght" (1199) is funny, racy, musical, and idiomatic in the original. A modern version would seem dull, prosy, perhaps ungrammatical, so the old spelling, either of *A* or *B*, must be retained. As we have seen, *B*'s text was based on a MS similar in orthography to *A*. Yet the compositor was sufficiently confused by the hand and spelling of his copy to make many errors. The editor who detects and emends these, even if *B* is his copy-text, must do so on the basis of *A* or *C*, itself a reprint of *B* corrected by reference either to *A* or a MS very like it. Editorial logic, that is, consistently leads towards *A*, whether an editor realizes it or not; and since the spelling of both *A* and of *B*'s copy seems to have been Skelton's, it is only logical that *A*'s spelling should provide the standard for the treatment of text from both *B* and *C*. Merely to defer to the text in hand will produce a noticeable and confusing mixture of styles.

In principle it is not difficult to make *A*'s spelling standard for the text of *The Laurel*. What is required is a concordance to *A*, which then provides a guide for the adjustment of *B* and *C*. *A*'s spelling, however, is typical of its period in being consistent in general principles, but inconsistent in certain details, and it would be misleading to produce a text that obscured this kind of variation. *With* for instance appears as *withe* (the predominant form), *with, wythe, wyth*, and *wᵗ*; and the spelling can vary in the same stanza. Similarly the ending *-il* can appear as *-ille* (most frequent), *-ill, -il, -ylle, -yl*, and even *-el*. These are not significant variations, of course, but they should be represented in the adaptation of *A*'s forms to *B*'s text. A more interesting kind of variation involves the letters that gave *B*'s compositor trouble, especially *a, e,* and *o*. Sometimes one of these letters is indistinguishable to a transcriber, who must decide the case upon probabilities. This is not always easy. *Work* (n.) appears as *worke, warke*, pl. *workis, workkis*. At 223 the vowel in *workkis* could be *a* or *o*, and there is no guidance to be had from the relative frequency of the spellings. Similarly we find *thonke, thonk, thanke*, and *thankkis*; and the vowel is equivocal in the last two, though more likely to be *a* than *o*. Both the spellings and the letter-forms lead one to wonder whether there is not an indeterminacy in the hand itself quite foreign to modern standards of notation.

It seems important that the text should represent this feature of *A*'s orthography, almost certainly Skelton's own, as well as its characteristic and unequivocal forms. The reader will know that variations in spelling stem from a single source, not a promiscuous confusion of sources, and that such indeterminacy as attaches to the adoption of *A*'s spelling for *B*'s text is a feature of the original itself.

PUNCTUATION. Modernized punctuation damages Skelton's text as badly as modernized spelling, breaking up his rhythm with unnecessary, sometimes misleading attempts at precision. *A*'s punctuation is light and usually, though not invariably, helpful. It consists of the *virga*, equal to the modern comma, the colon, and the period. Sometimes *virga* and colon are used together. Another habit of *A*, not convincingly reproducible in print, is to use spacing to represent punctuation.[31] The present text, more heavily punctuated, similarly restricts itself to comma, period, and colon. I have used the *virga*, but sparingly, to suggest or emphasize the rhythmical pattern where it might not be obvious.

FORMAT. *A*'s arrangements of lines and stanzas are preserved. Stanza numbers and the missing *capitulum* headings are supplied. Since the latter correspond to changes of scene in the narrative, and are also related to a numerological scheme of composition, this is not too difficult, although absolute certainty is not possible in some cases. I have also ignored a minor convention of modern printing that falsifies, if only slightly, Skelton's intention. Like any well-educated person of his time, Skelton was bilingual in English and Latin. There was a continual commerce between the two languages in his speech and writing—a fact of English life, incidentally, which Shakespeare was to represent comically in Holofernes, the schoolmaster of *Love's Labours Lost*, but which he represented in himself by the ease with which he, like his educated contemporaries, adapted his Latin vocabulary to English. It seems not to have occurred to Skelton to parade his Latin by writing or printing Latin phrases, proper names or titles in a distinctive script. He mixed the languages in his texts as in his vocabulary. I have not, therefore, distinguished Latin typographically because it is Latin, but because it is otherwise separate from the text, as when Skelton says of his Latin satire against an adversary that it is "interpolated" (741a).

Skelton's "bibliography" has also posed problems. A mixture of descriptive phrases and titles names the books listed by Occupacioun, and the difficulty is to tell the difference. "The Boke to Speke Wele or be Stille" might be a title, the book a translation of Alberto of Brescia's *Tractatus de doctrina dicendi et tacendi*. Yet Skelton says "or be Stille" not "and be Stille," so that the second phrase sounds more like an ironic comment than part of the title. MS *A*'s conventions of punctuation and capitalization leave the reader free to separate title from comment or not, as he pleases. Modern convention is inflexible, forcing an editor into decisions that either obscure the ambiguity or expose it too plainly, for example (1169):

The Boke to Speke Wele, or be stille.

This might remind a reader of line 82, "Better a dum mowthe than a braynles skulle," and so although the punctuation is unsubtle it is better than,

The Boke to Speke Wele or Be Stille

—which might sound like nothing but the title of a dull book.

EMENDATION. Since *A* is the basis of this text, readings from *B* and *C* are admitted only when *A* is apparently wrong. There are two exceptions. *B*'s *yone* (739) and *I make yow sure* (993), both probably revisions, are obviously superior to the *A* readings, and it would be inflexibility not to adopt them. *B* is treated more freely. It is not a good text, abounding in error. Editorial judgment, supported by the rhyme-test, suggests that in the nonrhyming portions of the text supplied by *B* there are some 50–60 substantial errors. Those of which I feel reasonably certain I have emended and noted. *C* supplies *B*'s omissions, corrects some of its errors, and supplies the Second Envoy. Because its corrections are based on a good MS, perhaps *A* itself, they are treated respectfully.

Finally, the marginalia printed in *B* are an important, often funny part of the text, consisting mostly of quotations in Latin from the Bible and classical authors. Since Skelton evidently quoted from memory he sometimes got a text or a reference wrong, and sometimes the compositor garbled his copy. These mistakes are corrected, their presence indicated by square brackets. Sometimes, though, Skelton altered a quotation for his own purposes, and these changes are kept. The correct form is noted in the commentary, where the reader will also find translations. Where possible I have given detailed references for all these quotations, always indicating non-Skeltonic matter by square brackets.

In a more perfect world, *A* would have survived intact, providing not only an excellent, authoritative text, but probably also telling the date of composition according to Skelton's private calendar.[32] As things are, any edition of *The Laurel* has to be a composite and a compromise. This one aims to reconstruct, as closely as the materials and the present state of knowledge allow, a text as similar as possible to Skelton's own.

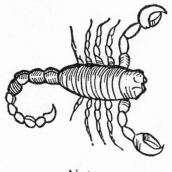

Notes

1. William Ringler, "John Stow's Editions of Skelton's *Workes* and of *Certaine Worthye Manuscript Poems*," *Studies in Bibliography* 8 (1956): 215–17. On f. 207v of MS *A*, someone practicing handwriting has written "Unto my coussin John ryche man of ⟨. . .⟩ London marchaunte taylor of Londo⟨. . .⟩". Stow was a merchant tailor.

2. Omitting 1185–1369, added ca. 1522–23, there are 193 lines to be accommodated, requiring 10 MS pages (1 quire), thus allowing 2 pages for concluding matter.

The revised version has 378 lines, needing 19-20 pages (2 quires), leaving 4 pages for the concluding matter.

3. First interpreted by Henry Bradley, "Two Puzzles in Skelton," *Academy*, 1 August 1896.

4. The quality of Skelton's suriving texts varies. In spelling, punctuation, and format, most represent the habits as well as some of the errors of compositors. Cotton Vitellius E.X. is a witness to Skelton's own conception of the MS format of one of his works.

5. Robert S. Kinsman and Theodore Yonge, *John Skelton: Canon and Census* (Renaissance Society of America: Monograph Press, 1971), 71.

6. "Linked error . . . is the only proof of derivative copy" (Gary Taylor, *Three Studies in the Text of "Henry V"* (Oxford: Clarendon Press, 1979), 54.

7. On this kind of authorial repetition, see Ernst Honigman, *The Stability of Shakespeare's Text* (Lincoln: University of Nebraska Press, 1965), 157: ". . . some writers, especially fast ones, tend to repeat words just as much as copyists." See also pp. 77, 86ff.

8. Rare in *B*. Other examples: *thankkis* (429), *turrettis* (459).

9. On Skelton's origins, see Edwards, 29 and n. 1; Pollet, 6ff.

10. E.g., *whyte/kyte* (*Elynour Rummynge*, 424-25). The pseudo-archaic spellings *wright* and *whight* show that genuinely archaic spellings such as *higth* and *hyght* do not represent Skelton's pronunciation.

11. *C*'s compositor was so confused that he printed stanza 48, line 5 in error for the fifth line of stanza 49. See textual note.

12. The envoy to *The Douty Duke of Albany* (1523) is so similar that the two must be contemporary. See Nelson, 201-2.

13. See Dyce, 2:317; Nelson, 196-205; also Nelson, "Skelton's Quarrel with Wolsey," *PMLA* 51 (1936): 385-96; Nelson and Edwards, "The Dating of Skelton's Later Poems," *PMLA* 53 (1938): 608-10; Pollet, 135-49.

14. Helen Stearns [Sale], "The Date of the *Garlande of Laurell*," *MLN* 5 (1928): 314-16.

15. Nelson, *PMLA* 51:386-88; Edwards, 228; also I. A. Gordon, *John Skelton* (Melbourne: Melbourne University Press, 1943), 57.

16. Melvin J. Tucker, "Skelton and Sheriff Hutton," *ELN* 4 (1967): 254-59.

17. "The Ladies in Skelton's 'Garland of Laurel,' " *RQ* 22 (1969): 333-45.

18. Owen Gingerich and Melvin J. Tucker, "The Astronomical Dating of Skelton's *Garland of Laurel*," *HLQ* 32 (1968-69): 207-20.

19. *HLQ* 32:212.

20. Leigh Winser, " 'The Garlande of Laurell': Masque Spectacular," *Criticism* 19 (1977): 51-69.

21. Nelson, 188-90, dates *Colyn Cloute*.

22. Nelson, 49, 54, 63.

23. Nelson, 158-74; Brownlow, "Speake Parrot," *ELR* 1 (1971): 7, n.11.

24. Dyce, 2:327.

25. See, however, R. S. Kinsman, "A Lamentable of Kyng Edward the IIII," *HLQ* 29 (1966-67): 95-108; also Carol M. Meale, "The Compiler at Work: John Colyns and BL MS Harley 2252," in Derek Pearsall, ed., *Manuscripts and Readers in Fifteenth-Century England* (Cambridge: D. S. Brewer, 1983), 82-103.

26. *ELR*, 1:7.

27. Dyce, 1:359-427; Eleanor Prescott Hammond, ed., "The Garland of Laurell," in *English Verse between Chaucer and Surrey* (Durham, N.C.: Duke University Press, 1927), 336-67; John Scattergood, ed., *John Skelton: The Complete Poems* (London and New Haven, 1983), 312-58.

28. Dyce's mistakes are few and insignificant, but when he makes them, Scattergood follows him, e.g., *lytell* for *lytyll* (285), *baudry* for *bawdry* (609). From this one infers that a copy of Dyce was the basis of Scattergood's text.

29. See appendix 2.

30. A. E. Housman, ed., *D. Iunii Iuvenalis Saturae* (London: Grant Richards, 1905), v: "This classic, like many more, had suffered some hurt from the reigning fashion of the hour, the fashion of leaning on one manuscript like Hope on her anchor and trusting to heaven that no injury will come of it."

31. E.g., 109: "How be it   it were hard to constru this lecture"

32. Nelson, 161–65.

Introduction 2

The Poem: Setting in Place and Time

Skelton was in his early thirties when he wrote *The Laurel* at Sheriff Hutton in 1495. He was a graduate of Cambridge who held the degree of Poet Laureate from Oxford and, apparently, Louvain, as well as Cambridge; and on the evidence of *The Laurel* he had already written a great deal in prose and verse. He was an energetic, brilliant young man, one of the best educated of English poets and, as Wordsworth said of him, "a demon in point of genius." Of this early work only three datable major examples survive: the translation of the *Historical Library* of Diodorus Siculus; a rhyme-royal lament for the earl of Northumberland (both written in 1489), and *The Bowge of Courte* (written after August 1482, and before 1495).[1]

This is virtually all that is known of Skelton's early life. Modern biographies, of which there are several, seem to know more, yet to an extent probably not realized by the biographers themselves, the life these works describe is largely a fiction extrapolated from Skelton's poems, many of them vaguely, even inaccurately dated. Skelton's biographers often confuse life and literature, their interest in the poetry mainly historical, their literary taste formed upon models very different from Skelton. There is not much evidence in the academic writing on Skelton of enjoyment of his poetry for its own sake. E. P. Hammond, who disliked Skelton and his poetry about equally, presents an extreme case; but others, who have derived great pleasure from research into his career, can be just as insensitive to his writing. Nelson, the most accurate and imaginative of Skelton students, was capable of emending *Few men* to *Fewmes* ("deer-droppings") in the line

> Few men can telle now where the hynde calf gose
>
> (26)

—ruining one of Skelton's most gracefully cadenced lines. H. L. R. Edwards laid a dead hand on the same stanza when he emended *mose* to *wose*. He did this because he was certain that Skelton's "decoration . . . is the purest tautology"; his emendation ensured that "silt of the miry wose [i.e. 'ooze']'' should be ''only a rhetorical triplication of the single notion 'mud'.'' Yet *mose* is a perfectly good word, represented in modern Northern English by ''moss,'' and not all mosses are miry, at least not all of the time.[2]

The best academic effort to give Skelton his due is still C. S. Lewis's, a model of well-meant, beautifully written incomprehension. Skelton's meter strikes Lewis as chaotic, his forms either labored or artless; naturally enough, there is little left for him to like except what appeals to him in the poet's character or the content of his writing. So with praise for his tenderness, playfulness, and whimsical charm, Lewis concludes that this most professional of early English writers was a gifted amateur, ''always in undress,'' but ''an unmistakable individual, a man we have met.''[3]

Not surprisingly, although Skelton has been a lively influence on English poetry in this century,[4] he remains little known to the makers of curricula and anthologies. He is the victim of the historicist's idea that the purpose of poetry is to tell us about the past. Applied to Skelton (or to anyone else), that notion only produces modern fictions. The truth of the matter is surely that the purpose of history is to explain such things as poetry. The poetry is the primary value. If, as Lewis says, Skelton ''stands out of the streamy historical process,'' this is not because he was an eccentric priest or, in some moods, a whimsical charmer who happened to write things down, but because he was a poet who made things that have proved remarkably lasting.

The Laurel is one of Skelton's most intricately contrived poems, meant to last, an apologia for, as well as a demonstration of, his poetic character. It is a poetic microcosm centered on its maker, *Poeta Skelton* as he calls him, who is narrator and chief actor in it. To make this little world, Skelton has drawn upon the whole range of his technique, so that to read *The Laurel* is to be introduced to the entire larger world of Skelton's poetry. Nevertheless, although *The Laurel* is very inclusive in one way, in another it is equally exclusive. It presents the world of *Poeta Skelton*, not of Skelton the priest (he was not yet ordained) or Skelton the schoolmaster, or even Skelton the man. The interests of these other Skeltons appear only insofar as they provide material for his writing or impinge upon his poetic career.

This distinction is important, and Dyce, who failed to make it, has misled generations of readers with a much-quoted, amusing, wrongheaded remark:

> In one respect the *Garlande of Laurell* stands without a parallel: the history of literature affords no second example of a poet having deliberately written sixteen hundred lines in honour of himself.

—or, more briefly, the poem is "unparalleled in its egotism."[5] This is not true. A poet's egotism is not proportionate to the number of lines he devotes to himself; and in any case much of *The Laurel* praises other people. Dyce must have thought the poem was simply about Skelton, a mistake he would never have made about, say, *The Prelude*. He read it as part allegory (without explaining the allegory), part autobiography, without noticing that whatever its relationship to real events, the poem is a fiction. He did not notice that *Poeta Skelton*, as we meet him in the poem, is a vulnerable, shy, rather timid man. His wonderful dream, possibly caused by too much drink, is as comical to him as it is moving and delightful, and he presents it with a complexity of tone that few readers in modern times have appreciated. Skelton the man may have been all that the jest-books and popular tradition say (though one may doubt it); *Poeta Skelton* is a different person. As an egotist, he is not in the competition with Dante, Milton, or Wordsworth.

The Laurel, then, is not autobiography communicated, through some quirk of the late medieval mind, in rhyme royal and a dream-vision. It is a work of art, much of it carefully hidden. Undoubtedly, like Boccaccio before him and Spenser after him, Skelton believed that poetry was a learned, even occult art, its true meaning and form always hidden from the casual or uninitiated reader. This was as true of the cosmos itself as it was of poetry; the poet who hid his meaning under a "dark conceit" was imitating the art of Dame Nature herself. The idea was a commonplace, and one of the most famous (and untranslatable) verses of the New Testament, expressed perfectly for medieval man the difficulties of reading in nature's book: "For now we perceive things as it were in a mirror, in a mystery" (1 Cor. 13:12). In Skelton's case, however, the general principle is more than a convention or a decorously accepted way of approaching certain subjects. By temperament and training he was prepared to take it up enthusiastically and seriously, and the ingeniously obscure forms of his major poems reflect a genuine fascination with the complexity of his material.

Superficially Skelton, like Lydgate, is a poet in the Chaucerian tradition; but he is the product of a different background. Chaucer was the child of prosperous parents, a Londoner, a diplomat, a civil servant, and a courtier. Skelton, on the other hand, was a northerner, probably from a modest family, perhaps trained in a monastic choir-school, and finally educated at Cambridge.[6] Although from time to time he tried without much success to be a courtier, he was always and most happily an intellectual, a poet, and later, a priest. Education was the basis of his life's career. He loved the learning that had made him. The allegorizing, typologizing habit of mind was bred into him, and with it a fascination for the intricate, the difficult, even for the occult.

The narrative of *The Laurel* is presented as a dream located precisely, though cryptically, in place and time. Skelton "studyously dyvysed" the whole poem at Sheriff Hutton castle in the Forest of Galtres in Yorkshire, but in the prologue to the vision itself, he says that the dream came to him outside the castle, in a wooded part of the forest. It is marshy ground underfoot, and there is a hunt in progress (st. 4). In some depression and turmoil of mind, musing upon the transitoriness of life and the uncertainty of fortune, he leans against the dead stump of a great oak, falls into a daydream, and—

> wheither it were of imagynacioune,
> Or of humors superflu, that often wille krepe
> Into the brayne by drynkkynge over depe,
> Or it procedid of fatalle persuasioune

(31–34)

—experiences the vision that is the subject of his poem.

The details of this setting signify time as well as place. The oak, emblem of the poet's condition, is dead not from age but the storms of misfortune, symbol of a career ended in the prime of life. It exemplifies the events that have caused the poet's depression as well as the brevity, uncertainty, and violence of life. Had Skelton fitted his whole poem with the kind of marginalia we find later on, he would probably have glossed these lines of his prologue with one or more of these biblical verses:

> Qui quasi flos egreditur et conteritur, et fugit velut umbra, et numquam in eodem statu permanet.
>
> (Job 14:2)
>
> Homo sicut foenum dies eius, tanquam flos agri sic efflorebit.
>
> (Psalm 102:15)
>
> Cum fueritis velut quercus, defluentibus foliis.
>
> (Isaiah 1:30)
>
> Non sit in recordatione, sed conteratur quasi lignum infructuosum.
>
> (Job 24:20)[7]

A long habit of thought thus relates the individual to the general pattern of life, and such, in general is the context in time of Skelton's vision. But does he time the vision more specifically? Another habit of thought, venerable in Skelton's time, associated the months of the year with certain scenes and activities: December, for instance, with hunting the boar (as in the illuminations to the *Grandes Heures du Duc de*

Berry).[8] Normally, one would expect such a stanza as Skelton's on the hunt to be part of a seasonal setting. This stanza, however, closely read, turns out to be peculiar.

"Thus stode I," says *Poeta Skelton*,

> Where harttis belluynge, embosid with distres,
> Ran on the raunge so longe that I suppose
> Few men can telle now where the hynde calf gose:
> Faire falle that foster that so wele kan bate his hownde. . . .

A great deal of hunting lore is contained in these four lines.[9] The hart, "the fairest hunting that any man may hunt after" (*MG*, 29), is a male deer at least six years old (*BSA*, Sig. E1v). He bellows when he is in rut:

> It is known that they begin to bellow fifteen days before grease time ends, especially old deer, and also if the end of August and September be wet and rainy (*MG*, 160).

Bellowing time, however, is not hunting time. That comes in grease time, when the harts are fat, which lasts from Midsummer Day (11 June in the old reckoning, St. Barnabas's day) until Holy Cross day, 14 September. With a little overlapping at either end, then, the hart season lasted from about the end of May until Michaelmas, 29 September (*BSA*, Sig. E5; *MG*, 254). The harts were then in rut, and dangerous, into October and November: wise people do not loiter in deer parks in bellowing time. Yet Skelton also tells us that the bellowing harts are "embosid with distres," exhausted, that is, with the chase, and foaming at the mouth: "When he is foamy at the mouth, we say he is *embost*" (*STH*, xxi).

Then we are told that the bellowing, embossed harts have run "on the raunge," i.e., in quest of food or the hinds, so long that no one knows where the hind calf is. This is even more perplexing.

The hind, or female deer, calves in May, and at that time, naturally they are not hunted. When the hind season opens with the closing of the season on harts, only the "barren" hinds are hunted, and the season lasts till Lent:

> And they which bear calves, in the morning when she shall go to her lair, she will not remain with her calf, but she will [keep] him and leave him a great way from her, and smiteth him with the foot and maketh him to lie down, and there the calf shall remain always while the hind goeth to feed. And then she shall call her calf in her language and he shall come to her. And that she doth so that if she were hunted her calf might be saved and that he should not be found near her. (*MG*, p. 35)

A lost calf, therefore, should mean that the hind is being hunted. The forester whom Skelton praises has so bated, or set, his hound at the game that he has engaged the whole herd, harts and hinds, simultaneously![10]

Either this is a disorderly hunt, unlikely in the royal forest of Galtres, or Skelton is writing nonsense. Or else he is doing something quite different, setting us a puzzle whose solution is that his vision is set in no one season of the year. Rather, his scheme embraces spring and fall together, represented by the mixed hunting seasons; and those two seasons stand, synecdochally, for the cycle of the whole year. Fifteenth-century readers, familiar with the hunt, would recognize the inconsistencies at once; and those attuned to Skelton's cryptic imagery might well sense in the poet's approval of the forester's odd behavior an allusion to his own approach to his subject. But in this context, what would the whole year's cycle mean?

With this puzzle in mind it is time to examine the first stanza in detail. Usually passed rapidly over as a bit of stately conventional rhetoric, it is actually a very precise description of the time of the vision:

> Arrectynge my syght toward the zodiak
> The signnys twelve for to behold afar,
> When Mars retrogradant reversid his bak,
> Lorde of the yere in his orbicular,
> Put up his sworde for he kowde make no war:
> And when Lucyna plenarly did shyne,
> Scorpioune ascenddinge degrees twiys nyne. . . .

Common as these astronomical-scientific passages are in late medieval English poetry,[11] this one is rather unusual because it gives no plain indication of the season—usually the one feature of these passages accessible to the modern reader. The opening of the *Canterbury Tales* is the classic example, and Skelton's own *Bowge of Courte* begins, "In Autumpne, whan the sonne in Vyrgyne. . . ." There is a peculiarity in the first two lines as well, for Skelton could not possibly behold the twelve signs as he stood on the wet ground leaning against his oak tree. The signs are the conventional emblems of the twelve divisions of the zodiac, sometimes called houses, and named after constellations which were once a good deal closer to them than they are now. The signs themselves are not visible. The tracts of sky they describe are only readily visible at night, and even then at the latitude of Sheriff Hutton (54°N), even at midsummer, Skelton could not see all twelve. Skelton is presenting himself as a medieval illuminator would paint him, as a figure in a stylized, symbolic landscape, and the zodiac he is looking at is the kind one finds painted on ceilings and walls, or written out on paper: it is a horoscope, a diagram of the heavens describing a significant moment in time.

The following features define the celestial configuration that Skelton sees before him: Mars is retrograde; the moon is full, and the sign Scorpio is rising 18° on the cusp of the first house, or ascendant. Taken separately and out of their Skeltonic context, these details might not mean much. Mars retrogrades, i.e., appears to reverse his motion, about every two years for about three months. During that time the moon will be full twice, and each day Scorpio will rise once. The stanza, read thus, seems to describe no specific time, not even a season.

To readers accustomed to astrological descriptions of time, however, Skelton's details would make good sense, yielding a season and a time of day even without calculations. The essential features of a horoscope are the positions of the sun, the moon, the ruling planet, and the ascending sign. Since Scorpio, the nocturnal house of Mars, is rising, Mars rules this chart; and although Skelton has not specified the positions of Mars and the moon, it is a natural inference that he has told us all we need to know, and that further detail would entail repetition. That being so, Mars and the moon must be in Scorpio together. Nor is it necessary to give the sun's position, because if the moon is full, then the sun is in opposition to it, setting in Taurus.[12] Since in Skelton's time Scorpio was rising 18° at sunset in early May, we have a season and a time of day. To know whether the horoscope is more precisely timed to a particular day, one must consult tables to find, first, whether Mars, during Skelton's active lifetime, was ever retrograde in Scorpio in early May, and whether the moon was full in Scorpio at the same time.[13]

The answer is that although Mars was retrograde in May several times, only once was it in Scorpio, and on that occasion the moon was full in Scorpio at the same time. The stanza, therefore, describes a fairly rare occurrence, and we can time the vision to between 7:00 and 7:30 P.M. on 8 May 1495.[14]

This is certainly very close to the date of composition, as we have already argued. Skelton, however, did not begin with a horoscope so that scholars could date the poem. Rather, the first stanza is part of the poem's setting upon the great stage of the world, "Whereon the stars in secret influence comment." It delineates a moment of great fortune, synchronous with the happy dream that turns the narrator's misery into rejoicing, and it is judged to the half-hour, not by a fallible mechanical clock, but by the great clock of the heavens. Why, though, having named so precise a time, should Skelton then jumble the seasons of the hunt?

The horoscope contains the answer. As Gingerich and Tucker noticed, the configuration it describes had occurred almost exactly thirty-two years earlier on 2 May, 1463. If one takes the horoscope for about half-past seven on that day at Sheriff Hutton (appendix 4, fig. 2), Mars retrograde is conjunct with a full moon in Scorpio, Scorpio ascending 18°. Venus, Mercury, and the sun cluster in the seventh house. These two groups of planets, one rising, the other setting, approach a "T-square" pattern, as astrologers now call it, formed by Jupiter and Saturn below the horizon in the third house. The significant difference between the configurations of 1463 and 1495 is in the position of Jupiter.

On 2 May 1463, Jupiter is in Aquarius, the diurnal house of Saturn, the greater infortune, with whom he shares it. He is also in square aspect to Mars, the lesser infortune, and the moon. Saturn, however, at 25° Aquarius occupies not only his own house, but the precise "term" of it ruled by Jupiter, and he is in trinal aspect, a very good one, to Mars. What all this means in general is that the benign and powerful influence of Jupiter, the greater fortune, is much constricted.

On 8 May 1495, Mars, the significator of the horoscope, and his co-significators sun and moon hold much the same positions; but the relative positions of Jupiter and Saturn have changed decisively. Jupiter is now in his exaltation in Libra, and approaching the midheaven, a position very favorable to him. He is also in almost perfect trinal aspect to the sun; and he is in opposition to Saturn, now subdued in Jupiter's nocturnal house, Pisces.[15]

Astrology is a drama of character, a *psychomachia* expressed in the spatial relationships of the heavens seen from a particular place at a particular time. It is a kind of heavenly chess game. In 1463 the cold, restrictive influence blocks the native's fortunes; in 1495, when the same essential configuration of sun, moon, ruler, and ascendant recurs, Jupiter radiates beneficent influence upon the horoscope.

The relationship of these two horoscopes is so striking that Skelton can hardly have chosen the moment of his vision unaware of it. Striking as the 1495 chart is by itself, it is far more dramatic in relation to its predecessor. It announces a moment at which great but previously obstructed capacities in the "native" are released, and when one considers that *Poeta Skelton*'s vision presents a similar pattern in the form of a poetic fiction, the conclusion is irresistible that the charts, like the poem, must have a personal significance. The horoscope of 1463 must describe Skelton's nativity: 2 May 1463 was his birthday.[16]

If this is so, then on 8 May 1495, he was just beginning his thirty-third year, a number of great symbolic import.[17] If that number did indeed coincide with the recurrence and resolution of his nativity, then Skelton—or any other scientifically educated contemporary—would have awaited the time with great anticipation. Extraordinary as the hypothesis seems, it is the only one that explains the astrology of the first stanza. In the absence of a recorded birth date, it is unprovable;

but its probability will be much strengthened if it should prove the means of revealing and understanding other hitherto unknown aspects of the poem—if, in a word, it should prove useful. Such is the case.

If Skelton was born 2 May 1463, then his poetic horoscope times the dream-vision of the poem to a moment placed in the context of his whole life's career which, like a narrative poem, has a beginning, a middle, and an end. The setting in time, that is, is also related to the form as well as the content of the vision, to the spatial as well as the temporal arrangement of its parts into a coherent whole.

An ancient tradition, wonderfully summarized in one of the most popular books of Skelton's age, *Le Grand Kalendrier des Bergiers*,[18] says that a calendar year is symbolic of the life of man:

Nous bergiers disons que leage de lhomme de lxxii. ans est comme ung an seul: comprenant tousiours six ans pour ch[aq]un moys de lan. (Sig. A3)

Four seasons of the life-year correspond to the seasons of the calendar year: "jeunesse" (spring), "force" (summer), "sagesse" (autumn), and "viellesse" (winter). Each season of the life-year equals eighteen calendar years. Seventy-two is the natural term of life, and thirty-six is the term of growth, "in beauty, strength, and vigour" (Sig. A2v). Scriptural tradition says that seventy is the term of life, but Skelton seems to have preferred the *Kalendrier*'s seventy-two.

Let us assume that the time of the vision, 8 May 1495, coincided with Skelton's entry into his thirty-third year. In the *Kalendrier*'s scheme, the thirtieth year corresponds to May whose emblem in the *Kalendrier* as elsewhere, is a young man with a hawk and scepter who says of himself, "Je suis le franc roy de lannee." If, following a precedent of the time, one combines the twelve months of the year with the signs of the zodiac to produce a zodiac of human life (appendix 4, fig. 3), then May, between the signs Taurus and Gemini, occupies a place corresponding to the tenth house. May's place in the cycle of the year, then, corresponds to Jupiter's position in the 1495 horoscope. Furthermore, as one sees very clearly from the diagram, the zodiacal point representing the thirty-third year occupies the center of the tenth house. Therefore, as Jupiter, the ruling planetary deity, dominates the horoscope from the tenth house, so May rules the calendar year, and the thirty-third year rules the "year" that is the life of man. All three, planet, month, and life-year, moreover, are "culminating," just antecedent, that is, to the zeniths of their respective spheres of motion.

So we see that *Poeta Skelton* places himself in relation to three concentric circles of time: of the year, of human life, and of the cosmos. He has set himself upon a stage of time as well as of place. As the first sentence of the canons prefixed to the Alfonsine Tables says, "Time is the measurement of the motion of the *primum mobile.*"[19] Time is place in motion.

Since the scheme centers so definitely upon May, why did Skelton not simply and unequivocally set the vision in that month? As we have seen, the hunting stanza mixes hart with hind season, spring with fall, youth with age.

May as culminating point of the personal and calendrical year, corresponding to Jupiter's position in the 1495 horoscope, has a past and a future contained in its present moment, a beginning and an end. If we continue to apply Skelton's astrological-calendrical thinking to the 1495 chart, we shall see that if Jupiter in the tenth house corresponds to May, then Saturn in the fourth corresponds to November. May and November, the spring and fall of the hunting stanza, are six months apart, 180° of the sun's yearly movement through the zodiac. Laid upon the diagram of the zodiac, they are in perfect opposition. In the human "year," November is the sixty-sixth year, prelude to the end. As the month says in the *Kalendrier*:

> Toute personne de facon
> Doit penser davoir vin et pain
> Et doit prier au souverain
> Roy des cieulx pour so saulvement.
> Car en mon temps il est certain
> Que tout meurt naturellement.
>
> (Sig. A3)

Saturn/November/death, then, is the end prefigured in the horoscopes. In 1495, the predictable movement of Jupiter into the tenth house attended the zenith of the native's fortunes: the equally predictable movement of Saturn is yet to occur.

The opposition of November and May concealed in the astrology of the first stanza of *The Laurel* stands explicitly revealed in the iconography of Fakes's 1523 edition, prefaced by two woodcuts. The first, based on a very ancient motif of the scribe or writer at work, shows an old man at a desk, pointing to a manuscript.[20] This is the old poet, the man in November, putting his book (also a symbol of his life) in order. Two people watch him from behind his great chair, and the windows of the handsome Gothic study reveal a landscape such as one might have seen from a window of Sheriff Hutton Castle. The second woodcut shows a gaily dressed young man in a garden, holding a branch and a flower. It illustrates the speech-heading "Skelton Poeta," and as anyone acquainted with the subject sees immediately, it comes

CA ryght delectable trea
tyse vpon a goodly Gar
lande oꝛ Chapelet of Laurell by mayster Skelton Poete
laureat studyously dyuysed at Sherythotton Castell. In
ȳ foꝛeste of galtres/wherein ar cõpꝛysyde many ꝗ dyuers
solacyons ꝗ ryght pꝛegnant allectyues of syngular plea
sure/as moꝛe at large it doth apere in ȳ ꝑces folowynge.

.A.

STC 22610, Sig. A1. By permission of the British Library.

from a series of cuts of the months. For this is April as he so often appears among the images of time—in the *Kalendrier* itself, for instance.[21] He should really be May, but Richard Fakes must have used the closest thing he could find to the poet's instructions.

One curious final development of Skelton's conceit of time remains. The conjunction of Mars retrograde with a full moon in Scorpio did not recur until 1542 when Skelton, had he lived, would have been seventy-nine, a number outside the scope of the scheme.[22] Nonetheless, having come so far, one naturally wonders whether, following the hints in the astrology of the first stanza, in the symbolism of the woodcuts and the hunting stanza, there is not a third horoscope to be cast, representing *Poeta Skelton*'s end as the others represent his beginning and his zenith, respectively. How significant, in relation to these other charts, is the predictable movement of Saturn?

Since May and November are beginning and end in Skelton's scheme, then an ending horoscope should probably be cast for some time in November. This will preserve the Scorpian character of the prior charts, because on 1 November in Skelton's time the sun was rising 18° in Scorpio; and this also suggests that just as the year has moved 180° through its cycle from May to November, so the time of day should be moved a similar distance through the circle of the day, from evening to morning. All that remains to be set is the year. Since the horoscope is to represent the end of *Poeta Skelton*'s life, it should be set for November 1535, when Skelton would have reached the *Kalendrier*'s term of life, seventy-two. What does a horoscope for 7:30 on that day reveal?

It is sunrise, and the sun is at 18° Scorpio (appendix 4, fig. 4). Mars, lord of the ascendant, is again the significator whose aspects and position portend the fortunes of the native or, in this case, the querent. So far the symmetries of this chart in relation to the others express the simple geometry of the calendar year. The surprising and rather chilling feature is that Saturn and Jupiter have now changed places. The two planets are in close opposition, Saturn elevated in the upper sky in Leo, Jupiter below the horizon in Aquarius, and the Saturnian influence is powerful and sinister.

In the jargon of astrology, Saturn is strong because he is elevated in the ninth house, but he is also "ill-dignified," being "in his detriment" in Leo, in square aspect to the sun, and in opposition to Jupiter. In this horoscope these positions aggravate his malignity. Once again he constrains Jupiter in his own diurnal house, Aquarius. Even more portentous, Jupiter at 28° Aquarius is close to a "transit" of Saturn's position in the 1463 chart. This is very threatening to the native; and whereas in 1495 at the zenith of his fortunes, Jupiter was trine to the

sun, mutually augmenting their good influence, Saturn is now square to the sun, suppressing its benign, life-giving power at the moment of sunrise.

In fact, all the planets are looking angrily in this chart. Except for the conjunction of the sun with Mercury, there is no good aspect in it. The native is isolated, bereft of vitality and friends; only his wit and his eloquence remain. Mars, his planet, is on the cusp of the eighth house, the house of death. This horoscope, therefore, describes the predicted movement of Saturn, and the pattern adumbrated in its predecessors is completed with a touch of grand celestial drama. (The opposition of Saturn to Jupiter in Aquarius, with the sun rising in Scorpio, had not occurred since November 1475: it is not a common pattern.)

As it happens, Skelton did not live to be seventy-two, but died on 21 June 1529. As the orthodoxy of his time said, the stars influence, but do not constrain.[23] The patterns that he concealed in the prologue to *The Laurel*, however, are objective, a matter of observation, measurement, and arithmetic. They are the foundation on which the form of the vision stands.

Before dealing with the poem's form, however, it remains to be shown that Skelton's astrology explains two curious details of the setting, one of them perplexing and important.

In the fourth stanza of the prologue, *Poeta Skelton* stands against his oak-stump, "Ensowkid with fylt of the myry moose"—an odd condition in which to fall into a "traunce or . . . an extasy." As Dyce knew, the forest of Galtres around Sheriff Hutton was marshy in places. The mode of the prologue, however, is not realistic. The real Skelton is no more dreaming in the mud than he is looking up at all twelve signs at once in broad daylight at sunset, in May during November! The reason for the detail is that if Skelton was born about 7:30 P.M. on 2 May 1463, his ascending sign was Scorpio, a "fixed sign of the watery triplicity." It is a cold, watery, nocturnal, phlegmatic, northern, feminine sign, says the seventeenth-century astrologer William Lilly, and its influence is potent in "Gardens, Orchards, Vineyards, ruinous Houses near Waters, muddy, moorish Grounds, stinking Lakes, Quagmires. . . ."[24] The marshy ground is part of a symbolically composed picture of the Scorpian native in his proper setting.

The other detail is more puzzling. The vision ends when *Poeta Skelton* is awakened by the cheering of the poets in his dream. There is no more mention of the marsh, the oak, or the hunt. He wipes his eyes and looks up "to the heven sperycal":

> Where I saw Janus with his dowbill chere
> Makynge his almanak for the new yere:

He turnnyd his tirrikis, his volvell ran faste:
Goode luk this new yere! the olde yere is paste!

There follow two Latin lines attributed in the margin to *vates*, i.e., the poet, presumably Skelton himself, not his fictional persona:

Mens tibi sit consulta petis: sic consule menti:
Emula sit Jani, retro speculetur et ante.

Some have thought this to mean that Skelton finished his poem on New Year's Eve,[25] but Janus is part of a fiction. Leigh Winser apparently believes that Janus is part of the décor of the room where *The Laurel* was first staged as a masque.[26] As he says, the new year was a favorite time for feasting and masques. He is probably right to visualize Janus as painted or drawn, and not as something in "the heven sperycal," where he has no place. The difficulty in saying he is part of a masque is that we actually find him in a narrative poem; one cannot make sense of him by explaining him as something left over from another occasion and another, hypothetical form of the material. Double-faced Janus is *in* the poem, not on somebody's wall or ceiling, even if Skelton imagines him (as he imagined the details of the prologue) as if drawn by a contemporary artist.

Janus is another figure from the *horae* and calendars where, however, he does not show off his mastery of astronomy, but sits down to a hearty meal by a big fire.[27] Skelton's Janus is not presented as the month of January, but as guardian of the year, god of beginnings and endings, of entrances and exits. Evidently, he presides over the end of the poem because it too is a beginning as well as an ending. *Poeta Skelton*, waking from his dream as the recital of his works reaches a climax in the present moment with *The Laurel* itself, reenters his own waking life and its "new year." Two-faced Janus parallels the backward- and forward-looking horoscope of the first stanza; he is an iconographical version of the ancient motto-paradox, "In my beginning is my end." Skelton's distich comments on the structural significance of the parallelism, too: "You ask what well-considered meaning this might have for you? Then give your mind some consideration. Let her be like Janus. He looks before and after." What, however, is Skelton's "new year"? A poet so precise in working out his patterns of life and form must mean more than something merely metaphorical.

There is an answer to this question, but first the form of the poem must be elucidated.

The Poem: Form

Poems are made of more than words. The most obvious nonverbal element of poetry is its music, either the explicit music of melody and a singing voice or the implicit music of the speaking voice, its pitch, tone, and rhythm. There is also a silent, constructive music of the poetic form itself, most easily apparent in stanzas and lines which are often the verbal equivalent of musical phrases; but it was a general belief of the learned from the Christian culture of late antiquity to the Renaissance that the constructive music of poetry was, like the form of actual, practical music, an imitation of the form, order, reason, and proportion of creation itself. In this sense the music of poetry, as of architecture, painting, or practical music, is essentially a matter of number.[28]

When A. Kent Hieatt announced his discovery of the musico-numerical form of Spenser's *Epithalamion*,[29] the reaction of some readers was that such a form, if it really existed and was not a figment of the scholar's imagination, was not really part of the poem, being either merely decorative, and so frivolous, or else so well-hidden as to be irrelevant. The same objection can be made against the astrological and calendrical symbolism so far revealed in Skelton's poem: it is not all "in" the poem, for one thing; and insofar as any of it actually is "in" the poem, it is irrelevant to the average reader's expectations of the art of poetry. Anyone who takes for granted such a basic tenet of humanist criticism as the belief that poetry should be "simple, sensuous and passionate" is bound to be repelled by scholarship that implies the contrary: that in some cases at least, it can be hermetic, rational, and mathematical. Yet much in the artistic forms of the medieval world is encoded metaphor, and poems and musical compositions thus make statements to the initiated that are nonverbal and nonmusical, respectively. Numerical form in particular is not literary; it is found in all forms of art, literature among them, and its appearance in a work of literature, therefore, does not necessarily derive from a literary antecedent. An author's general education in the seven liberal arts, or his knowledge of a specific art, such as music or architecture, may underlie his use of numerical form.

The numerical form of *The Laurel* is an example. According to conventional literary history, *The Laurel* is a dream-allegory in the Chaucerian tradition. Yet Chaucerian precedent explains comparatively little in the poem, including its form. According to John MacQueen, there is little sign of real numerological interest in Chaucer.[30] He makes a "decorative" use of number in *The Parliament of Fowls*, but he does not express his theme numerically, neat and graceful as his numbers are. In fact, says MacQueen, "The most interesting and elaborate British examples of literary numerology in the period come from areas well to the north and west of the metropolitan culture within which [Chaucer] flourished" (96). This might relate Skelton's numerology to his own northern background; yet even so, there is no evidence that he knew such numerically composed works as *Pearl, Sir Gawain*, and *The Kyngis Quair*.[31] Skelton's use of number in *The Laurel* is just as likely to be derived from his education and from other interests, especially music and alchemy. Numerical form in music of Skelton's era is well-documented, and musicians whom Skelton knew composed numerically, among them the remarkable John Browne who set "Woffully Araid" (probably by Skelton) in the Fayrfax manuscript.[32] Skelton was musically trained himself.[33] He was also interested in alchemy, as the alchemical phrases that turn up in his work prove. Alchemy provided Skelton (in *Speke, Parrot*) with a metaphor for the mystery of poetic making, and it seems also to have been an important source of his understanding of poetic form, according to which number is one aspect of the formal principle.[34] Thomas Norton's *Ordinall of Alchemy* (1477), one of the most influential alchemical poems of Skelton's age, is surprisingly clear on this subject. According to Norton, in the process of the alchemical "work" called *Conjunction*, the artist must combine his elements grammatically, rhetorically, logically, arithmetically, musically, and astrologically. Grammar ensures concordance, rhetoric gives the tincture purity and beauty, and logic joins "trewe kindes not sophisticate." Arithmetic joins the elements "By suttill Numbers proportionally." Music brings harmony to the proportions, and astrology "fortunes" the workings of the elements.[35]

It is a pity that Norton omits geometry from his scheme; otherwise this passage of his poem is a very neat expression of the widespread idea that the seven liberal arts encompass unity of knowledge, unity of the cosmos (i.e., of the thing known), and unity of the thing made from knowledge, the work of art. What Norton says of the alchemist's art also applies to all other major forms of medieval art. As a principle it was most obviously visible to the educated eye in the architecture of the greater churches and cathedrals. Educated readers would have perceived it at work in *The Divine Comedy*, and it looks as if Skelton expected readers to see it in *The Laurel*. For there is no doubt that each of the liberal arts has its role in the deployment of Skelton's materials. The *trivium* (grammar, logic, and rhetoric) governs the poem's language; the *quadrivium* (arithmetic, music, astronomy, and geometry) governs its numbers, and to these we now turn.

One of Skelton's strongest signals to a reader about his poem's numbers has never been generally available. During the preparation of the now-fragmentary MS, Skelton began to include headings indicating the division of the poem into parts called *capitula*. Three of these survive (I, VIII, IX), enabling one to see that the *capitula* correspond to the major incidents of the vision, and that there must be eleven of them. (The argument leading to this conclusion, which is fairly complicated, is given in appendix 1.)

The number eleven is not a favourite with numerologists because in the standard authorities it stands for transgression of the law and sin.[36] It has some poetic standing, however, because in Psalm 118 there are twenty-two sections, one for each letter of the Hebrew alphabet, which the makers of prayer books arranged in eleven pairs; hence the number twenty-two was a sacred number, much used in the grouping of parts of works, i.e., of books, chapters, stanzas, and lines.[37] In *The Laurel*, eleven and its multiples appear in ways that cannot be accidental. Of the eleven *capitula*, II–IV seem to consist of twenty-two, eleven, and eleven stanzas. In the main part of the poets' procession, presented in nine stanzas, there are thirty-three poets, and in the poem's revised version *cap.* XI has thirty-three stanzas. In these instances, as in *cap.* VI (about the garden of poetry), which has nine stanzas, and in the devotion of *cap.* IX to the ladies' poems, the numbers nine and thirty-three will symbolize poetry and the Muses. And although there are five *capitula* in the poem's first part, one cannot be sure of the exact division points and stanza counts. Yet there are also eleven poems presented to eleven ladies, and the number of works in Skelton's "bibliography" in the final text (1523) is probably fifty-five.

These elevens, however, continually turn into twelves. The *Prologue* added to the *capitula*, and Skelton added to the ladies, both make twelve. Less obviously, the three English poets added to the preceding thirty-three make thirty-six, a multiple of twelve. The eleven *capitula*, too, fall into two well-distinguished parts disposed about the central one, VI, and the number of narrative stanzas in each part is a multiple of twelve, eighty-four in the first, and sixty in the second, the two parts in the proportion 7:5.

Centricity is an important principle, too. In the poets' procession, nine stanzas deploy the main body of poets, and in the fifth, central stanza we are told that "blessyd Bacchus was in ther company" (355). In the whole procession, moreover, with the English poets in the place of honour at the rear, Bacchus is in the exact center, eighteen poets before him, eighteen after. *Cap.* VI, about the garden of poetry, comes at the center of the vision, thus imitating its archetype the Garden of Eden, reputed to be at the center of the world.

Skelton's most delicate and imaginative deployment of number, order, and centricity is reserved for the countess of Surrey and her ladies. *Poeta Skelton* offers her a rhyme-royal poem in four stanzas comparing her to six famous ladies. Her two young unmarried daughters by the earl come next, and each receives a two-stanza poem. The elder,

Lady Elizabeth, is given three ladies to compare herself with, her younger sister Muriel just one. Then the countess's married daughter by a previous marriage, Lady Anne Dacre of the South, receives two stanzas and four ladies. In number of ladies, therefore, she precedes both Lady Muriel and Lady Elizabeth, although she yields to them both in position. All three as sisters share the same social rank, and receive the same kind of poem in the noble rhyme-royal stanza. The poems' form, then, symbolizes the exact precedence of these ladies. Lady Anne's age and marriage put her in one way next after her mother, but her half-sistership makes her yield place to the two younger girls.

Of the seven ladies-in-waiting, each receives a poem in a form specific to her. They too appear in order of precedence, but because Skelton evidently preferred some ladies to others, and put many individualizing touches into the poems, their forms and their order seem natural, even accidental. C. S. Lewis treats these poems as examples of Skelton's "real artlessness," but that is a mistaken estimate of them.[38]

First, simple numbers. In the MS, the waiting-ladies' poems number a hundred and seventy-four lines, a number whose digits add up to twelve. The seven poems are grouped three and three about the central one, addressed to Isabell Pennel. The first three poems contain sixty-seven lines, a number whose digits add up to thirteen: the second group of three contains seventy-six lines, and again the digits equal thirteen.[39] Sixty-seven is a mirror reflection of seventy-six and, as we shall see, imitates the physical arrangement of the ladies about their mistress and her daughters. Stanza numbers are also significant. The first group of poems has five plus four plus two stanzas, eleven in all. The second group has four plus three plus four, also eleven.

The central poem of the seven is made of nine three-line stanzas, plus four lines imitating bird-song. Nine and three are the numbers of poetry and perfection, and here the form symbolizes the little girl's beauty. The four lines of bird-song have a peculiar effect. Since the nine-stanza poem is a finished little work, the bird-sounds do not give an impression of something incomplete just trailing off, but of something ecstatically prolonged, an experience out of the usual dimension of time. The line-total of this poem, thirty-one, also "reflects" the number thirteen, found in the line-totals of the flanking poems. And it is certainly surprising that those totals, seventy-six and sixty-seven, add up to a hundred forty-three, the multiple of eleven and thirteen!

Since as the numbers tell us, the ladies are grouped symmetrically about Isabell Pennel, they are not presented in simple linear order, but in two groups of three, with Margery Wentworthe leading the first group, Margarete Hussey the second. The lovely poem that Skelton wrote for Mistress Margarete suggests that she also stood high in his personal order of precedence. He arranges her poem in elevens: the lines of her stanzas are two plus eleven plus two plus eleven plus two. In the 1523 text, the lines are rearranged, by whom one cannot say, and the couplets turned into quatrains. This changes the total number of lines in the set of poems to one hundred and eighty, and simplifies the numerological design without much change in its effect. For in both versions, by means of his numbers, Skelton has grouped his ladies about their mistress and her daughters in a half-circle. In the MS version, the reversed numbers seventy-six and sixty-seven show that the "wings" of the semicircle reflect each other. With the quarto's change to one hundred eighty lines, this effect is lost, but the half-circle is more obvious.

The really important thing is that in both versions, *Isabell Pennel is the center, and in both, the meaning of the arrangement emerges from the central line of her poem:*

> Star of the morow gray
>
> (988)

Asked to make some return to the ladies who have so gracefully saluted his poetic gift, Skelton has turned them into a constellation twinkling about their mistress:

> I wille my self apply
> Trost me intentyvely
> Yow for to stellify
>
> (961–63)

—as he tells Jane Hasset. But the vision itself centers upon a star. Admitted to the garden of poetry in *Cap*. VI, *Poeta Skelton* hears one of the legendary poets, Virgil's Iopas, singing to his harp. His song is of the sun, the moon, and the stars, of the earth and its seasons; and at the center of *his* song we find:

> . . . that pole artike whiche dothe remayne
> Behynde the tayle of Ursa so clere.
>
> (695–96)

This is the central image and symbol of the poem, for as Skelton also says in his prefatory verses:

> Eterno mansura die dum sidera fulgent
> Equora dumque tument hec laurea nostra virebit.

"As long as the everlasting stars shall shine in eternal day . . . so long my laurel will flourish." To be a star is to last forever, to exist fully realized, perfect, beyond time and mutability. In the natural sphere the condition is intimated in symbols of perfection like the song of the nightingale prolonging Isabell Pennel's poem.

The meaning of Skelton's numbers, then, is that eleven, standing for the imperfect, human, time-bound order, is also Skelton's own number because his beginning, his horoscope tells us, is in May, the fifth month, his end in November, the eleventh. As the number of deficiency and sin, eleven also aptly represents the dangers of his nativity and character, continually threatened by strains of malignity within and without (see appendix 4). For this very reason, however, for Skelton eleven is also the number of possibility and of poetry revealing beauty and perfection in the forms of time. This is why the structure of the poem is based on a continual equivocation between the numbers eleven and twelve, which is the number of completion, perfect order and permanence, standing for the circles of the years and the zodiac. These are the measure of time, but they are also the symbols of eternity.

If the grand theme of the poem is that poetry is a creative, redemptive art that defeats time, then the entire vision should be formed in twelves as well as elevens. As the ladies form a constellation within it, so it should form a poetic zodiac. At first this seems not to be so. Since there are eleven scenes, one would expect the twelves (the more hidden numbers in this scheme) to appear in the stanza count, as indeed is the case in *caps*. I–V (eighty-four) and VII–XI (sixty), one hundred forty-four altogether, flanking the central scene as the ladies group themselves about Isabell Pennel. But in the whole vision, subtracting the prologue and the rhyme-royal stanzas to the ladies which are not part of the vision-narrative, there are one hundred fifty-three stanzas, and this number seems to have no connection with twelve.

Every now and again a hypothesis in literary scholarship behaves as a hypothesis should. The reader will remember that in dating the poem, we identified a group of nine later stanzas which Skelton interpolated in the 1523 text. If we remove these, one hundred forty-four stanzas of narrative remain in the vision, and twenty-four in *cap*. XI, the recital of Skelton's list of works on which his claim to fame is based. Thus the hypotheses of date and number corroborate each other, a satisfying result. By adding nine stanzas, Skelton lost the neatness of the original total, but the idea of perfection remained in his new number; for one hundred fifty-three is "one of the best-known of all symbolic numbers," the number of fish that Peter catches (John 21:11), hence in its simplest interpretation symbolic of the number of the saved who enter into everlasting life.[40]

Moreover, since the stanzas of the two sets of *capitula* flanking the central one now form multiples of twelve, and add up to the square of twelve, it is more clearly apparent the form of the vision is not the same as its simple linear narrative. Just as the *Kalendrier*'s human year of twelve six-year months forms the cycle of human life, so Skelton's narrative forms a cycle, a kind of poetic day turning about its center, the garden of poetry, where Flora and the Muses dance about the laurel where the phoenix burns. This must be why the awakening poet sees Janus, and advises himself to look behind and before. The vision symbolizes a whole career, with a beginning, a middle, and an end; and so its proper form is the circle, image of completeness and perfection.

Skelton's interest in numerical form was so strong that it affected his life as well as his poetry. His adoption of eleven as a personal number, certainly connected with the role of the eleventh month in his astrological scheme, may also be related to the odd fact that if one applies to his own name the number-code under which he attacked Roger Stathum (751a,b), the result (9.4.8.13 / 18.10.2.11.19.4.13) adds up to one hundred eleven. Numbers also affected the private calendar by which he dates his poems. It began between 29 October and 17 November 1488, and it has been thought that it commemorated either his first laureation or his entry into royal service.[41] Yet it may be connected with neither. As we can now see, the time of year, when the sun is in Scorpio, is connected with Skelton's own horoscope. The number 1488, moreover, equals three times four hundred ninety-six, another of the perfect numbers.[42] Skelton may have singled out that year to begin his calendar as much for the importance of its number as for the special significance of its events. It is also significant that on 3 November 1488, the moon was successively in conjunction with Mercury, the sun, and Venus in Scorpio.

Whatever Skelton's reason for choosing 1488 to begin his calendar, if his new year's day fell about 1 November, it must be related to the number and calendar symbolism of *The Laurel*. As we have seen, Skelton equivocates about the time of the vision. The astrological date sets it precisely in early May, but the hunting stanza mingles spring and fall, and Janus's presence at the end (1509) indicates the start of a new year. The explanation must be that Janus inaugurates Skelton's own new-year, starting about 1 November, the day we have identified as *Poeta Skelton*'s putative deathday. This will seem rather macabre to the modern reader. In Skelton's time, however, as in the Church today, a saint's true birthday was considered to be the day of his death.[43] And so the May-November, or birthday-deathday, opposition found in the horoscopes, the hunt, and the woodcuts appears also in the framing of the poetic vision, with the introduction of Janus, expressive of the motto, "In my beginning is my end."

So Skelton had two personal calendar years, the usual one beginning on his birthday, 2 May 1463, the other on or very near to 1 November 1488. Although this second calendar kept the record of Skelton's poetic career, it did not date its beginning. By 1488 Skelton was already well embarked as a writer. Why did he begin it when he did? On the whole, it is unlikely that so private a calendar expressing so profound a sense of personal destiny, would mark some merely topical or public event, such as entry into royal service. It might have marked his laureateship, to which he attached great importance, but if it did, then I think we have to allow the probability that Skelton adjusted the date of the ceremony to fit the time-patterns of his life as he understood them.

A rather more likely explanation, I think, would link Skelton's calendar to his involvement in the fortunes of his patrons, the Howards. John Howard, duke of Norfolk, his first patron, was killed at Bosworth, and his son Thomas was imprisoned in the Tower. At the same time, Skelton's own early career must have come to a sharp end, and he may even have been in personal danger himself. His career began anew in late 1488 precisely when Thomas Howard was establishing himself in Henry VII's confidence. Howard's reward was release from the Tower, restoration to his earldom and to some, at least, of his family's estates. The reward of his family's poet was the restoration of his career as poet and writer. In both cases, life was born again out of death, and this would explain the peculiar private calendar with its beginning and end in the death month of November. It would also explain the symbolism of the phoenix, the sign of rebirth, ablaze in a fire of olive-wood, enthusiastically praised by Skelton as the wood of peace (670–75).

In Christian orthodoxy all men have a supernatural destiny. Skelton, however, seems to have been unique in his time in identifying the signs of supernatural grace with the signs of his calling as a poet, and in studying its workings in such detail. In ways not easily grasped by us his sense of personal identity was invested in his poethood, and the experience of being simultaneously John Skelton and John Skelton, poet, was evidently tinged for him with feelings of the numinous and miraculous. One even wonders whether he was especially pleased to publish *The Laurel* in 1523 because the year's digits add up to eleven! In that year he was also sixty, and his personal life-year entered its eleventh and, according to his scheme, its last month—which in fact it proved to be, since he died in 1529, in his sixty-sixth year. And since that number is a multiple of eleven whose digits add up to twelve, Skelton in death exemplified the numerical mystery that had underlain his life and poetry. As they had done all his life, to his great wonderment, patterns both overt and occult converged.

The Poem: Allegory, Tone, Technique

Medieval and Renaissance allegory speaks for a temper of mind epitomized in St. Augustine's great sentence from the first book of *The Confessions*: "Fecisti nos ad te et inquietum est cor nostrum, donec requiescat in te"; for allegory characteristically expresses a yearning for a stability and perfection of being that transcend the limitations of space, time, and matter. The great difference between the medieval allegorist and the Romantic poet who may share the same apparently instinctive longing is that the medieval man already lived in a world that was itself a symbol of the transcendent and the eternal. He did not need to make his symbols up or to find them in his own experience. They were already there for the reading in the two great books of God, the Bible and the Creation. His works, whatever the specific occasion or subject, imitate in their forms the lineaments of nature. The result, whether on the grand scale of *The Divine Comedy* or the comparatively small scale of *The Laurel*, is always at bottom a kind of meditation upon, or adoration of, the creator through his creation.[44]

The form of *The Laurel* imitates the movement of the heavens and the seasons, and their perfect motion is the symbol of its poet's longing. He wants the immortality of a life beyond this one, both the thing itself in another existence, and its analogy, the achievement of poetic fame in this one. Other dreamers long for an ideal love or for the beatific vision; this one wants to write the kind of poem that will last. In this respect he has rather more in common with Spenser and Shakespeare than with his predecessors. For the typical medieval allegorist hoped to succeed in his longing or his quest by submitting himself to the will of another, to God, for instance, or to his lady. Skelton, however, means to succeed by imitating the creator. He will make a world, a microcosm of the great world, and in it he will deal out rewards and punishments, confer fame, good and bad. His little world must also imitate the great world in its beauty and intricacy, prove worthy of the demands he makes of it, support the kind of life he wants it to have, and back up the claims he makes for it. *The Laurel*, among other things, is a challenge to criticism, meant to set standards.

The poem, then, is not an assemblage of parts, a series of conventions, an exercise in a genre, but a highly finished, very original work of the poet's art, inhabited and presented by its creator as his masterpiece and the culmination of his poetic ambition.

Such is the general outline of Skelton's allegory. It lives in the details that use and master the experiences of a particular time and place in the forms of the allegorical narrative. In great measure, too, it has done what it was supposed to do, for *The Laurel* really has immortalized the ladies and its creator, even though generations of anthologists and readers have not known how it was done. Those much reprinted lyrics were never meant to stand alone, but as part of a set in a specific setting, where they gain in beauty as well as in effect from the context. As one of the whole constellation of seven, Mistress Hasset's more modest star shines as brightly in its way as Isabell Pennel's or Margarete Hussey's.

As we meet him in the prologue, *Poeta Skelton*, haunted like dreamers before him by feelings of melancholy, failure, and hopelessness, falls into what seems to him the dull semisleep of exhaustion and depression. What he thought was the nadir of his fortunes, however, proves to be their zenith, and to his amazement the wonderful dream begins with the vision of Dame Pallas in her pavilion, talking about him to another lady, the Queen of Fame.

These two characters are the work of a writer who was also a practiced dramatist, and there is much social comedy in their exchange. They are also aspects of the discontented, unhappy narrator himself. The Queen of Fame stands not only for reputation, good and bad, but also for the longing for it; and when she complains that *Poeta Skelton*, although enrolled in her books, has lost his right to his place because he is not writing, we realize that this is one side of a debate in the author's mind.

Fame complains in particular because he has not been writing in praise of ladies, an understandable and amusing debating point in a poem written for an audience of women. Pallas, however, understands the complaint to apply to the whole range of his writing. She, as goddess of learning, is *Poeta Skelton*'s sponsor in the Palace of Fame, and on his behalf she tells the queen that she has no understanding of a writer's difficulties. If he writes poems of praise in beautiful English, he is blamed for lies and flattery; if he tells the plain truth, he is called stupid, and threatened with punishments. So the ambitious writer is in a quandary. To be well-known, he must put himself forward and write, but writing draws unwelcome attention to him. The upshot of the debate is that the ladies decide to hold a Court of Fame to find out how the poet will speak for himself. So ends the first *capitulum*.

When Eolus blows his trumpet at the opening of *cap*. II, all sorts of people come running to the sound. They are a motley crowd, driven crazy by the longing for fame. There are apparently no poets among them, nor does Skelton join them. He stands back watching, for insofar as a writer is merely ambitious he is no different from others. If he wants fame, this is the market, these his fellow shoppers. *Poeta Skelton* seems to know this, and is not going to make a fool of himself.

The two little woodcuts illustrating the quarto at the beginning of *cap*. I (p1.6) make a nice comment on these two ladies. Fame is a beautiful girl with luxuriant blonde hair (were the cut colored, it would probably be reddish-blonde); Pallas is a middle-aged woman whose figure has gone, and she holds the taper of understanding instead of Fame's rose of love. A severe-looking lady, she is the poet's sponsor, but Fame is the image of what most men desire, standing for a life that, for a time at least, can look attractive: the company of the very successful. Skelton's characterization of Fame also includes a perennial feature of such clubs when Fame tells Pallas that success alone does not bring entry to her palace. Her clients are all hard-working and virtuous as well as successful; she has high standards and a keen sense of responsibility.

The truth is that she has little of either. The rabble who come running to her trumpet do not change character simply because she admits them. They are, on the whole, a rude, stupid lot, and the whole performance is a sham. Fame is not really very clever at all, and the only real keeper of standards is Pallas, who is old and plain, and whom few men run after. Left to run her court in her own way, Fame is incompetent and destructive. Pallas's rebuke to her is severe:

> Bot whome that ye favor I se wele hathe a name
> Be he never so litille of substance,
> And whome ye love not ye wold put to shame:
> Ye counterway not evynly youre balaunce.

(176–79)

Her court is unjust, and so, by implication, are her complaints about Skelton. Someone else will have to settle his case.

And whether it were of ymagynacyon
Or of humors superflue that often wyll crepe
In to the brayne by dzynkyng ouer depe
Or it procedyd of fatall persuacyon
I can not tell you what was the occasyon
℃But sodeynly at ones as I me aduysed
As one in a trans or in an extasy
I sawe a pauylyon wondersly disgysed
Garnysshed fresshe after my fantasy
Enhachyde with perle and stones precyously
The grounde engrosyd and bet with bourne golde
That passynge goodly it was to beholde
℃within that a pryncess excellente of porte
But to recounte her ryche abylyment
And what estates to her did resorte
Therto am I full insuffycyent
A goddesse inmortall she dyd represente
As I harde say Dame Pallas was her name
To whome supplyed the royall quene of fame

℃The quene of Fame.   To dame Pallas

PRynces moost pusant of hygh preemynence
Renownyd lady aboue the sterry heuyn

One of the charms of *The Laurel* is that despite the firmness and intricacy of its construction, the narrative proceeds with something like the associational logic a real dream might have. Eolus's trumpet, besides drawing all the usual seekers after reputation, has the unexpected effect of summoning to the scene the entire college of poets, living and dead. They have decided to interest themselves in the case, and as Fame's debate with Pallas expressed the difficulties of the poet's situation in one way, the poets' procession expresses it in another. They appear in triumph, splendidly dressed, many of them holding their most famous books, all of them quaffing the wine that Bacchus generously hands out among them. Yet as the song of their leader Apollo tells us, the progress of poetry does not begin in triumph. Their perfectly tuned music, their magnificent language, and the grand range of their subject matter all began in response to pain and failure. Their laurels, which he also wears, are the sign of Apollo's hopeless love for Daphne. According to this part of the allegory, pain, not fame, is the spur that pricks the poet on to write. Apollo's lines, closely imitated from their originals in Ovid, express his inability, though a physician and the inventor of medicine, to heal himself; and they also apply to poets in general. In his bibliography, *cap.* XI, Skelton lists many works of good advice, moral, spiritual, and political, and they probably helped him very little in the crises of his life.

The poets stand for a real though mysterious and joyful achievement that is independent of Fame's standards, though she apparently recognizes it. If she is the president of the university, then the poets constitute an independent college within it that runs its own affairs. They send to *Poeta Skelton* his three English predecessors, Gower, Chaucer, and Lydgate, to assure him that there is a place for him in the college, and that by vote of the whole body they are going to present him to Fame's Court (stanza 60). They also send him the most delightful character in the allegory, the Lady Occupacioun, "a goodely mastres" who is Fame's registrar, the person who actually does the work of the court. She is an old friend to *Poeta Skelton*, whom she has helped out of difficulties before:

> Of youre aqueintaunce I was in tymis past,
> Of studiows doctryne when at the porte salu
> Ye fyrste aryvyd, when broken was youre mast
> Of worldly troste: then dyd I yow rescu,
> Youre storme dryven shippe I repayrid new,
> So wele entakeld / what wynde that ever blow,
> No stormmy tempeste your barge shalle over throw.

(Stanza 78)

Occupacioun is the poet's calling, the time he actually spends at his desk, and she is his best friend. She can also be very hard on him, and the first thing she does (*cap.* V) is to show him a terrible vision of the life of mere ambition.

The walled field of the world, the gates of the nations, past and present, the gate called *Anglia* surmounted by the royal leopard with its strange verses of warning: this is a picture of the life of affairs and politics lived in the world of time and history where things merely rise and fall, flourish and decay. It is also quite specifically a picture of the dangers of life around the English court, and it is as personal as anything else in the poem. When *Poeta Skelton* says he was "no thynge prowde / Of that aventure" (648-49), the implication is that he was not just a spectator of it. Occupacioun has shown him something he knows at first hand; he has been one of the callers and knockers at the gate, perhaps one of the pitifully wounded whom the guns bang so cruelly. Like Drede in *The Bowge of Courte*, *Poeta Skelton* has wanted to be a courtier. Because Occupacioun shows him this ugly scene, turning his dream briefly into a nightmare, we must conclude that *Poeta Skelton*, forsaking his true vocation, has mixed himself in matters that were none of his proper business. The unpleasant results served him right. The grotesque and pathetic little figure of stanza 89, who has his hat and his brains blown away by a gun-stone, is probably a projection of the poet himself. An audience at a reading who happened to know of some unhappy experience at court in the poet's past would certainly take it that way.

After this experience, a mist obscures the vision of the field, and when it clears, Occupacioun has brought the dreamer into an enclosed garden with a fountain, a fishpool, alleys, and arbors of roses and vines. Here in a laurel tree the phoenix continually immolates itself in a fire of olive-wood; the Muses led by Flora dance and play about the tree; Apollo plays his harp, and Iopas the Carthaginian poet from the *Aeneid* sings his great cosmological song of the heavens and the earth. This scene, as already explained, is the center of the vision, the point about which the narrative turns. It is the center of the poet's life, the garden of poetry where things are new made. Iconographically, it is a typical paradise-garden, reminiscent of others like it in art and literature. In this vision it stands, like the walled field, for an activity and a state of mind. It is the condition of the poet at work, an image of a way of life open to him in this existence, always there, only a step away. That is why Occupacioun, his own vocation speaking to him, asks:

> How say ye: is this after youre appetite?
> May this content yow and your myrry mynde?

Here dwellithe plesure withe lust and delight:
Contynualle counforte here ye may fynde,
Of welthe and solace no thynge left behynde.

(Stanza 101)

Enclosed and reclusive as it is, the garden is not immune from intrusion. *Poeta Skelton* notices a building from which he hears very bad music played on an out-of-tune fiddle (stanzas 102–105). The experience, he says, is one he will get over, but nonetheless he would like to know the name of the intruder. Whereupon Occupacioun tells him that the tenant of the "pyle" is Envious Rancour, a troublemaker whom the dreamer should avoid. *Poeta Skelton* recognizes a man he knows in the features of the type, and launches an "interpolated satire" against him, attacking him as an unintelligent nuisance who pries into poets' affairs because he thinks that knowledge of poetic secrets brings power and influence.

The numbers attached to the satire conceal the name Rogerus Stathum,[45] and it is a reasonable inference that he was connected, probably as husband, with Mistress Geretrude Statham, the lady whose poem (1032–55) suggests that she had curious sexual tastes. The satire itself takes us into a long-lost world where the aura of magic still hovers about the man of learning. To Roger Statham, Skelton's Latin, his astrology, alchemy, numerology, even his grammar and command of language, are signs of mysterious power. Roger and his satire, however, are not part of the vision, but a gloss upon it. As far as Occupacioun knows, the intruder's name is Envious Rancour. Yet the placing of the scene is important: the garden of poetry is flanked on one side by court violence, on the other by personal ambition and jealousy. By this means Occupacioun gives her poet a sharp warning against errors and follies he could easily fall into himself.

In *cap.* VIII, *Poeta Skelton* and his guide arrive via a winding staircase in a chamber where they find the countess of Surrey, her three daughters, and seven ladies, about to weave a garland for "Skelton my clarke." With this scene, the vision seems to have changed from a drama enacted between embodied states of mind into a portrayal of real people. However charming the scene, it seems to be a surprising shift in the mode of the narrative: "To introduce the Countess of Surrey among the mythical characters who make up the rest of the cast is not exactly consistent art."[46]

It could be argued that the change is not as abrupt as it seems because the countess and her ladies are also part of the vision. Her chamber is not in her own castle but somewhere in the purlieus of Fame's castle. This is not convincing simply because all readers feel that in *cap.*

VIII they are reading about a social scene in a great household. The sequence is detailed and concrete, even if it is not realistic (the ladies could not weave, design, and embroider the garland in one sitting). Another argument might be that the dream is a confused one, and so the mixture of styles is intentional. If this is so, the poet gives no hint of the fact in the scene itself, and the numerological construction of the ladies' poems is proof that confusion of any kind was not in Skelton's mind.

The answer to the difficulty has partly to do with genre, partly with content. Whether the poem ever existed as a masque, as Winser believes, cannot be known; nor can one argue that it did on the basis of a similarity between its modes of presentation and narrative and those of the contemporary drama. In any age a writer will imitate the visual conventions of his day. In a modern novel we find the conventions of the cinema, just as in the *Waverley Novels* we find the conventions of picturesque landscape painting. Skelton was as happily, and no doubt as unconsciously, bound by the visual conventions of his time as any poet before or since. *The Laurel*, however, did not have to be a masque to be performed, for like Chaucer, Skelton wrote for reading aloud. Many of the poet's cues to a reader for tone and implication appear only in live reading. This being so, *The Laurel* is, with all its complexities of construction, a social poem, and the introduction of the countess, far from being a confusion, is at least half the point of the whole performance. The mutual compliment that passes between her and her poet is the climax, and the allegorical machinery is there to motivate it.

What needs explanation is not the transformation of the poem by the countess, but the transformation of the countess by her introduction into an allegorical poem. In the structure of the narrative her role is similar to Pallas's. She too is the dreamer's sponsor, as well as a dignified older woman. She also interferes (with Occupacioun's connivance) in Fame's affairs, bestowing the garland that turns *Poeta Skelton*'s trial into a triumph. By her sponsorship she gives him the occasion to be a true poet and so earn the immortality he craves. In return he bestows poetic immortality upon her and her ladies. That, in simple outline, is the fiction of the poem as a social celebration. It implies that the countess is a godlike figure whom her poet worships, whose real place is with the other mythical beings whom she supplants, not with mere mortals. She is the deified star around whom the constellation of ladies twinkles. *The Laurel* is an apotheosis of the countess, and as she appears in it she is no more a real person than the "Lady" in *Comus* is simply Lady Alice Egerton. Indeed, the masque and other forms of decorative, social art provide innumerable analogies to Skelton's treatment of the countess.

A particularly good example is the famous picture at Windsor Castle, *Queen Elizabeth and the Three Goddesses*, attributed to the painter known as "the Monogrammist 'HE'," and dated 1569.[47] In this picture, Queen Elizabeth as Paris adjudicates the contest between Juno, Minerva, and Venus. Minerva armed, Juno crowned, and Venus nude occupy the right-hand side of the picture, painted in a recognizably classicizing style. The queen, normally dressed, painted in the stiff, rather archaic style of English sixteenth-century social painting, occupies the left. The contrast in styles is so strong that it is rather comical; but it is we, brought up on neoclassical standards of aesthetic unity, who make the joke. The monogrammist, like Skelton, knew no such rules. In the story that his picture tells, the queen awards the prize to herself, thus assuming the qualities of the discomfited deities, who are therefore understood to represent aspects of the queen herself. The point is made by the resemblance between the faces: the goddesses all have the same face, an idealization of the queen's.

In *The Laurel*, a similar conceit gives the countess the qualities of Pallas, and were the poem to be read in a semidramatic style, it seems likely that the countess might read Pallas's part as well as her own. When her ladies shine around her, the effect should recall Fame's first address to Pallas: "Renowmmyd lady above the starry heven" (51).

The dual presentations of the garland and the poems over, the serious business of the poem is complete, and what remains is recreation, a grand, comic performance of the poet's bibliography. Master Newton, the household's resident artist, records the scene of the presentations, and *Poeta Skelton*, led by his English masters, passes into the Court of Fame. Here the queen can only ratify, not very generously, the countess's decision. Occupacioun opens her beautiful book, and reads the long list of her friend's works. When she arrives at the most recent, *The Laurel* itself, the assembled poets break into wild applause. The dreamer awakes, wipes his eyes, and gives himself a new-year greeting—the new-year being, as we have suggested, a personal one, the whole poem the celebration of a very important birthday.

In the present state of Skelton scholarship, understanding the poet is difficult. Much of the information in print is wrong, or seriously misinterpreted, and virtually all of the criticism is based upon mistaken notions of the poet's forms, techniques, and ideas. His mastery and his personality are so strong that individual passages will always make some effect, but to understand a whole poem a reader must be prepared to move slowly at a task rather like restoring a picture buried under layers of varnish. So approached, *The Laurel* begins to emerge, one hopes, looking somewhat like the poem Skelton originally made, learned, intricate, graceful, and exquisitely civilized.

Undoubtedly personal experience underlies the poem. The details are irrecoverable, but in general it seems that at a time of reverses and disappointments, Skelton had the good fortune to find himself in the protection of a lady who was one of the great patronesses of literature, a woman of dignity, charm, imagination, and taste. She encouraged Skelton to write for her, and in return—perhaps as part of a household recreation conceived in common with him—rewarded him with his beautiful garland.

Skelton's poem of acceptance expresses the happiness of a world in tune, of an existence centered and fulfilled in a time and a place. The ideal has for a time become real: the garden of poetry is in bloom in a Yorkshire castle. According to the poetics of *The Laurel*, poetry renews, remakes, and ennobles the world. It also remakes the poet; and one of the strongest emotions one senses in the poem (e.g., 533–643) is relief, from danger, disappointment, and hurt. Consequently, the Skelton of *The Laurel*, comfortable and at his ease, is a different person from the usual Skelton of the literary histories. The learning, the exuberance, and the inventiveness are familiar; but the civility, the confident and attractive social manner, are a surprise.

The Laurel, then, is a moving and beautiful poem. It is also often a funny one that does not take itself too seriously. One cannot always be sure of responding to earlier literature as its authors would wish, and it is as easy to miss comedy entirely as to find it where none was meant. Skelton's own marginalia, however, are a reliable guide, and they continually encourage one to laugh. Any reader who attends to the first, fragmentary note (to stanza 7) will find it hinting at comedy in the dialogue between Pallas and Fame: "Egida concussit p[ariter] dea pectore porta[ns]" ("The goddess smote the aegis she wore at her breast"). This note, based on Ovid, *Metamorphoses* 2.755, is like a stage direction instructing us, first, to see that Pallas is deeply perturbed, and second, to smile because her emotion is out of all proportion to the cause. Why should she be so moved because Fame says that Skelton has been lazy? The same vein of histrionic irony appears, in the dialogue itself this time, when the ladies actually talk:

> The sum of your purpose, as we ar avysid,
> Is for that our servaunte is sumwhat to dulle. . . .
>
> (78–79)

Or:

> To passe the tyme in slawthfulle idylnes
> Of youre roialle palace it is not the gise. . . .
>
> (120–21)

The irony of the first example is in the placement and tone of "sumwhat"; of the second in the stress placed on "not." Angry as they are, these two great ladies raise their eyebrows, not their voices.

Other examples of the same dramatic comedy are *Poeta Skelton*'s courteous refusal of the English poets' invitation to go with them to Pallas's pavilion ("Under the forme as I saide to fore"), and his reunion with Occupacioun:

> I saw hir smile, and I then did the same:
> Withe that on me she kest her goodely loke. . . .
>
>   (530–31)

The funniest scene is probably the last, when *Poeta Skelton* arrives at the Court of Fame wearing his new garland for a hat. One irritated glance from the queen cuts off the chatter of the other poets, who have never seen so beautiful a laurel before:

> She lokid hawtely and yave on me a glum:
> There was not a worde amonge them then bot mum.
>
>   (1111–12)

This ironic, understated comedy is characteristic of *The Laurel*, the work of a poet who was also a dramatist with an ear for dialogue and situation. The effects depend upon poet and audience sharing certain perceptions, and there is little, if any, of the broad comedy of burlesque and exaggeration. At first Eolus, blowing his trumpet until his eyes stare and the world is in ruins, looks like an exception. But the effect of this scene also depends upon a shared perception of irony, because Eolus and his trumpet are certainly meant to remind us of the Last Judgment. When the great throng of poets cheers *The Laurel* at the end of the poem, Skelton's marginal note links the scene with the apocalypse of Daniel:

> . . . thousand thousands ministered unto him, and ten thousand times ten thousand stood before him: the judgment was set, and the books were opened. (Dan. 7:10)

Similarly Pallas recalls, in some detail, the biblical Wisdom; the garden of poetry recalls true paradise, past and to come. For the modern reader, these implied or explicit references are hard to assess. Pallas may gain some dignity from the association with Wisdom; nonetheless, she is a character designed to be part of a fiction, and her language is proper to that role, not to the role of Wisdom. Similarly, when Skelton relates the Court of Fame to the Last Judgment, we are not at all sure—if we are candid—of the effect, whether either or neither is inflated or deflated.

A fifteenth-century reader, however, who took it for granted that outside the poem and its imitative fictions there really is a Wisdom, an Eden, an angel trumpeter, and a Last Judgment, would not fall into our error of confusing fiction and scriptural reality. His reading, therefore, would necessarily be a comic one. He would know that the poet was handling very serious themes playfully, that time and eternity, reputation and judgment, wait upon the real John Skelton and himself as the Court of Fame awaits the fictional *Poeta Skelton*. For the reader so much at ease in Zion, laughter and seriousness are compatibles, in Skelton as in Chaucer his master: indeed, the comic emotion is the more profound for being exercised upon serious matter. This principle, so completely at odds with neoclassical ideas of decorum, requires (no doubt for reasons of taste) that a firm boundary be marked between the fictional and the true.

Skelton, therefore, continually reminds the reader of his artifice. His poem is a world of art made by art, celebrating art, and it is as self-reflective as a play by Shakespeare. In this respect, Skelton's self-projection as narrator is the center of the performance, its high point the reading of his bibliography.

The thirty-three stanzas of bibliography epitomizing Skelton's career (twenty-four in the earlier version) are the counterpart to the thirty-three stanzas of the poets' procession epitomizing the poetic calling; and when Occupacioun begins to read from her gorgeously illuminated register, the vision, the poem, and the performance become simultaneous events. Her register is the actual poem that we are reading, and the lines describing its physical makeup also describe the ideal, never-realized form of the book in our own hands. Occupacioun, the poet's vocation, thus metamorphoses into the poet's readership, a transformation wrought by art and laughter in which Envious Rancour, the intruder in the garden of poetry, can have no part. As the countess's garland is for the poet, the cluster of poems for the ladies, so the whole book and the life is for the readers, and it is a fine gift:

> The margent was illumynid alle withe golden raillis
> And byse: enpycturid with gressoppis and waspis,
> With butterfliys and freshe pokok taylis,
> Enflorid with flowris and slymy snaylis,
> Envyvid picturis wele towchid and quikly. . . .

(1151–55)

Like the garland and, no doubt, Master Newton's picture, this description of a manuscript expresses a taste for virtuosity and intricate splendor also found in the art, music, and architecture of the fifteenth century. As for the bibliography it contains, it is perhaps the most exuberant list in English literature.

If we accept the poet's gift, then we join our applause to his fellow poets', assenting to his claim upon our attention, and simultaneously validating another claim, made by Skelton in a striking sentence prefixed to the manuscript text of *Speke, Parrot*: "Lectoribus auctor recipit opusculy huius auxesim"—"From his readers the author receives an augmentation of this little work." *Auxesis* is one of Skelton's rare Greek words, a rhetorical term that means "a kind of amplification or increment that grows by degrees."[48] What the sentence really means, therefore, is, "This little work will grow in the minds of its readers." It is obviously true of *Speke, Parrot*, which requires the most energetic cooperation of its readers; but it is also true of *The Laurel*. In the "bibliography," for instance, whole lost poems, such as the story of Marion Clarion (1433), come to life in the reader's mind in the spaces made for them between Skelton's descriptions and the marginal glosses upon them. These two things are the coordinates of a space Skelton invites us to fill, and if we do not know the poem named, then in a curious way, so much the better. We invent it out of the materials given us. This is true of the whole poem. *The Laurel* is a microcosm of a life's career, but the form, range, scope, and kind of that larger world hardly exist until the reader has found them out.

Politics and The Laurel

Artful as *The Laurel* proves to be, it would be a mistake to let that discovery color one's reading of the poem retrospectively, turning it into a self-contained world of art, isolated from contact with realities. For there are realities in it that only the poet's art can safely communicate. As Pallas tells Fame, plain speaking is dangerous: "Ovyde was bannysshid for soche a skille' (93). It is also crude, as vulnerable to criticism as its opposite, flattery (83–88). In contrast, art is the poet's "protectyon, his pavys, and his wall," as Parrot says of allegory in *Speke, Parrot* (208), behind and within which he practices a freedom of speech not otherwise to be presumed upon.

Nelson (198–205), Edwards (229–33), and Pollet (145) all detected an undercurrent of political comment in *The Laurel*. Passages of satire against the court and its hangers-on recur, for instance, in the speech of Pallas to Fame (169–210), and in the descriptions of Fame's suitors (*cap*. IV). *Cap*. V, the nightmare scene of the walled field and the gate called *Anglia*, is obviously political in general intent, though riddling in its particulars. Edwards noticed the poet's emphasis, in *cap.* VI, upon the olive, the symbol of peace. There the phoenix, symbol of the mystery of poetry, immolates itself in a fire of olive-wood, which seems to be Skelton's addition to the myth, since the detail appears neither in Ovid nor Claudian, his most likely sources. Skelton, moreover, draws attention to the olive with a marginal gloss. Does his treatment of the myth mean that poetry is reborn in times of peace, away from the court?

The mistaken dating of *The Laurel* has invalidated previous attempts to relate its political passages to specific times and events. Since we now have an accurate date, we can distinguish between the politics of the poem as first written in 1495, and as revised and presented to the King and Cardinal Wolsey in 1523. Even so, it is unlikely that we shall ever be able to do more than interpret Skelton's political allegory in general terms, and this may be what he intended.

To have some feeling for the politics of the original *Laurel*, one needs to know that in 1495 Skelton was a poet of the Howards, as he had been since the beginning of his career. "Power's Quay," the house or inn where the dreamer of *The Bowge of Courte* has his nightmare, belonged to John Howard, duke of Norfolk, and the date of the poetic dream, encoded in the poem's first stanza, is 19 August 1482.[49] Young Skelton, therefore, began his career in the ambience of the Yorkist court of Edward IV. His first Howard patron was "bannerer" at the funeral of Edward IV, and that may be why Skelton wrote his fine lament for the king. At Bosworth Field in 1485, John Howard was killed fighting for Richard III, and his son and heir, Thomas Howard, earl of Surrey, was wounded, captured, attainted, stripped of his estates, and imprisoned in the Tower. He succeeded, after some time, in persuading the first Tudor king, Henry VII, of his loyalty and of his value to the crown; and his first important commission as a servant of the Tudors, after his release in early 1489, was to put down the northern rebellion in which the earl of Northumberland, acting for the King, had been killed. Once again, Skelton followed his Howard patron's lead: his first known poem for the Tudors is his elegy on the death of Northumberland.[50]

By 1495, Surrey, installed in Richard III's former castle of Sheriff Hutton, was one of the most effective and trusted of Henry VII's servants. Yet although the King had restored him to his earldom, he had kept most of the forfeited lands, and Surrey did not recover his dukedom until after the Battle of Flodden Field. Obviously, the decade 1485–95 had its difficulties for the Howards, their friends, and dependents. In *The Laurel* there are several veiled references to political misfortune, and their presence implies that in the privacy of the Howard household Skelton could express a covert, implicit kind of criticism of the new regime. For instance, he compares his patroness the countess—no doubt to her own satisfaction—with Queen Thamyris and Agrippina. The first defended her country against invasion by Cyrus, and avenged her son's death at his hands. The second, the wife of Germanicus, died of self-starvation in defiance of Tiberius. Like Thamyris she is an emblem of resistance to tyranny. Both comparisons must reflect the attitude, perhaps the demeanor, of the countess in the years after Bosworth, and congratulate her upon it (see 857–60 and note, and appendix 6).

The comparison of Margarete Hussey to Hypsipyle, famous for devotion to her father, and for exile, is also politically significant (1021 and note). Elsewhere in the poem there are also references to arbitrary government in the words *mayntenans* (193), *extorcioun* (194), and *credence* (1127). Fame's court, where these vices (all of them characteristic of tyrannical government) flourish, is in some respects a more sharply, specifically critical image of the royal court than we have hitherto realized. Had the decision been left to Fame, Skelton would not have been admitted to her court. No doubt these are some of the details that led Pollet to perceive an "undercurrent of rancour and hostility towards the Government . . . in the critical passages of *The Laurel*" (145). Yet sometimes the political comment can be comical. The proverbs of stanzas 149 and 150, accompanied by the marginal instruction, "Observe!" and Horace's famous line, "Friends, can you contain your laughter?" certainly imply an amused acceptance of the inevitable:

> He is not wise ageyne the streme that stryvithe:
> Dun is in the myre, Dame, reche me my spurre:
> Nedis most he ryn that the develle dryvithe:
> When the stede is stolyn, spar the stabyl durre:
> A jantylle hownde shuld never play the kurre:
> It is sone aspiyd where the thorne prikkithe,
> And wele wotithe the cat whos berde she likkithe.

The best of Skelton's proverbs, and apparently his own invention, certainly indicates beautifully his own ironic style in the presence of these dangerous matters, as well as the complicity of his audience:

> Yit when the rayne raynithe and the gose wynkkith,
> Lytille wotithe the goslyng what the gose thynkithe.
>
> (1424–25)

In this context of scattered and covert political reference, some of it fairly pointed, the gate *Anglia* of *cap.* V, its leopard and scroll sound very bitter indeed. The difficult, riddling Latin attacks the crown directly for rapacity and violence, and we realize that the peace of the garden of poetry is a refuge from real nastiness. Edwards argued (231) that the countess must have presented Skelton with his chaplet as a reward for services, presumably political, in the form of poetry, but from what we now know of the date, form, and content of the poem, this no longer follows. As we have seen, the celebration between countess and poet is mutual, and its theme seems to be the new peace and security of the whole great household, Skelton included in it.

Why, however, should a poem centering upon a celebration of John Skelton's poetic career at its zenith, and representing it in microcosm, do so in the context of the fortunes of the Howards? There is no answer to this question except the general one, that his career was apparently dependent upon that family's protection. We do not know why or how Skelton came to be so closely involved with them. The connection lasted throughout his life, and took precedence over all others. It is also apparent, on the evidence of *The Laurel* itself, that Skelton was a welcome, respected, and well-liked member of the household. How one wishes that Garnesche's attack on Skelton's ancestry had survived (*Against Garnesche*, 3.63)! It would probably explain a good deal.

These political elements in *The Laurel* may also underlie a feature of the poem's myth or fiction more mystifying and more profoundly personal to Skelton than these biographical insights, interesting and important though they are. A. C. Spearing, who ends his account of medieval dream poetry with *The Laurel*, describes it as the last major exemplar of a long tradition, and he compares Skelton to T. S. Eliot:

> Skelton's relationship to literary tradition is somewhat similar to T. S. Eliot's. Both are poets who value tradition very highly precisely because their sensibilities and their works are (in relation to their respective pasts) modern.[51]

Unlike Lydgate, who "follows tradition because the possibility of doing otherwise never occurs to him," Skelton "invokes the idea of tradition very consciously, and makes it serve the purposes of his individual talent." There is truth in this, and it is not much affected by the new dating of Skelton's poem, putting it before, not after, Douglas's *Palace of Honour* (1501), which it must have influenced. Spearing's perception may explain why many modern readers, including poets, have found Skelton congenial. Like them he inherited a fair weight of intellectual and artistic tradition, and in principle should have had little difficulty orienting himself, making his way. Yet also like them, he found himself at odds with his times. As a writer he found matters of form and style problematic, a situation that led in his case to a remarkable development of what we recognize in later sixteenth-century writing as mannerism. In Skelton's work, however, literary individualism has to find expression for the most part outside any consensus upon acceptable literary modes.

This, presumably, is what Spearing means by "modern." It is also true, as he implies, that the medieval past explains a great deal in Skelton's poetry. *The Laurel*, for instance, will appear to a reader looking for tradition to be a reworking of material from Chaucer's *House of Fame*.[52] Yet attributing to Skelton too self-conscious an attitude to tradition will turn him into a reflection of ourselves. Our understanding of history and our canon of medieval literature shape our version of Skelton's tradition, and it is not the same as his. Moreover, belief that Skelton wrote in a tradition has a way of obscuring his originality. Although he may owe to Chaucer his idea of a dream of Fame, even his treatment of himself as a self-deprecating narrator, little else in *The Laurel* comes from Chaucer. Ovid is a far stronger influence. Skelton's conception of poetry as a transforming agency that defeats time and suffering owes more to his trained Latinist's reading of the *Metamorphoses* than to anything in the native tradition of poetry. Our own education in Latin is so deficient that we do not know most of the literature Skelton knew best, and no amount of reading in Skelton (or Chaucer) can tell us that *The Laurel* owes more to Skelton's Latin than to his native past. Yet it does, and Skelton's first Envoy commends the poem to "Latin men" (1539), not to mere English readers.

The presence of Ovid in *The Laurel*, and especially of his theme of transformation, sheds a fascinating, if tantalizing light upon Skelton's fiction, particularly its political and autobiographical undertones. The transformation of suffering into song, allegorized in the episode of Apollo and Daphne (stanzas 42–46), is based on *Metamorphoses* 11.452ff. It has its parallel in the fiction with the transformation of the walled arena of the world into the closed garden of poetry (*capitula* V, VI). Skelton's gift of fame to the countess and her ladies, which Skelton describes as "stellification" (964), echoes the transformation of Caesar (*Met*. 15.843–51) into a star shining immutable beyond the moon's orbit. By entering his own poem as *Poeta Skelton*, Skelton even transforms himself into a work of art. His presentation of himself and his poem in Fame's palace echoes Ovid's *opus exegi*,[53] a claim he makes specific in the verses preceding and following his poem, prophecies of fame that internalize, so to speak, one of the grandest themes of Latin epic: the eternity of Rome and the poetry that celebrates her.

At the center of *The Laurel*, Skelton has placed the phoenix, the one creature that does not undergo these changes. As Ovid says of it, "una est, quae reparet seque ipsa reseminet, ales": "one bird there is, which renews and regenerates itself" (*Met*. 15.392). In a fire of olive-wood in the laurel tree, it undergoes its strange renewal; the Muses, dryads, and shepherdesses, led by Flora, celebrate the miracle with their dance, which Iopas harmonizes with the dance of the cosmos about the pole star. This scene symbolizes the mysteries of poetry. Skelton, however, does not claim phoenix-like qualities for himself. Instead, he identifies himself twice with Adonis: "Everywhere Skelton will be commemorated, another Adonis," and "Say that Skelton was your Adonis" (prefatory verses, and 1517).

In the *Metamorphoses* (10.708–39), Orpheus sings the story of Adonis, the young huntsman loved by Venus, killed by a boar, whom the goddess transforms into an anemone. The standard tradition of interpretation told Skelton that Adonis was the sun, his death and transformation a seasonal myth; but Skelton no more intends this meaning than he intends the phoenix to be an allegory of Christ, another standard interpretation.[54] In both cases, he has gone to the Latin sources, Ovid and (for the phoenix) Claudian, and he has used the material for his own purposes. We have to interpret his symbols in their context. If we do that, it appears that Skelton's rather bookish symbolism must adumbrate some personal experience linked to his knowledge that he is a poet and that to be a poet is to be a most unusual kind of person.

Adonis neglects sound advice, and exposes himself to the wrath of the boar. As an "enduring monument" (10.725) of her grief, Venus turns his blood into the anemone, which becomes, paradoxically, a symbol of the brevity of human life and beauty. I have already suggested, on the basis of Skelton's calendar and numerology and of the siege of the gate called *Anglia*, that some traumatic experience interrupted his life and career. Does his self-identification with Adonis imply that in the political violence of the 1480s Skelton came very close to actual death? That he not only lost his friend and patron, but came near to losing his own life as well?

To speak in the mythical terms that the subject and Skelton's symbolic handling of it require, he seems to have experienced in his own life a motif of epic and ballad, the descent into the underworld. Whatever it was, the experience seems to have drawn a line across his life. Like the famous medieval Scots poet Thomas of Erceldoune (whose ballad Skelton, a northerner, must have known: he apparently imitates it in one of his own poems),[55] he began his life again with a sense that he was singled out to be a poet of prophetic power. The peculiar, and very original myth of Parrot the popingay, which we can now date from the same period as *The Laurel*, communicates the same feeling of uniqueness: Parrot is an exile from Paradise, living in the world of time, where he is a ladies' pet, and squawks oracular prophecies to an uncomprehending audience. Only he and his mistress the lady Galathea know what he is and what he means.

A passage in Skelton's very late *A Replycacion* (359–78) reveals that one of the lost books mentioned in the first version of Occupacioun's "bibliography," *The Boke of Goode Avysemente*, was—in part at least —about poetry. In it, Skelton described a theory of poetic inspiration:

> . . . of divyne myseracion
> God maketh his habytacion
> In poetes which excelles,
> And sojourns with them and dwelles.
>
> (*Replycacion*, 375–78)

In itself, this was not unusual.[56] His association of poetry with suffering, found in *The Laurel*, was far less usual. If, as Parrot, the phoenix, and Adonis all seem to imply, Skelton thought that poets and poetry were things that, like the grain of wheat, had to die in order to live again, then that was as unusual as he said it was:

> Sunt infiniti, sunt innumerique sophiste,
> Sunt infiniti, sunt innumerique logiste,
> Innumeri sunt philosophi, sunt theologique,
> Sunt infiniti doctores, suntque magistri
> Innumeri: sed sunt pauci rarique poete.
>
> (*Replycacion, ad fin.*)

If this is indeed the occult significance of Skelton's symbolism, and the poetic meaning of the political and autobiographical elements in *The Laurel*, then Skelton's experience has a modern coda as strange as itself. Of Skelton's modern followers, the most sympathetic was Robert Graves, to whom Skelton was the type of the true poet.[57] In 1915, Graves was a twenty-year-old officer of the Royal Welch Fusiliers, stationed in France. In his autobiography he describes a cricket match played between officers and sergeants, with a piece of rafter for a bat, a rag tied with string for a ball, and "a parrot cage with the clean dry corpse of a parrot inside" for a wicket. "I recalled a verse of Skelton's," says Graves, and quotes one of the most striking stanzas from *Speke, Parrot*:

> Parrot is a fayre byrd for a lady:
> God of his goodnes him framed and wrought:
> When Parrot is ded, she dothe not putrefy:
> Ye, all thyng mortall shall torne unto nought,

Except mannes soule, that Chryst so dere bought,
That never may dye nor never dye shall:
Make moche of Parrot, the popegay ryall.[58]

(211–17)

It seems, though, that Graves has backdated his knowledge of Skelton. Elsewhere he says that he first encountered Skelton in 1916, on leave from France, and this is the more likely date.[59] For in the meantime, a most extraordinary thing had happened to him. In the Battle of the Somme, on 20 July 1916, four days before his twenty-first birthday, he was severely wounded and given up for dead. His commanding officer and the Army Council notified his parents that he had died of wounds; the *Times* announced his death, and his bank closed his account. Back in England, out of danger, he had the *Times* retract its notice, and as he convalesced, he affected to treat his "death" as a joke. But it affected him profoundly. "I *did* die on my way down to the Field Ambulance," he wrote to a friend. As his biographer says, the experience was traumatic:

Many of his poems dealing with the theme of death-in-life—a notion which has always obsessed him—draw on the experience of actually having been reported 'dead', though not directly so; rather, they gain their power from the experience.[60]

Graves probably discovered Skelton while he was recovering from these wounds, and the association of the lines from *Parrot* with the dead parrot of the 1915 cricket match—"When Parrot is ded, she dothe not putrefy"—must have originated then. Whether the experiences underlying Skelton's rhyme-royal poems from the period ca. 1483–95 (*The Bowge of Courte*, the original *Speke, Parrot*, and *The Laurel*) was, like Graves's, an actual event, or whether it was some more inward experience, it provided the mythos by which he shaped his life into art. It also gave him the obligation and the freedom, paradoxical as that sounds, to be the poet we know and whom Graves recognized as a fellow being, a survivor, a mind set free of commitments, except those to its own deepest allegiances, in particular to poetry.

A generation after he completed *The Laurel*, between November 1522, when he finished *Why Come Ye Nat to Courte?* and October 1523, when he published a revised version of *The Laurel*, Skelton returned to his poem, adding nine stanzas of "bibliography" to bring it up to date, and presenting dedication copies to Henry VIII and to Cardinal Wolsey. For some six years, beginning with the writing and performance of *Magnyfycence* in about 1516, Skelton had been writing openly and covertly against Wolsey, no doubt with Howard encouragement. We cannot reconstruct with certainty the events leading to the abandonment of that campaign, and any attempt at explanation will be speculative. The revised *Laurel*, however, calls *Colyn Cloute* a "trifel"; it does not mention *Why Come Ye Nat to Courte?* at all, and it describes *Speke, Parrot* as a poem about ladies—which it no doubt was, in part at least, when first written. Evidently, Skelton is pretending that his attacks on Wolsey never happened; and although this may be an elaborate joke, it is evident from the tone and the wording of "L'Autre Envoy" attached to *The Laurel* that Skelton abandoned his attack as a result of agreement on both sides. For he reminds the King to reward poets who praise him, and he very pointedly reminds the Cardinal to keep his promise of a prebend:

> Go, book, lowly reverence the famous King, Henry the Eighth, resonating his rewards of praise. Equally, with the same reverence, you should salute the Lord Cardinal, legate *a latere*, and pray him remember the prebend he once promised to consign to me. . . .

Surely, in the light of what we now know about the composition and meaning of *The Laurel*, this revised, rededicated version of the old poem must be seen as a decidedly ironic gift? Read as a new poem, it would show Skelton as an elderly man, eager for peace, delighted to have peace, anxious only to put his affairs in order and look serenely to the future. This will not have seemed very convincing to Wolsey, the recent recipient of *Why Come Ye Nat to Courte?* Besides, king and cardinal must have known that the poem was not new, the mood it expressed not recent. Read as a poem nearly thirty years old, *The Laurel* has nothing to do with Henry VIII and his minister. Moreover, it only mentions the court as a place of nightmarish violence to be avoided by any sane man. Instead of offering praise to king and cardinal, it celebrates a gracious and civilized provincial world, and no dedication can change the obvious fact that the poem belongs entirely to the ambience of the Howards.

Read thus, the dedication is as extraordinary as the turnabout it records. Even as Skelton submits to the crown and its minister (in surprisingly uneffusive language, incidentally),[61] he presents them with a poem telling them, if they wished to work it all out, exactly who he is, what his deepest allegiances are, and why he writes. In effect, he tells them that history, as usual, has repeated itself, and that poetry has better things to do. "I make my peace with you as I made it with your predecessors," he says, "and I am the same man now that I was then."

It is important to remember, finally, that Skelton was a northerner. *The Laurel* is the last major product of that chivalric and Catholic northern culture eradicated by the Tudors. By 1523 it was a conscious archaism, even in the context of its author's own poetry, ironically, perhaps defiantly offered, fit coda to a tradition.

Conclusion

Several major conclusions emerge from this study in the form of an edition, bearing upon Skelton's life as well as his poetry.

First, John Skelton apparently served three generations of Howards and through them, two dynasties of English kings. As Tucker suspected, his literary career began in the ambience of John Howard, duke of Norfolk and, therefore, of the last Plantagenet kings, Edward IV and Richard III. He then served Thomas Howard I, the victor of Flodden, in whose household he wrote *The Laurel*. If Edwards is right to identify the Galathea of the concluding parts of *Speke, Parrot* with Elizabeth née Stafford, countess of Surrey, then he also served Thomas Howard II, whose wife she was. Skelton was in some way very closely connected with the Howards; his loyalties were theirs, and his fortunes followed theirs.

From this a second biographical conclusion follows, that Skelton had two careers, one as a young man of great energy and promise under the Plantagenets, and a second, longer one under the first two Tudors. Some early poems denied to him on rather flimsy arguments (based upon comparisons with his later style and employments) can therefore be restored to him, notably his fine elegy for Edward IV, and the religious lyric "Wofully Arayd" (see note to *Laurel*, 1412). *The Bowge of Courte*, whose vision is dated 19 August 1482 (note to *Laurel*, 1177, and appendix 4), becomes one of these early works. Even if it was written a few years later than the date of the vision, it shows a young Skelton ambitious for service and reward at Edward IV's court.

Finally, *The Laurel* is not an old man's retrospective gesture to the world and the styles of his youth, but a poem from the midpoint of Skelton's career, a Janus-faced work looking before and after, like the poetic persona who narrates it. It is an elaborately contrived work, the art of its making drawn from the whole curriculum of the seven liberal arts. This kind of structure, according to John MacQueen, is charac-teristic of "Other World" narratives of the kind to which *The Laurel* belongs,[62] and indeed, lighthearted as *The Laurel* is for the most part, it seems to draw upon biographical experiences of profound impor-tance to its poet, and it makes, by implication, enormous claims for the authority and independence of poets and poetry.

We can now see, too, that *The Laurel* was Skelton's last major poem in the rhyme-royal, allegorical style. It also appears that the three major rhyme-royal poems—*The Bowge, Parrot*, and *The Laurel*—all origi-nate from the same period of Skelton's life. Whether in fact they form a sequence, a kind of Skeltonic Inferno-Purgatorio-Paradiso, it is too soon to say;[63] but it does seem likely that *The Laurel* was a conscious summation of Skelton's achievement at the time of its writing, possi-bly with valedictory implications.

Naturally, these discoveries have consequences for the reader of Skelton. The John Skelton who became so strong an influence on En-glish poetry after the First World War was always irreconcilable with either the swaggering Tudor cutup of legend or the academics' rheto-rician and court-server. This new Skelton, however, a self-conscious, highly original poet, learned, quirky, independent, and absolutely true to his poetic instincts is decidedly a poet from whom his modern fol-lowers could learn new ways to write when the old were suddenly dis-credited. We fall so easily into the habit of assuming that because poetry has been written, it has always been easy for poets, at least, to write it. Things have always looked very different from the poet's end, where every poem is a new beginning, and every word of it a matter of choice.

All this being so, it is also pleasant to report that, almost as a by-product of the examination of *The Laurel*, we now have a birthday for Skelton: 2 May 1463. It is a little later than one might have expected, the "ca. 1460" of the standard works having made a strong impression on everyone's mind. Yet more than forty years ago, William Nelson said that if Skelton was indeed the young man who became a Bachelor of Arts at Cambridge in 1480 (which is very likely), and if he was the normal age of sixteen or seventeen, then he must have been born in 1463 or 1464.[64] The astrological evidence for 1463 is very strong be-cause no other year in the vicinity of 1460 provides the features of a nativity required by the elective horoscope of *The Laurel*. Once again, therefore, separate strands of evidence combine to make a single conclusion: Skelton's birthday was 2 May 1463.

Notes

1. Pollet, 6–11, 21–22, and Edwards, 29, have summaries of facts and arguments relating to Skelton's early life. Like other older scholars, they date the beginning of Skelton's career too late. On the early date of *The Bowge of Courte*, see Melvin J. Tucker, "Setting in Skelton's *Bowge of Courte*: a Speculation," *ELN* 7 (1970): 168–75, and Brownlow, "The Date of *The Bowge of Courte* and Skelton's Authorship of 'A Lamentable of Kyng Edward the IIII,'" *ELN* 22 (1984): 12–20. Wordsworth's comment is in *Letters: The Later Years*, ed. E. de Selincourt (Oxford, 1939), 1:129.

2. Hammond, 336–40 passim: "He took satisfaction in his smartly colloquial and ribald writing. . . . He was a man of coarse, vigorous, and restless fibre, of huge vanity, bad temper, and no self-control. . . . He has no outlook on life or letters in the true sense. His style shows in the same way the lack of balance in his nature . . . a temperament has run away with an intellect. . . . Skelton's vain and violent temperament. . . ." Nelson, *PMLA* 51:388, n. 42a; Edwards, 26.

3. *English Literature in the Sixteenth Century* (Oxford: Clarendon Press, 1954), 142–43.

4. Anthony S. G. Edwards, ed., *Skelton: The Critical Heritage* (London: Routledge & Kegan Paul, 1981), 27ff.

5. Dyce, 1:xlix, xl.

6. Nan C. Carpenter, "Skelton and Music: A Gloss on *Hippates*," *ELN* 8 (1970): 96, says it is "likely that the laureate had his early training in a choir school, for his many musical allusions are based upon various aspects of practical music—the system of solmization, the Gregorian chant, the secular song, and instrumental performance—and in all these he is thoroughly at home." See also her *John Skelton* (New York: Twayne, 1967), 114–22.

7. "He cometh forth like a flower, and is cut down: he fleeth also as a shadow, and continueth not" (Job 14:2). "As for man, his days are as grass: as a flower of the field, so he flourisheth" (Psalm 102:15). "For ye shall be as an oak whose leaf fadeth" (Isaiah 1:30). "He shall be no more remembered; and he shall be broken like an unfruitful tree" (Job 24:20).

8. New York: Braziller, 1971.

9. The quotations following are from Edward, Duke of York, *The Master of*

Game (*MG*), ed. William A. and F. Baillie-Grohman (London: Chatto and Windus, 1909); Sir Thomas Cokaine, *A Short Treatise of Hunting* (*STH*), ed. W. R. Halliday (Oxford: Oxford University Press, 1932); Dame Juliana Berners, *The Boke of St. Albans* (*BSA*) (London: Eliot Stock, n.d.).

10. The word *bate* indicates that this is the behaviour of hunted, not rutting animals: "When a stagge is hot he desireth the water, at which time you are to bate your six couple of fresh hounds that have him in the water to break the bay" (*STH*, Sig. C3).

11. Rosamund Tuve, *Seasons and Months: Studies in a Tradition of Mediaeval English Poetry* (Paris: Librairie Universitaire, 1933), 170-91.

12. Owen Gingerich and Melvin J. Tucker, *HLQ* 32:207-20, first explicated this horoscope. A reader wishing to learn the basics of the necessary calculations may consult Helen Weaver, ed., *Larousse Encyclopedia of Astrology* (New York: New American Library, 1980), s.v. "Chart Calculation"; Alan Leo, *Casting the Horoscope*, 3d ed. (London: 1912; reprint, New York: Astrologer's Library, 1978); Neil F. Michelson, *The American Book of Tables* (San Diego, Calif.: Astro Computing Services, 1982).

13. Readily available modern tables are Bryant Tuckerman, *Planetary, Lunar, and Solar Positions,* A.D. *2 to* A.D. *1649 at Five-Day and Ten-Day Intervals* (Philadelphia: American Philosophical Society, 1964); Herman H. Goldstine, *New and Full Moons, 1001* B.C. *to* A.D. *1651* (Philadelphia: American Philosophical Society, 1973). For the year 1495, Skelton could use the first printed ephemeris, the *Ephemerides* of Regiomontanus, or Johann Müller of Königsberg, a daily ephemeris for 1475-1506 published at Nuremburg, 1474. Later editions began the tables in the year of publication, so for years before the date of his edition or after 1506, Skelton would have had to make his own calculations from a version of the Alfonsine Tables, e.g., *Tabulae Astronomicae* (Venice, 1483).

14. Scorpio would have been rising 18° at about 7:00 P.M. The moon at 19° Scorpio would then have been still below the horizon. Since Skelton is timing the vision by a horoscope derived from tables, not from observation, this does not matter. The actual moment of the vision is an ideal one. For the moon and Mars, very bright during retrogression, to be visible in conjunction, we would have to advance the clock about half an hour, when Scorpio would no longer be rising 18°.

15. Convenient descriptions of the traditional aspects, and of the relationships of planets, signs, and houses, are to be found in William Lilly, *Christian Astrology* (London, 1647).

16. Pollet, 10, gives the year of birth as 1460 or 1461, "the date commonly assigned to it by tradition." "Tradition" here means Dyce, who said, "The time of his birth, which is left to conjecture, cannot well be carried back to an earlier year than 1460" (1:v). No records of Skelton's early life survive. The first reference to him is by Caxton, who mentions his laureation at Oxford in the preface to *The Boke of Eneydos* (1490).

17. Thirty-three is traditionally Christ's age at his crucifixion. See Caroline D. Eckhardt, "The Number of Chaucer's Pilgrims" in *Essays in the Numerical Criticism of Medieval Literature* (Lewisburg, Pa.: Bucknell University Press, 1980), 178. The idea that the circle of life has its zenith is expressed by Prospero, *The Tempest*, 1.2.181-84.

18. First published in Paris, 1493, and translated into English as *Kalendayr of the Shyppars* (1503; *STC* 22407). I consulted the Beinecke Library copy, published at Lyons, 1510.

19. "Tempus est mensura motus primi mobilis" (*Tabulae Astronomicae* [Venice, 1483]).

20. Compare the famous miniature of St. Matthew in the Lindisfarne Gospels, which shows the evangelist writing and an enigmatic nimbed figure watching him from behind a curtain. Janet Backhouse, *The Lindisfarne Gospels* (Oxford: Phaidon Press, 1981), 47, says that "This arrangement is very reminiscent of that in later Mss of the *Registrum Gregorii* . . . where the attendant deacon manages an illicit glimpse of Pope Gregory the Great while he is being inspired by the Holy Dove." There is no agreement about the Saxon figure. Concerning the Skelton cut, which repeats the ancient design, Hodnett, 54, only says that it is "neither new nor interesting." If the implication of such a design is that the writing figure is divinely inspired, then the cut is very interesting.

21. Hodnett, 54, finds the same design in Marchant's 1498 edition of John of Holywood's *Sphera Mundi*, but does not mention its calendrical meaning. Tuve, *Seasons and Months*, 162–63, gives several instances of the design.

22. On 29 April 1542, the moon was full at 18° Scorpio, Mars retrograde at 8° Scorpio.

23. A common saying, e.g., "Influencies doo not constraine but incline" (Reginald Scot, *The Discoverie of Witchcraft* [London, 1584], bk. 11, cap. 21).

24. Lilly, *Christian Astrology*, 97.

25. E.g., Edwards, 228–29.

26. *Criticism* 19 (1977): 52.

27. Chaucer, *The Franklin's Tale*: "Janus sit by the fyr, with double berd, / And drynketh of his bugle horn the wyn" (523–24). See Tuve, *Seasons and Months*, 157ff.

28. Standard texts on music as number and allegory for Skelton's time were Boethius, *De institutione musica*, and St. Augustine, *De musica*. See James Anderson Winn, *Unsuspected Eloquence: A History of the Relation between Poetry and Music* (New Haven: Yale University Press, 1981), 30–73, especially 39ff. On the Pythagorean background, see S. K. Heninger, Jr., *Touches of Sweet Harmony: Pythagorean Cosmology and Renaissance Poetics* (San Marino, Calif.: Huntington Library, 1974), 71–145.

29. *Short Time's Endless Monument* (New York: Columbia University Press, 1960).

30. *Numerology: Theory and Outline History of a Literary Mode* (Edinburgh: Edinburgh University Press, 1985), 95–96.

31. On the numerology of these works, see MacQueen, *Numerology*, 70–71, 96–99; A. Kent Hieatt, "Sir Gawain: Pentangle, *Luf-lace*, Numerical Structure," in Alastair Fowler, *Silent Poetry* (London: Routledge & Kegan Paul, 1970), 116–40; and "Numerical Structures in Verse: Second-Generation Studies Needed," in Eckhardt, *Essays*, 65–78.

32. On John Browne, an elusive figure, and his music, see Hugh Benham, *Latin Church Music in England, 1460–1575* (London: Barrie and Jenkins, 1977), 82–89. Two of his pieces from the Eton Choirbook, *Stabat Mater* and *Stabat Iuxta Christi Crucem*, are very beautifully performed by The Sixteen in "Music from the Eton Choirbook" (Meridian E77062). On structure in English fifteenth-century music, see Benham's chapter 4, "Musical Form and Structure." Brian Trowell, "Proportion in the Music of Dunstable," *Proceedings of the Royal Musical Association* 105 (1978–79): 100–141, gives an intricate analysis of Dunstable's numerically ordered forms. John Stevens, "Rounds and Canons from an Early Tudor Songbook," *Music and Letters* 32 (1951): 29–37, solves some musical enigmas set by Skelton's friend William Cornish, Jr.: "The intellectual complication of most of these rounds," he remarks, "belongs to the age of the puzzle-canon. . . . The composers were of one mind with John Skelton, laureate, whose songs they sometimes set" (36–37).

33. See above, p. 49, and n. 6.

34. Brownlow, *ELR* 1:12–16.

35. Elias Ashmole, *Theatrum Chemicum Britannicum* (London, 1652), 59–61. A modern edition of Norton's *Ordinal* by John Reidy for the *Early English Text Society* (no. 272: 1975) has a helpful introduction. Norton (?1433–1513 or 14) had appointments at the courts of Edward IV and Henry VII (Reidy, xxxviii–ix), so Skelton could have known him.

36. Isidore of Seville, *Liber Numerorum*, 12, "De undenario numero" (Migne, *PL* 83: col. 191): "In scripturis autem undenario numero transgressio praecepti significatur, sive diminutio sanctitatis. Unde et undecimus psalmus sic inchoat, dicens: Salvum me fac, Domine, quoniam defecit sanctus." See also Peck, "Number as Cosmic Language," in Eckhardt, *Essays*, 15–64. On the symbolism of the 22 letters of the Hebrew alphabet and its influence on the forms of biblical books, see MacQueen, *Numerology*, 1–25.

37. E. R. Curtius, *European Literature and the Latin Middle Ages*, trans. W. R. Trask (New York: Pantheon Books, 1953; reprint, Harper, 1963), "Excursus xv: Numerical Composition," 501–9.

38. *English Literature in the Sixteenth Century*, 142.

39. The numbering of the MS differs slightly from the Quarto's.

40. Alastair Fowler, *Triumphal Forms* (Cambridge: Cambridge University Press, 1970), 184–86, 189; "The number 153 was famous as the total catch of fish in John xxi 11, fulfilling the prophecy of Ezekiel xlvii and the parable of Matthew xiii 47f. . . . It had attracted many interpretations from the Church Fathers and from arithmologists, the dominant theme being symbolism of the elect. By Shakespeare's time, most commentators understood the distinctive mathematical feature of 153 to reside in its triangularity." As Fowler says, citing Pietro Bongo, *Numerorum Mysteria*, p. 594, 153 is the sum of the first 17 natural numbers, and forms an equilateral triangle on a base of seventeen.

41. On Skelton's calendar, see Nelson, 161–65, who relates it to the poet's laureation. Edwards, 38, prefers to base it on his entry into royal service.

42. Perfect numbers equal the sum of their aliquot parts, e.g., $1 + 2 + 3 = 6$. They are very rare, there being only 7 of them between 1 and 40,000,000 (6:28:496:8,128: 130,816:2,096,128:33,550,336). The final digits alternate between 6 and 8. "A 'perfect' number stands appropriately for the *terra repromissionis sanctorum* the perfect land reserved for the redeemed at the end of the world" (MacQueen, *Numerology*, 55).

43. See the wording of the collect of the Mass *Sacerdotes Dei* for a martyr bishop: "O God, who makest us glad with the yearly festival of blessed N. the Martyr and Bishop: mercifully grant that as we now observe his heavenly birthday, so we may likewise rejoice in his protection" (*The Anglican Missal* [Mount Sinai, N.Y.: The Frank Gavin Liturgical Foundation, 1961], 572). If Skelton's "heavenly birthday" was November first or second, then it fell, properly enough, upon either the feast of All Saints (1 Nov.) or All Souls (2 Nov.).

44. The conviction that art is worship underlies the pre-Renaissance author's pleasure in lists, a marked feature of Skelton's work that we read in purely rhetorical terms as a figure of speech, and often a tiresome one at that. The best-known lists in pre-Reformation England were the various litanies. The archetypal liturgical list is the canticle "The Song of the Three Children," an apocryphal addition to the Book of Daniel, sung in Skelton's time at Lauds on feast-days, and in the reformed Church of England at Matins, where its use has always been optional (though it remained popular, as did the other traditional canticles Magnificat and Nunc Dimittis, despite Protestant aversion). An author who celebrates things by naming them also imitates Adam

(Gen. 2:19): "And out of the ground the Lord God formed every beast of the field, and every fowl of the air; and brought them unto Adam to see what he would call them: and whatsoever Adam called every living creature, that was the name thereof."

45. Edwards, 31, 236–38, identifies Roger as the husband of Gertrude Statham, née Anstey, daughter of John Anstey, of Stow-cum-Quy, Cambridgeshire. They married in 1482. Tucker, *RQ* 22:339–40, adopts Edwards's identification as well as his romantic speculation that Skelton as a student at Cambridge had been in love with Gertrude, who turned him down for Roger. There is no evidence whatever for this. The identification is not certain, and even if one adopts it, Skelton's lyric for Gertrude is not a poem of love, whether happy or rejected. One suspects that Gertrude's hardheartedness, whatever its occasion, was more recent thatn 1482, and well-known in the countess's household.

46. Edwards, 229.

47. The picture, attributed (but doubtfully) to Hans Eworth, is reproduced and commented upon in Oliver Millar, *The Tudor, Stuart, and Early Georgian Pictures in the Collection of Her Majesty the Queen* (London and New York: Phaidon, 1963), 69 and plate 32.

48. R. S. Kinsman, ed., *John Skelton: Poems* (Oxford: Clarendon Press, 1969), 160.

49. Tucker, *ELN* 7:168–75; Brownlow, *ELN* 22:12–20.

50. On the Northumberland poem, see Edwards, 41–43. On the first two Howard dukes of Norfolk, see *DNB*, s.vv. "Howard, John," and "Howard, Thomas"; also Tucker, *The Life of Thomas Howard, Earl of Surrey and Second Duke of Norfolk* (The Hague: Mouton, 1964).

51. *Medieval Dream Poetry* (Cambridge: Cambridge University Press, 1976), 212.

52. Ibid., 73.

53. "And now I have finished a work that neither Jove's anger, nor fire nor sword nor devouring age will destroy" (*Met.* 15.871–72).

54. Boccaccio, *Genealogia*, book 2, cap. 53, was the readiest source available to Skelton on Adonis as the sun, a late classical tradition stemming from Macrobius, *Saturnalia*. Adonis was also a common type of male beauty, used by Skelton in "A Lawde and Prayse Made for Our Souereigne Lord the Kyng" (Dyce, 1:x): "Adonis of freshe colour, / Of yowthe the godely flour." It is unlikely that Skelton meant this when he called himself Adonis. On the phoenix as Christ, see T. H. White, trans., *The Bestiary* (New York: Putnam's, 1960), 126.

55. "My darlyng dere, my daysy floure" (Dyce, 1:22–23). Compare lines 15–17 ("The ryuers rowth, the waters wan, / She sparyd not to wete her fete; / She wadyd ouer, she found a man . . .") with a passage in the ballad of Thomas the Rymer, variously phrased in the different versions, in which Thomas and the Queen of Elf-hame cross a river in the dark, e.g., "O they rade on, and farther on, / And they waded thro rivers aboon the knee" (C version, Child, 1:325, stanza 15). The ballad, story, and prophecies of Thomas were known throughout the north and the Border country (see Child's introduction, 1:317ff.). For Skelton the archetypal story of a poet's descent to the underworld would be the story of Orpheus, which he would know from many sources, e.g., Virgil *Georgics* 4.453, Ovid *Met.* 10.1ff., Boethius *De cons. phil.* 3.12. It is very interesting that Skelton's admonition to the trees in *The Laurel* (1597–1609) imitates Orpheus's summons to the trees (*Met.* 10.86ff.) after his return from the underworld.

56. Boccaccio, *Genealogia*, bk. 14, cap. 7, provides the classic statement. Skelton's lines on the rarity of poets, quoted below, are based on Boccaccio. See also Curtius, *European Literature*, Excursus 8, "The Poet's Divine Frenzy," 474–75.

57. Graves wrote on Skelton in "The Dedicated Poet," in *Oxford Addresses on Poetry* (London: Cassell, 1962), 3–25; also in *The Crowning Privilege* (London: Cassell, 1955), 11–13, 21–22, 76.

58. Robert Graves, *Goodbye to All That*, Rev. ed. (New York: Anchor Books, 1957), 116. I have emended *he* in the quotation to *she*.

59. *Oxford Addresses*, 5.

60. Martin Seymour-Smith, *Robert Graves* (New York: Holt, Rinehart and Winston, 1982), 51.

61. A point well made by Edwards, 232.

62. *Numerology*, 26.

63. Although it has not been noticed (I believe) by Skelton's commentators, the word *bowche* or *bowge* in the title *Bowge of Courte*, meaning as Dyce said a courtier's dietary allowance, is the English equivalent of Dante's *bolgia*, his name for the "pockets" of deep Hell, the *Malebolge* where the courtierlike sins of fraud are punished. If Skelton, like Chaucer, knew Dante, he was certainly philologist enough to appreciate the irony in the fact that the word he used to mean "reward," derived from the pouch or bag in which the courtier put his rations, could also mean the pouch in Hell where a greater power might put the courtier himself. Similarly, since the same word underlies Modern English *bulge*, a literate infantryman in the last European war might have thought the Battle of the Bulge was aptly named.

64. Nelson, 60.

The Book
of The Laurel

A
RYGHT DELECTABLE TRATYSE
UPON
A GOODLY GARLANDE OR CHAPELET OF
LAURELL
BY
MAYSTER SKELTON POETE LAUREAT
STUDYOUSLY DYVYSED
AT
Sheryfhotton Castell in the Foreste of Galtres,
where in ar comprysde many & dyvers solacyons
& ryght pregnant allectyves of syngular pleasure,
as more at large it doth apere
in the proces folowynge.

ETERNO MANSURA DIE DUM SIDERA FULGENT
EQUORA DUMQUE TUMENT HEC LAUREA NOSTRA VIREBIT:
HINC NOSTRUM CELEBRE ET NOMEN REFERETUR AD ASTRA
UNDIQUE SKELTONIS MEMORABITUR ALTER ADONIS.

PROLOGUS

POETA SKELTON

1

ARRECTYNGE my syght toward the zodiak
The signnys twelve for to behold afar,
When Mars retrogradant reversid his bak,
Lorde of the yere in his orbicular,
Put up his sworde for he kowde make no war:
And when Lucyna plenarly did shyne,
Scorpioune ascenddinge degrees twiys nyne:

2

In place alone then musinge in my thowght
How alle thynge passithe as dothe the sommer floure,
On every half my resons forthe I sowght   10
How often fortune variythe in an howre,
Now clere wedder, forthwithe a stormmy showre:
Alle thynge compassid, no perpetuyte,
Bot now in welthe, now in adversite.

3

So depely drownnyd I was in this dumpe,
Encrampisshed so sore was my conceyte,
That me to rest I lent me to a stumpe
Of an oke, that sumtyme grew ful streite,
A myghtty tre and of a nobille heyghte,
Whos bewte blastid was withe the boysters wynde: 20
His levis lost, the sap was frome the rynde.

103

4

Thus stode I in the fryththy forest of Galtres,
Ensowkid with fylt of the myry moose,
Where harttis belluynge, embosid with distres,
Ran on the raunge so longe that I suppose
Few men can telle now where the hynde calf gose:
Faire falle that foster that so wele kan bate his hownde:
Bot of my proces / now turne we to the grownde.

5

Whils I stode musinge in this meditacioune,
In slumbrynge I fille and halfe in a slepe,   30
And wheither it were of imagynacioune,
Or of humors superflu, that often wille krepe
Into the brayne by drynkkynge over depe,
Or it procedid of fatalle persuasioune,
I kan not wele telle yow what was the occasioun:

6

Bot sodenly at onys as I me avysid,
As one in a traunce or in an extasy
I saw a pavylioune wonderly disgisyd,
Garnnysshid freshe, after my fantasy,
Enhachid with perle and stonys preciowsly,   40
The grounde engrosid and bet with burne gold,
That passinge goodely it was to behold:

7

Withe in it a prynces, excellente of porte,
Bot to recounte her riche habilymente,
And what astatis to her did resorte,
There to am I fulle insufficiente:
A goddes immortalle she did represent,
As I hard say, Dame Pallas was her name,
To whome suppleyd the roialle Quene of Fame.

Egida concussit p[ariter] dea pectore porta[ns]. [Ovid. *Met*. 2, 754–5]

CAPITULUM PRIMUM

THE QUENE OF FAME. TO DAME PALLAS.

8

PRYNCES mooste pusaunt, of higth prehemynence,   50
Renowmmyd lady above the starry heven,
Alle other transcendinge of verey congruence:
Madame Regent of the Scyence Sevene,
To whos astate alle nobilnes most lene:
My supplicacioune to yow I arrecte,
Where of I beseke yow to tender the effect.

9

Not unrememberd it is unto your grace
How ye yave me in roialle commaundment
That in my cowrte Skelton shuld have a place
By cause that his tyme he studiowsly hath spent   60
In your servyce: and to the accomplishment
Of your request, regesterd is his name
Withe Laureate Tryumphe in the Courte of Fame.

10

Bot goode madame, the acustome and usage
Of auncyent poetis ye wote ful wele hathe bene
Them self to enbissy withe alle ther hole corage
So that ther workkis myght famowsly be sene,
In figure where of they were the laurelle grene:
Bot how it is, Skelton is wonder slak,
And as we dare, we fynde in hym grete lak,   70

11

For ne were only he hathe your promocioune,
Owte of my bokis fulle sone I shulde hym race:
Bot sithe he hathe tastid of thensugerd pocioune
Of Elyconys wel, refresshid withe your grace,
And wille not endevoure hym self to purchace

The favor of ladys with worddis electe,
It is syttynge that ye most hym correcte.

DAME PALLAS. TO THE QUENE OF FAME.

12

The sum of your purpose, as we ar avysid,
Is for that our servaunte is sumwhat to dulle:
Where in this aunswere for hym we have comprysid,   80
How ryvers ryn not tille the sprynge be fulle,
Better a dum mowthe than a braynles skulle:
For if he gloriowsly pullishe his matter,
Then men wille say how he dothe bot flatter:

13

And if hym fortune to wright trew and playne,
As sumtyme he mooste vicis remorde,
Then sum wille say he hathe bot litille brayne,
And how his worddis with reson wille not corde:
Beware, for writynge remaynnythe of recorde,
Displese not an hunderd for on mannys plesure: 90
Who writithe wisely hathe a grete tresure.

14

Also to furnnyshe better his excuse,
Ovyde was bannysshid for soche a skille,
And many mo whome I kowde enduse:
Juvenalle was thret, parde, for to kylle
For that he enveiyd: yit wrate he none ille,
Savynge he rubbid sum on the galle:
It was not for hym to byde the tryalle.

15

In generalle wordis, I say not gretely nay,
A poete sumtyme may for his plesure taunt,   100
Spekynge in parabols: how the fox, the gray,
The gander, the goose, and the huge oliphaunt

Went with the pokok agayne the fesaunt:
The lesarde kam lepynge and said that he must,
Withe helpe of the ram, ley alle in the dust.

16

Yit dyverse that be industriows of reson
Sumwhat wold gadder in ther conjecture
Of soche an enderkkid chapiter sum seson:
How be it, it were hard to constru this lecture:
Sophisticatid craftily is many a confecture: 110
Another mannys mynde diffuse is to expound,
Yit harde is to make / bot sum fawte be fownd.

THE QUENE OF FAME. TO DAME PALLAS.

17

Madame, with favor of your benygne sufferaunce,
Unto your grace then make I this motyve:
Whereto made ye me hym to avaunce
Unto the rowme of laureat promotyve,
Or where to shuld he have that prerogatyve,
Bot if he had made sum memorialle
Where by he myght have a name immortalle?

18

To passe the tyme in slawthfulle idylnes   120
Of youre roialle palace it is not the gise,
Bot to do sumwhat eche man dothe hym dres:
For how shuld Cato els be callid wise
Bot that his bokis whiche he did devise
Recorde the same? Or why is had in mynde
Plato, bot for that he left wrytinge behynde

19

For men to loke on? Aristotille also,
Of philosophers callid the pryncipalle,
Olde Dyogenes with other many mo,

Dymostenes that Orator Roialle   130
Whiche yave Eschynes soche a cordialle
That bannysshid was he by his proposicion,
Ageyne whome he kowde make no contradiccion—

DAME PALLAS. TO THE QUENE OF FAME.

20

Softe, goode my sister, and make there a pause:
And was Eschynes rebukyd as ye say?
Remember yow wele: poynte wele that clause:
Wherefor then rasid ye not away
His name? Or why is it I yow pray,
That he to your courte is goynge and commynge,
Sithe he is sclaunderde for defaute of konynge?   140

THE QUENE OF FAME. TO DAME PALLAS.

21

Madame, your opposelle is wele inferrid,
And at your avauntage quykly it is
Towchid, and hard for to be debarrid:
Yit shalle I awnswere your grace as in this,
Withe youre reformacioun if I say amys:
For bot if youre bownte did me assure,
Myne argument els kowd not longe endure.

22

As towchinge that Eschynes is rememberd,
That he so shuld be / me semythe it is syttynge,
Alle be it grete parte he hathe surrenderd   150
Of his honor: whos dissuasyve in writynge
To korage Demostenes was moche excitynge
In settinge owght freshely his crafty persuasioun
Frome whiche Eschynes had noone evasioun.

23

The cause why Demostenes so famowsly is brutyd
Only procedid for that he did owtray
Eschynes: whiche was not shamefully confutid
Bot of that famows orator, I say,
Whiche passid alle other: wherefor I may
Amonge my recorddis suffir hym namyd,   160
Sithe thowthe he were venquisshid, yit was he not shamyd:

24

As Jerome in his preambille *Frater Ambrosius*
Frome that I have saide in no poynte dothe vary,
Where he reporttithe of the coragiows
Wordis, that were moche consolatory,
By Eschynes rehersid / to the grete glory
Of Dymostenes that was his utter fo:
Few shalle ye fynde or noone that wille do so.

DAME PALLAS. TO THE QUENE OF FAME.

25

A thonke to have, ye have wele deservyd,
Your mynde that kan mayntene so apparently,   170
Bot yit a grete parte ye have reservid
Of that most folow then consequently,
Or els ye demene yow inordynatly:
For if ye laude hym whome honor hathe opprest,
Then he that dothe worst / is as goode as the best.

26

Bot whome that ye favor I se wele hathe a name
Be he never so litille of substance,
And whome ye love not ye wold put to shame:
Ye counterway not evynly youre balaunce:
As wele foly as wisdome ofte tyme ye avaunce,   180
For reporte risithe many dyverse waiys:
Sum be moche spoken of for makinge of fraiys,

27

Sum have a name for thefte and brybery,
Sum be callid crafty that kan kit a purse,
Sum men be made of for ther mokery,
Sum karefulle kokolddis, sum have ther wyvis kurse,
Sum famows wetewolddis, and they be moche wurse,
Sum liddurns, sum losellis, sum nowghtty pakkis,
Sum facers, sum bracers, and sum make grete krakkis:

28

Sum drunkon dastarddis with ther dry sowllis,   190
Sum sluggishe slovens that slepe day and nyght:
Ryote and revelle be in your courte rollis:
Mayntenans and myscheif, theis be men of myght:
Extorcioun is kounttid withe yow for a knyght:
Theis pepille by me have noone assignement,
Yit ryde they and ryn they from Karlyle to Kente.

29

Bot litille or no thynge shalle ye here telle
Of them that have vertu by reson of konyng,
Whiche sovereynly in honor shuld excelle:
Men of soche maters make bot a mummyng,   200
For wisdom and sadnes be set owte a sunnyng:
And soche of my servaunttis as I have promotid,
One fawte or other in them shalle be notid:

30

Eyther they shalle say he is to wise,
Or els he kan nowght bot when he is at skole:
Prove his wit, saithe he, at karddis or dise,
And ye shalle fynde wele he is a verrey fole:
Twishe, set hym a chayre or reche hym a stole
To syt upon, and rede Jak-a-thrummys bibille:
For truly it were pyte that he sat idylle!   210

THE QUENE OF FAME. TO DAME PALLAS.

31

To make repugnaunce ageyne that ye have said,
Of verey dewte it may not wele acorde,
Bot your benyngne sufferaunce for my discharge I laid,
For that I wold not withe yow falle at discorde:
Bot yit I beseke your grace that recorde
May be browght forthe, soche as kan be fownde,
Withe laureate tryumphe why Skelton shuld be krownd.

32

For els it were to grete a derogacioun
Unto your palace, oure nobille Courte of Fame,
That any man, under supportacioun,   220
Withe owght deservynge shuld have the best game:
If he to the ampille encrese of his name
Can ley any workkis that he hathe compilyd,
I am contente / that he be not exilid

33

Frome the laureate senate, by force of proscripcioun:
Or els ye know wele, I kan do no les,
Bot I most bannyshe hym frome my jurisdiccioun,
As he that aquayntithe hym with idelnes:
Bot yf that he purpose to make a redres,
What he hathe done, let it be browght to sight: 230
Graunte my peticioun: I aske yow bot right.

DAME PALLAS. TO THE QUENE OF FAME.

34

To your request we be wele condiscendid:
Calle forthe, let se, where is your claryonar
To blow a blast withe his longe brethe extendid?

Eolus your trumpet, whiche knowen is so far,
That bararag blowithe in every marcialle war?
Let hym blow now, that we may take the vew,
What poetis we have at oure retenew,

35

To se if Skelton dare put hym self in prece
Amonge the thikkest of alle the hole rowghte: 240
Make noyce inowthe, for claterars love no pece:
Let se my sister, now spede yow, go abowght:
Anon I say! This trumpet were fownd owte!
And for no man hardly let hym spare
To blow bararag brag / til bothe his ien stare!

CAPITULUM SECUNDUM

POETA SKELTON

36

FORTHWITHE there rose amonge the thronge
A wonderfulle noyce, and on every syde
They presid in faste: sum thowght they were to longe,
Sum were to hastyve and wold no man byde,
Sum whisperd, sum rownid, sum spake, and sum cryde: 250
Withe hevynge and shovynge, have in and have owte,
Sum ranne the nexte way, sum ranne abowte.

37

There was suyng to the Quene of Fame:
He plukkid hym bak, and he went afore,
Nay, holde thy tunge, quod another, let me have the
     name:
Make rowme, sayde another, ye prese alle to sore:
Sum sayd holde thy pece, thow gettest here no more:
A thowsande thowsande I sawe on a plumpe:
Withe that I hard the noyce of a trumpe,

38

That longe tyme blew a fulle timorows blast   260
Lyke to the boryalle wynddis when they blow,
That towris and townis and trees downe cast,
Drive clowddis togedder lyke dryfttis of snow:
The dredefulle dinne drove alle the rowght on a row:
Sum tremblid, sum girnid, sum gaspid, sum gasid,
As pepille halfe pevyshe, or men that were masid.

39

Anon alle was whyst, as it were for the nonys,
And eche man stode gasyng and staryng upon other:
Withe that there com in wonderly at onys
A murmur of mynstrallis, that soche another   270
Had I never sene, sum softer, sum lowder:
Orpheus the Traciane harpid melodiowsly
Withe Amphion and other musis of Archady,

40

Whos hevenly armony was so passynge sure,
So truly proporcionyd and so wele did gre,
So duly entunyd withe every mesure,
That in the forest was noone so grete a tre
Bot that he daunsid for joy of that gle:
The huge myghtty okys them selfe did avaunce,
And lepe frome the hyllis / to lerne for to daunce.   280

41

In so moche the stumpe where to I me lente
Sterte alle at onys an hunderd fote bak:
Withe that I sprange up toward the tente
Of nobille Dame Pallas / where of I spak,
Where I saw com after / I wote ful litille lak
Of a thowsande poetis assembilde to gedder:
Bot Phebus was formest of alle that kam thedder,

42

Of laurelle levis a cronelle on his hede,
Withe heris encrispid yalowe as the golde,
Lamentynge Daphnis whome withe the darte of lede   290
Cupyde hathe strykken so that she ne wold
Concente to Phebus to have his harte in holde:
Bot for to preserve her maydenhode clene,
Transformyd was she in to the laurelle grene.

43

Meddelyd with murnnynge the mooste parte of his muse,
O thowghtfulle harte, was evermore his songe:
Daphnis my darlynge, why do yow me refuse?
Yit loke on me that have yow lovyd so longe:
Yit have compassyoun upon my paynnis stronge!
He sange also / how the tre as he did take,   300
Betwene his armys he felt her body quake.

44

Then he assurdid in to his exclamacyoun
Unto Dyana the goddes immortalle:
O merciles madame, hard is your constellacioun,
So close to kepe your cloyster virgynalle:
Enhardid adyment the sement of your walle:
Alas, what ayle yow to be so overthwharte,
To bannyshe pyte owte of a maydens harte?

45

Why have the goddys shewid me this cruelte,
Sithe I contryvid fyrst prynciplis medicynabil?   310
I helpe alle other of ther infirmite,
Bot now to helpe my selfe I am not habille:
That profytithe alle other is no thynge profytabille
Unto me: Alas that herbe nor gresse
The fervent axys of love kan not represse!

46

O fatall Fortune! What have I offendid?
Odiows Disdayne! Why raist thow me on this facioune?
Bot sithe I have lost now that I entendid,
And may not atteyne it by no medyacioune,
Yit in remembraunce of Daphnis transformacioun   320
Alle famows poetis ensewynge after me
Shalle were a garlande of the laurelle tre.

47

This sayd, a grete nowmbyr folowyd by and by
Of poetis laureat of many dyverse naciouns:
Parte of ther namys I thynke to specefye:
Fyrste olde Quintiliane with his Declamacyouns,
Theocritus withe his bucolycalle relacyouns,
Esiodus the Iconomicar,
And Homerus the freshe historiar:

48

Prynce of eloquence / Tullius Cicero,   330
Withe Sallust ageyne Lucius Catelyne,
That wrate the history of Jugurta also:
Ovyde enshrynid withe the musis nyne:
Bot blessid Bacchus the plesant god of wyne,
Of closters engrosid with his ruddy flotis
Theis orators and poetis refresshid ther throtis.

49

Lucan withe Stacius in Achilliedos,
Percius presid forthe withe problemys diffuse,
Virgill the Mantuane withe his Eneidos,
Juvenalle satirrar that makithe men to muse: 340
Bot blessyd Bacchus that no man dothe refuse,
Of closters engrosid with his ruddy flotis
Theis orators and poetis refresshid ther throtis.

50

There Titus Lyvius hym selfe did avaunce,
Withe decadis historiows whiche that he mengithe
Withe matters that amounte the Romayns in substaunce,
Enyus that wrate of marcialle war at lengthe:
Bot blessid Bacchus, potencialle god of strengthe,
Of closters engrosid with his ruddy flotis
Theis orators and poetis refresshid ther throtis.   350

51

Aulus Gelius that nobille historiar,
Orace also withe his new poetry,
Master Terence the famows comicar,
Withe Plautus that wrate fulle many a comedy:
Bot blessyd Bacchus was in ther company:
Of closters engrosid with his ruddy flotis
Theis orators and poetis refresshid ther throtis.

52

Senek ful soberly wit his tragediis,
Boyce recounfortid withe his philosophy,
And Maxymiane withe his mad ditiis,   360
How dotynge age wold jape withe yonge foly:
Bot blessid Bacchus moost reverent and holy,
Of closters engrosid with his ruddy flotis
Theis orators and poetis refresshid ther throtis.

53

There kam John Bochas with his volumys grete,
Quintus Cursius fulle craftily that wrate
Of Alexander, and Macrobius that did trete
Of Scipions dreme what was the trew probate:
Bot blessyd Bacchus, that never man forgate,
Of closters engrosid with his ruddy flotis   370
Theis orators and poetis refresshid ther throtis.

54

Poggeus also, that famows Florentyne,
Musterde there amonge them withe many a mad tale,
Withe a frere of Fraunce men calle Sir Gagwyne,
That frownnyd on me fulle angerly and pale:
Bot blessid Bacchus that bote is of alle bale,
Of closters engrosyd with his ruddy flotis
Theis orators and poetis refresshid ther throtis.

55

Plutarke and Petrarke: two famows clarkis,
Lucilius and Valerius, Maximus by name,   380
With Vincencius in speculo that wrate nobille warkis,
Propercius and Pisandros, poetis of nobille fame:
Bot blessid Bacchus that mastris ofte dothe frame,
Of closters engrosid with his ruddy flotis
Theis notabille poetis refresshid ther throtis.

56

And as I thus sadly amonge them avysid,
I saw Gower that fyrst garnisshid oure Englyshe rude,
And Master Chawser that nobly enterprysid
How that oure Englyshe myght freshely be enneude:
The monke of Bury then after them ensuyd,   390
Dane John Lydgate: theis Englyshe poetis thre,
As I ymagynid, repayrid unto me,

57

To gedder in armys as brethern enbrasid,
Ther apparelle far passinge beyonde that I kan telle:
With diamauntis and rubis ther taberdys were trasid,
Noone so ryche stonys in Turkey to selle:
Thei wantid no thynge bot the laurelle,
And of ther bownte they made me goodely chere
In maner and forme as ye shalle after here.

CAPITULUM TERTIUM

MASTER GOWER. TO SKELTON.

58

BROTHER Skelton, youre endevorment   400
So have ye done, that meretoryowsly
Ye have deservid to have an enplement
In oure collage above the starry sky
By cause that ye encrese and amplify
The brutyd Britons of Brutus Albion
That welny was lost when that we were gon.

POETA SKELTON. TO MASTER GOWER.

59

Master Gower, I have nothynge deservid
To have so lawdabyl a commendacioun:
To yow thre this honor shalbe reservid,
Arrectynge unto youre wyse examinacioun   410
How alle that I do is under reformacioun:
For only the substance of that I entende
Is glad to plese and lothe to offende.

MASTER CHAWSER. TO SKELTON.

60

Counterweiyng yowre besy diligence
Of that we began in the supplement,
Enforcid ar we yow to recompence
Of alle oure hole collage by the agreament
That we shalle brynge yow personally present
Of nobille Fame before the Quenys Grace,
In whos courte appoyntid is youre place.   420

POETA SKELTON. TO MASTER CHAWSER.

61

O nobille Chawser whos pullisshyd eloquence
Oure Englyshe rude so freshely hath set owte
That bownde ar we withe alle du reverence
With alle oure strengthe that we kan brynge abowte
To ow to yow oure servyce, and more if we mowte:
Bot what shuld I say? Ye wote what I entende,
Whiche glad am to plese, and lothe to offende.

MASTER LYDGATE. TO SKELTON.

62

So am I preventid of my brethern twayne
In rendrynge to yow thankkis meritory,
That welny no thynge there dothe remayne   430
Wherwithe to yeve yow my regraciatory,
Bot that I poynte yow to be prothonotory
Of Famys Courte by alle oure hole assent,
Avaunsid by Pallas to laurelle preferment.

POETA SKELTON. TO MASTER LYDGATE.

63

So have ye me far passinge my merittis extollyd,
Master Lydgate, of youre acustomabille
Bownte, and so gloriowsly ye have enrollid
My name, I know wele, beyonde that I am habille,
That bot if my warkis thereto be agreabille
I am els rebukid of that I entende,   440
Whiche glad am to plese, and lothe to offende.

64

So finally when they had shewyd ther devyse,
Under the forme as I saide to fore,
I made it straunge and drew bak onys or twyse,
And ever they presid on me more and more,
Tille at the last they forcid me so sore
That with them I went where they wold me brynge,
Unto the pavylioune where Pallas was sittynge.

65

Dame Pallas commaundid that they shuld me convay
In to the riche palace of the Quene of Fame: 450
There shalle he here what she wille to hym say
When he is callid to aunswere to his name:
A cry anon / forthwithe she made proclame,
Alle orators and poetis shuld thidder go before,
Withe alle the prece that there was, lesse and more.

66

Forthwithe, I say, thus wandrynge in my thowght,
How it was, or els withe in what howris,
I kan not telle yow, bot that I was browght
In to a palace with turrettis and towris,
Engalarid goodely, withe hallis and bowris,   460
So kuriowsly, so kraftily, so konyngly wrowght
That alle the worlde, I trow, and it were sowght,

67

Soche another there kowde no man fynde,
Where of partly I purpose to expounde
Whils it remaynnythe freshe in my mynde:
With turkis and grossolitis enpavyd was the grownde,
Of birralle enbosid were the pyllars rownde,
Of oliphauntis tethe were the palace gatis,
Enlosengyd withe many goodely platis

68

Of golde enhachid withe many a preciows stone: 470
An hunderd steppis mountynge to the halle,
Oon of jasper, another of whalis bone:
Of dyamauntis poyntid was the rokky walle:
The carpettis withe in / and tappettis of palle,
The chaumbers hangid withe clothis of Arace:
Envawtid with rubis the vawte was of this place.

CAPITULUM QUARTUM

69

THUS passid we forthe, walkynge unto the pretory,
Where the postis were enbulyond with saphiris indy blu,
Englasid, glittrynge / withe many a clere story:
Jacinctis and smaragdis owte of the florthe they grew: 480
Unto this place alle poetis there did su,
Where in was set of Fame the nobille Quene,
Alle other transcendynge, most richely besene,

70

Under a gloriows clothe of astate,
Fret alle withe oryent perlys of garnate,
Enkrownde as empres / of alle this worldly fate,
So ryally, so richely, so passingly ornate,
It was excedynge by yonde the commowne rate:
This hows envyrowne was a myle abowte:
Yf .xii. were let in, .xii. hunderde stode with owte.   490

71

Then to this lady / and sovereyne of this place
Pursevaunttis there presid in withe many a dyverse tale:
Sum were of Poyle, and sum were of Trace,
Of Lymerik, of Loreyne, of Spayne, of Portyngale:
Frome Napuls, frome Navern, and frome Rouncevale,
Sum from Flaunders, sum fro the se coste,
Sum frome the Mayne Lande, sum fro the Frensche hoste:

72

Wythe, how dothe the Northe? What tydingis in the
   Sowthe?
The West is wyndy: the Est is metely wele:
It is hard to telle of every mannys mowthe,   500
A slipper holde the tayle is of an ele,
And he haltithe often that hathe a kyby hele:
Sum shewid his salfe cundight, sum shewid his charter,
Sum lokid fulle smothely, and had a fals quarter.

73

Wythe, Syr I pray yow / a litille tyne stande bak,
And let me kum in to delyver my lettre:
Another tolde how shyppis went to wrak:
There were many worddis, smaller and gretter,
Withe, Ay, as goode as thow! Ay, faythe, and no better!
Sum came to telle trowthe, sum came to lye,   510
Sum came to flatter, sum came to spye.

74

There were I say / of alle maner of sortis,
Of Dertmowthe, of Plummouthe, of Portismouthe also,
The burgeis and the ballyvis of the .v. portis,
Withe, Now let me com / and, Now let me go:
And alle the tyme wanderde I thus to and fro,
Tille at the laste theis nobille poetis thre
Unto me sayde / Lo Syr, now ye may se

75

Of this higthe cowrte the dayly besines:
From yow most we, bot not longe to tarry: 520
Lo hidder commyth a goodely mastres,
Occupacioun, Famys regestary,
Whiche shalle be to yow a sufferayne accessary,
Withe singular plesurs to dryve away the tyme,
And we shalle se yow ageyne / or it be pryme.

76

When they were past, and went forthe on ther way,
This jantylwoman that callid was by name
Occupacioun, in ryght goodely aray
Cam towarde me and smilid halfe in game:
I saw hir smile, and I then did the same: 530
Withe that on me she kest her goodely loke:
Under her arme me thowght she had a boke.

OCCUPACIOUN. TO SKELTON.

77

Lyke as the larke upon the sommers day,
When Titan radiaunt burnisshithe his bemys bright,
Mountithe on higthe with her melodiows lay,
Of the sone shyne engladdid withe the lyght,
So am I supprysid with plesure and delight
To se this howre now that I may say
How ye ar welcum to this courte of aray.

78

Of youre aqueintaunce I was in tymis past,   540
Of studiows doctryne when at the porte salu
Ye fyrste aryvyd, when broken was youre mast
Of worldly troste: then dyd I yow rescu,
Youre storme dryven shippe I repayrid new,
So wele entakeld / what wynde that ever blow,
No stormmy tempeste your barge shalle over throw.

79

Welcum to me as hartly as harte kan thynke,
Welcum to me with alle my hole desire:
And for my sake spare neyther pen nor ynke:
Be wele assuryd I shalle aquyte your hire,   550
Youre name recountynge beyonde the lande of Tyre,
Frome Sydony to the Mount Olympyan,
Frome Babille Towre to the hyllis Caspian.

CAPITULUM QUINTUM

POETA SKELTON. TO OCCUPACIOUN.

80

I thankkid her moche of her most nobille offer,
Affyaunsinge her myne hole assuraunce
For her plesure to make a large profer,
Enprintynge her worddis in my remembraunce,
To ow her my servyce with trew perseveraunce:
Com on withe me, she sayd, let us not stande,
And withe that worde she toke me by the hande.   560

81

So passid we forthe in to the forsayd place
Withe soche communicacyoun as cam to oure mynde:
And then she saide, whils we have tyme and space
To walke where we list, let us sumwhat fynde
To passe the tyme withe, bot let us waste no wynde:
For idyl jangelers have bot litille brayne:
Wordis be sworddis, and hard to calle agayne.

82

Into a fylde she browght me, wyde and large,
Enwallid abowte withe the stony flint,
Strongly enbateld, moche costiows of charge: 570
To walke on this walle she bad I shuld not stint:
Go softly she sayd, the stonys be ful glint:
She went before and bad me take goode holde:
I saw a thowsand gatis new and olde.

83

Then questionnyd I her what thos gatis ment,
Wherto she aunswerde and brevely me tolde
How frome the est unto the occident,
And frome the sowthe unto the northe so colde
Theis gatis, she sayde, whiche that ye beholde,

Be issuis and portis from alle manner of naciouns: 580
And seriowsly she shewid me ther denominaciouns.

84

They had wrytinge, sum Greke, sum Ebrew,
Sum Romayne letters, as I understode:
Sum were olde wryttyn, sum were writtyn new,
Sum carectis of Caldy, sum Frensche was fulle goode:
Bot one gate specyally where as I stode
Had gravyn in it of calcydony a capytalle A:
What gate calle ye this? And she saide, Anglia.

85

The byldynge therof was passinge commendabill,
Where on stode a lybbarde krownde withe golde and
   stonys,   590
Terribille of countenaunce and passinge formidabill,
As quikly towchid as it were flesshe and bonys,
As gastly that glaris, as grimly that gronis,
As fersly frownnynge as he had bene fyghtyng:
And withe his forme fote / he shoke forthe this writynge:

FORMIDANDA NIMIS JOVIS ULTIMA FULMINA TOLLIS:
UNGUIBUS IRE PARAT LOCA SINGULA LIVIDA CURVIS
QUAM MODO PER PHEBES NUMMOS RAPTURA CELENO: *Cacosyntheton ex industria.*
ARMA, LUES, LUCTUS, FEL, VIS, FRAUS, BARBARA TELLUS:
MILLE MODIS ERRAS ODIUM TIBI QUERERE MARTIS: 600
SPRETO SPINETO CEDAT SALIUNCA ROSETO.

86

Then I me lent and lokid over the walle:
Innumerabille pepille presid to every gate:
Shet were the gatis: they myght wele knok and calle
And turne home ageyne, for they cam alle to late:
I her demaundid of them and ther astate:
Forsothe quod she, theis be haskarddis and rebawddis,
Dysars, kardars, tumblars withe gambawddis,

87

Furdrers of love / withe bawdry aqueintid,
Brainles blinkarddis that blow at the kole,   610
Fals forgers of mony for kownnage atteintid,
Pope holy ypocritis as they were golde and hole,
Powle hatchettis that prate wille at every ale pole:
Ryot, reveler, rayler, brybery, thefte,
With other condicyouns that wele myght be lefte.

88

Sum fayne them selfe folys and wold be callid wyse,
Sum medelynge spiys by craft to grope thy mynde,
Sum dysdaynows dawkokkis that alle men dispyse,
Fals flaterars that fawne the, and kurris of kynde,
That speke fayre before the, and shrewdly behynde: 620
Hidder they com crowdyng to get them a name,
Bot hailid they be homward with sorow and shame.

89

Withe that I hard gunnis russhe owte at onys,
Bowns, bowns, bowns, that alle they owte criyde:
It made sum lympe leggid, and broisid ther bonis:
Sum were made pevyshe, porishly pynk iyde,
That ever more after / by it they were aspiyde:
And one ther was there, I wonderde of his hap,
For a gun stone, I say, had alle to-jaggid his cap:

90

Raggid and daggid and konyngly cut,   630
The blast of the byrnston blew away his brayne:
Masid as a Marche hare he ranne lyke a scut:
And Sir, amonge alle me thowght I saw twayne:
The one was a tumblar that afterwarde agayne
Of a dysowre a devyl way grew a jantilman:
Pers Prater the seconde, that quarrillis began.

91

With a pellit of pevishnes they had soche a stroke
That alle the daiys of ther lyf shalle styk by ther rybbis:
Foo, foisty bawdias! Sum smellid of the smoke:
I saw dyverse that were cariyd away thens in cribbis,   640
Dasyng dotrellis after, lyke drunkardis that dribbis:
Theis titivyllis with taumpynnis were towchid and tappid:
Moche mischeife, I hyght yow, amonge them there happid.

CAPITULUM SEXTUM

92

SUM tyme as it semyth when the mone light
By menys of a grosely endarkyd clowde
Sodenly is eclipsid in the wynter nyght,
In lyke maner of wice a mist did us shrowde:
Bot wele may ye thynke I was no thynge prowde
Of that aventure / whiche made me soore agast:
In darknes thus dwelt we tille at the last   650

93

The clowddis gan to clere, the mist was rarifiyde:
In an herber I saw, browght where I was,
There birddis on the brere sange on every syde,
Withe alys ensandid abowte in compas,
The bankkis enturfid withe singular solas,
Enrailid withe rosers and vinis engrapid:
It was a new counfort of sorowis escapid.

94

In the middis a coundight that kuriowsly was cast,
Withe pypis of golde engusshinge owte stremis:
Of cristalle the clerenes theis waters far past,   660
Enswimmyng with rochis, barbellis, and bremis,
Whos skalis ensilverd ageyne the sone bemis
Englisterd that joyows it was to beholde:
Then furthermore abowght me my syght I revolde,

95

Where I saw growyng a goodely laurelle tre,
Enverdurid withe levis contynually grene:
Above in the top a birde of Araby
Men calle a Phenix: her wyngis betwene
She bet up a fyre withe the sparkkis fulle kene,
Withe braunchis and bowghis of the swete olyve   670
Whos flagrant flowre was chefe preservatyve

Oliva speciosa in campis. [Ecclus. 24.19]

96

Ageyne alle infeccyons withe kancor enflamyd,
Ageyne alle baratows broisiours of olde:
It passid alle bawmmys that ever were namyd,
Or gummys of Saby, so derely that be solde:
There blew in that gardynge a softe piplyng colde
Enbrethyng of Zepherus with his plesant wynde:
Alle frutis and flouris grew there in ther kynde.

Nota excellentiam virtutis in oliva.

97

Dryadis there daunsid upon that goodely soyle
Wit the nyne musis, Pierides by name: 680
Phillis and Testalis ther tressis withe oyle
Were newly enbybid: and rownde abowte the same
Grene tre of laurelle moche solacyous game
They made, withe chapelettis and garlanddis grene:
And formest of alle, Dame Flora the Quene

98

Of sommer, so formally she fotid the daunce:
There Cintheus sat twynklyng upon his harpe stringis,
And Iopas his instrument did avaunce,
The poemis and storis auncient inbryngis
Of Athlas astrology and many nobille thyngis,   690
Of wandryng of the mone, the course of the sone,
Of men and of bestis / and where of they begone:

99

What thyng occasionyd the showris of rayne,
Of fyre elementar in his supreme spere,
And of that pole artike whiche dothe remayne
Behynde the tayle of Ursa so clere:
Of Pliades he prechid / with ther drowsy chere,
Immoysturid withe mislynge, and ay droppynge dry,
And where the two Trions a man shuld aspy,

100

And of the wynter daiys that hy them so fast,   700
And of the wynter nyghtis that tary so longe,
And of the sommer daiys so longe that dothe last,
And of ther short nyghtis: he browght in his songe
How wronge was no ryght and ryght was no wronge:
There was counteryng of carollis in meter and verse,
So many / that longe it were to reherse.

CAPITULUM SEPTIMUM

OCCUPACIOUN. TO SKELTON.

101

HOW say ye: is this after youre appetite?
May this content yow and your myrry mynde?
Here dwellithe plesure withe lust and delight:
Contynualle counforte here ye may fynde,   710
Of welthe and solace no thynge left behynde:
Alle thynge covenabill here is contryvyd
Where withe youre spiritis may be revivid.

POETA SKELTON. TO OCCUPACIOUN.

102

Questionles no dowght of that ye say:
Juppiter him self this lif myght endure:

This joy excedith alle worldly sport and play:
Paradyce this place is / of singular plesure:
O wele were hym that here of myght be sure,
And here to inhabite, and ay for to dwelle:
Bot goodely mastres, on thynge ye me telle.   720

OCCUPACIOUN. TO SKELTON.

103

Of your demaunde shew me the content,
What it is, and where upon it standdis:
And if there be in it any thynge ment
Where of the awnswere restithe in myne handdis,
It shalle be losond fulle sone owte of the banddis
Of scrupulows dowght: wherefor your mynde discharge,
And of your wille the playnnes shew at large.

POETA SKELTON. TO OCCUPACIOUN.

104

I thanke yow goodely mastres to me moost benygne
That of your bownte so wele have me assuryd:
Bot my request is not so grete a thynge   730
That I ne force what thowthe it be discuryd:
I am not woundid bot that I may be kuryd:
I am not ladyn of liddurns withe lumpis,
As dasid dotarddis that dreme in ther dumppis.

OCCUPACIOUN. TO SKELTON.

105

Now what ye mene I trow I conjecte:
God geve yow goode yere, ye make me to smyle!
Now by yowre faythe is not this the effecte
Of youre questioun ye make alle this whyle,

To understande who dwellythe in yone pyle,
And what blunderar is yonder that plaiyth diddil didille?   740
He fyndithe owght fals mesuris of his fond fyddille.

Interpolata, que industriosum postulat
interpretem, satira in vatis adversarium.

TRESSIS AGASONIS SPECIES PRIOR, ALTERA DAVI:
AUCUPIUM CULICIS, LIMIS DUM TORQUET OCELLUM,
CONCIPIT ALIGERAS, RAPIT, OPPETIT, ASPICE MUSCAS:
MAIA QUEQUE FOVET, FOVET AUT QUE JUPPITER, AUT QUE
FRIGIDA SATURNUS, SOL, MARS, VENUS, ALGIDA LUNA,
SI TIBI CONTINGAT VERBO AUT COMMITTERE SCRIPTO,
QUAM SIBI MOX TACITA SUDANT PRECORDIA CULPA:
HINC RUIT IN FLAMMAS, STIMULANS HUNC URGET ET ILLUM,
INVOCAT AD RIXAS, VANOS TAMEN EXCITAT IGNES,   750
LABRA MOVENS TACITUS, RUMPANTUR UT ILIA CODRO.

Nota Alchimian et 7. metella.

Ryght truly theys versis.

.17.   4.   7.   2.   17.   5.   18.
.18.   19.   1.   19.   8.   5.   12.

106

Hys name for to know if that ye lyst,
Envyows Rancor truly he hyght:
Beware of hym, I warne yow, for and ye wist
How daungerows it is to stop up his sight,
Ye wolde not dele with hym thowthe that ye myght,
For by his devillishe dryfte and graceles provysioun
An hole reme he is habille to set at dyvysioun.

107

For when he spekithe fayrest then thynkkithe he moost il,
Ful gloriowsly kan he glose thy mynde for to fele: 760
He wille stir men to brawlyng, and syt hym self stil,
And smyrke lyke a smytthy kur at sparkkis of stele:
He kan never leve warke whils it is wele:
To telle alle his towchis it were to grete wunder:
The develle of helle and he / be seldome asunder.

CAPITULUM OCTAVUM

108

THUS talkynge we went forthe in at a posterne gate,
Turnnyd on the right hand by a wyndynge stayre:
She browght me in to a goodely chaumber of astate
Where the nobille Countes of Surrey in a chayre
Sat honorably: to whome did repayre   770
Of ladis a bevy with alle du reverence:
Syt downe fayre ladis and do your diligence,

109

Com forthe jantilwomen, I pray yow, she sayde:
I have contryvyd for yow a goodely warke,
And who kan worke best now shalle be asaiyd:
A cronelle of laurel withe verduris light and darke
I have devisid for Skelton my clarke:
For to his servyce I have soche reygarde
That of oure bownte we wille hym rewarde.

110

For of alle ladis he hathe the library,   780
Ther namys recountynge in the Courte of Fame:
Of alle Jantylwomen he hathe the scruteny,
In Famys courte reporttynge the same:
For yit of women he never sayd shame
Bot if they wer counterfettis that women them calle,
That liste of ther lewdenes withe hym for to bralle.

111

Wythe that the tappettis and carpettis were layd,
Where on theis ladis softly myght rest,
The saumplar to sow on, the lasis to enbrayd:
To weve in the stole sum were fulle prest,   790
Withe slaiys, withe tavellis, with heddellis wele drest:
The frame was browght forthe withe his wevynge pyn:
God yeve them goode spede ther worke to begyn!

112

Sum to enbrawder put them in prece,
Wel gydyng the glutton to kepe streyght ther sylke:
Sum pyrlynge of golde ther worke to encrese,
Withe fynggers smale and handdis whyght as mylke:
Withe, Reche me that skene of Tuly silke,
And, Wynde me that botum of soche a hu:
Grene, rede, tawny, whyght, blak, purpulle, and blu: 800

113

Of broken workis wrowght many a goodely thynge,
In castinge, in turnnynge, in florisshinge of flowris,
Withe burris rowthe and buttuns surfullinge,
In nedel warke reisinge bothe birddis and bowris,
Withe vertu enbesid alle tymys and howrys:
And truly of ther bownte thus were they bente,
To worke me this chapelet by goode avysemente.

OCCUPACIOUN. TO SKELTON.

114

Beholde and se in youre advertisement
How theis ladis and Jantilwomen alle
For yowre plesure do ther endevorment,   810
And for youre sake how fast to worke they falle:
To youre remembraunce wherefor ye most calle,
In goodely worddis plesantly comprisid,
That for them sum goodely conceyte be devysid

115

Wythe proper captaciouns of benyvolence,
Ornatly pullisshid after your faculte,
Sithe ye most nedis afforce it by pretence
Of youre professioun unto humanyte,
Commensynge your proces after ther degre,
To eche of them rendrynge thonkkis commendabill,   820
Wythe sentence fructuows and termmys covenabill.

POETA SKELTON.

116

Avaunsynge my self sum thonk to deserve,
I me determynd for to sharpe my pen,
Devowtly arrectynge my prayer to Mynerve,
She to vowche save me to enforme and ken:
To Marcury also hartly praiyd I then,
Me to supporte, to helpe, and to assist,
To gyde and to governe my dredefulle tremlyng fyst.

CAPITULUM NONUM

SUPER HEROICA COMMENDACIONE

117

AS a maryner that masid is in a stormmy rage,
Hardly bestad / driven is to hope   830
Of that the tempestuows wynde wille aswage,
In troste where of / counforte his harte dothe grope,
Frome the ankker he kyttithe the gabille rope,
Commyttithe alle to God and lettithe his ship ride:
So I beseke Ihesu now to be my gyde.

TO THE RIGHT NOBILLE COUNTES OF SURREY

After alle duly orderd obeisaunce,
In humbille wice as lawly as I may,
Unto yow madame, I make reconusaunce
My lif enduringe I shalle bothe wright and say,
Recounte, reporte, reherce withe owte delay   840
The passinge bownte of your nobille estate,
Of honor and worship whiche hathe the formar date.

Lyke to Argyva by juste resemblaunce,
The nobille wif of Polymytes kynge,
Prudente Rebecca of whome remembraunce

The bibille makithe: withe whos chast lyvynge
Your nobille demenor is counterweiynge,
Whos passinge bownte and right nobil astate,
Of honor and worship it hathe the formar date.

The nobille Pamphila, Quene of the Grekis land,   850
Habilymenttis roialle fownd owte endustriowsly:
Thamar also wrowght withe her goodely hand
Many dyvisis passinge kuriowsly,
Whome ye represent and exemplify,
Whos passinge bownte and right nobille astate,
Of honor and worship it hathe the formar date.

As Dame Thamaris whiche toke the kinge of Perce,
Cyrus by name, as writithe the story:
Dame Agrippina also I may reherce,
Of jantylle corage the parfight memory: 860
So shall your name endure perpetually,
Whos passinge bownte and right nobille astate,
Of honor and worship it hathe the formar date.

TO MY LADY ELISABETHE

To be your remembrancer, Madam, I am bownd:
Lyke to Aryna maydenly of porte,
Of vertew and konyng the wel and parfight grownd,
Whome Dame Nature, as wele I may reporte,
Hathe freshely enbewtid withe many a goodely sorte
Of womanly feturis: whos florisshinge tender age
Is lusty to loke on, plesant, demure, and sage.   870

Goodely Creisseyda, fairar than Polycene,
For to envyve Pandarus appetite:
Troylus, I trow, if that he had yow sene,
In yow he wold have set his hole delight:
Of alle your bewte I suffice not to wright,
Bot as I sayde your florisshynge tender age
Is lusty to loke on, plesant, demure, and sage.

TO MY LADY MYRRYEL

My lytille lady I may not leve behynde,
Bot do her servyce nedis now I must,
Benygne, kurteise, of jantille harte and mynde,   880
Whome Fortune and Fate playnly have discust
Longe to enjoy plesure, delight, and luste:
Enbuddid blossome withe rosis rede of hu,
The lylly whight your bewte dothe renew.

Compare yow I may to Cydippes the mayd,
That of Aconcyus when she fownd the bille
In her bosom, Lorde how she was afraiyd:
The ruddy shamefastnes in her visage fylle,
Whiche manner of abashemente becam her not il:
Right so madame, the rosis rede of hu   890
Withe lyllis whight your bewte dothe renew.

TO MY LADY DAKERS

Zeuxes that enpycturid fayre Elene the Quene
Yow to devyse his craft were to seke,
And if Apelles your countenaunce had sene,
Of porturature whiche was the famows Greke,
He kowde not devyse the lest poynte of your cheke:
Prynces of yowthe and floure of goodely porte,
Vertew, konynge, solace, plesure, counfort.

Paregalle in honor unto Penolope,
That for her trowthe is in remembraunce had,   900
Fayre Dyanyra surmountynge in bewte,
Demure Dyana, womanly and sad,
Whos lusty lokis make hevy harttis glad:
Prynces of yowthe and flowre of goodely porte,
Vertew, konyng, solace, plesure, conforte.

TO MASTRES MARGERY WENTWORTHE

Wythe mageran jantel
The flowre of goodlihode

Enbrawderd the mantel
Is of your maydenhode.

Playnly I kan not glose: 910
Ye be as I dyvyne
The praty prymerose
The goodely columbyne.

Withe mageran jantel
The floure of goodlihode
Enbrawderd the mantel
Is of your maydenhode.

Benygne, curteise, and meke
Withe wordis wele devysid
In yow who list to seke   920
Be vertewys wele comprisid.

Wythe mageran jantyl
The floure of goodlyhode
Enbrawderd the mantyl
Is of youre maydenhode.

TO MASTRES MARGARETE TYLNNEY

I yow assure   Phedra ye may   940
Fulle wele I know   Wele represente,
My besy cure   Intentyve ay
To yow I ow,   And diligente,
930 Humbly and low   No tyme mysspent:
Commendinge me   Wherefor delight
To your bounte.   I have to wright

As Machareus   Of Margaryte
Fayre Canace   Perle oryente
So I / iwus   Lodestar of lyght
Endevour me   Moche relucent: 950
Youre name to se   Madame Regent
It be enrold   I may yow calle
Wryttyn with gold.   Of vertuys alle.

TO MASTRES JANE HASSET

What thowthe my pen wax faynte
And hathe smalle lust to paynte
Yit shalle there no restraynte
Cause me to cese
Among this prese   Your goodely name.   960
For to encrese

I wille my self apply
Trost me intentyvely
Yow for to stellify:
And so observe
That ye ne swerve   The Courte of Fame.
For to deserve

Sythe Mastres Jane Hasset
Smale flowris helpt to set
In my goodely chapelet   970
Therefor I render of her the memory
Unto the legend of fayre Laodomy.

TO MASTRES ISABELL PENNEL

By Seynte Mary my lady
Youre mammy and your dady
Browght forthe a goodely baby:
My maydyn Isabel
Reflayringe rosabel
The flagrant camamel:
The ruddy rosary
The sovereyne rosemary   980
The praty strawbery:
The columbyne, the nept
The jeloffer wele set
The proper vyolet:
Ennewyd her colour
Is like the daisy flour
After the Apryle shour:
Star of the morow gray
The blossom on the spray
The fresshest flour of May.   990

Maydenly demure
Of womanhode the lure
Wherefore I make yow sure
It wer an hevenly helthe
It wer an endles welthe
A lif for God hym selfe
To here this nytyngale
Amonge the byrddis smale
Warbolynge in the vale
Dug dug   1000
Jug jug
Goode yere and goode luk
Wyth chuk chuk, chuk chuk—

TO MASTRES MARGARETE HUSSEY

Myrry Margarete as mydsomer floure
Jantylle as fawkon or hauke of the towre
Withe solace and gladnes
Moche myrthe and no madnes
Alle goode and no badnes
So joyowsly
So maydenly   1010
So womanly
Her demenynge
In every thynge
Far far passinge
That I kan endight
Or suffice to wright
Of myrry Margaret as mydsomer flowre
Jantille as faukon or hawke of the towre.
As pacient and as stille
And as fulle of goode wille   1020
As the fayre Isyphill
Colyaunder
Swete pomaunder
Goode Cassander
Stedfast of thowght
Wele made, wele wrowght
Far may be sowght
Erst than ye kan fynde
So kurteise, so kynde

As myrry Margarete the mydsomer flowre   1030
Jantille as fawkon or hawke of the towre.

TO MASTRES GERETRUDE STATHAM

Thowthe ye were harde harttid
And I withe yow thwartyd
With worddis that smarttid
Yit now dowtles ye geve me cause
To wright of yow this goodely clause
       Mastres Geretrude
       With womanhode endude
       With vertew wele renewde.
I wille that ye shalle be   1040
In alle benygnyte
Lyke to Dame Pasiphe
For now dowtles ye geve me cause
To wright of you this goodely clause
       Mastres Geretrude
       With womanhode endude
       Withe vertew wele renewde.
Partly by your counselle
Garnnysshid withe laurelle
Was my freshe coronelle   1050
Wherfor dowtles ye geve me cause
To wright of yow this goodely clause
       Mastres Geretrude
       Withe womanhode endude
       Withe vertu wele renewde.

TO MASTRES ISBELL KNYGHT

Bot if I shulde aquyte your kyndnes
Els say ye myght
That in me were grete blyndnes
I for to be so myndles
And kowde not wright   1060
Of Isbel Knyght:

It is not my kustome nor my gyse
To leve behynde

Her that is both maydenly and wise
And specially whiche glad was to devyse
The mene to fynde
To plese my mynde:

In helpynge to warke my laureel grene
Withe silke and golde:
Galathea the maide wele besene   1070
Was never half so fayre as I wene
Whiche was extolde
A thowsand folde

By Maro the Mantuane prudent
Who list to rede:
Bot and I had leysor competente
I kowde shew yow soche a presedente
In verey dede
How ye excede.

OCCUPACIOUN. TO SKELTON.

118

Wythdraw your hand, the tyme passithe fast,   1080
Set on your hede this laurelle whiche is wrowght:
Here ye not Eolus for yow blowithe a blast?
I dare wele say that ye and I be sowght:
Make no delay, for now ye most be browght
Before my ladis grace the Quene of Fame,
Where ye most brevely aunswere to your name.

CAPITULUM DECIMUM

POETA SKELTON.

119

CASTINGE my sight the chaumber aboute
To se how duly eche thinge in order was,
Toward the durre as we were komynge owte
I saw Master Newton sit withe his compas,   1090

His plummet, his penselle, his spectakils of glas,
Devysinge in picture by his industryows wit
Of my laureell the proces every whit.

120

Forthwith upon this, as it were in a thowght,
Gower, Chawser, Lydgate, theis iii.
Before rememberd, kurteisly me browght
In to that place where as they left me
Where alle the saide poetis sat in ther degre:
Bot when they saw my lawrelle rychely wrowght,
Alle thos that they ware were counterfettis, they thowght,   1100

121

In comparison of that whiche I ware:
Sum praisid the perle, sum the stonys bright:
Wele was hym that there upon myght stare:
Of this worke they had so grete delight,
The silke, the golde, the flowris freshe to sight,
They saide my laureel was the goodelyest
That ever they saw: and wrowght it was the best.

122

In her astate there sat the nobille Quene
Of Fame: perceyvynge how that I was kum,
She wonderde, me thowght, at my laurelle grene: 1110
She lokid hawtely and yave on me a glum:
There was not a worde amonge them then bot mum,
For eche man harkend / what she to me wold say,
Where of in substance I browght this away.

THE QUENE OF FAME. TO SKELTON.

123

My frynde, sithe ye ar before us here present
To aunswere unto this nobille audyence,

Of that shalle be resond yow ye most be content:
And for asmoche as by the higthe pretence
That ye have now thorow preemynence
Of laureat promocioun, your place is here reservyd,   1120
We wille understand how ye have it deservid.

POETA SKELTON. TO THE QUENE OF FAME.

124

Right higthe and myghtty prynces of astate,
In famows glory alle other transcenddinge:
Of your bownte the acustomabille rate
Hathe bene fulle oftene, and yit is entendinge
To alle that to reson is condiscendynge,
Bot if hastyve credence by mayntenaunce of myght
Fortune to stande bytwene yow and the light:

125

Bot soche evydence I thynke for me to enduce
And so largely to ley for myn indempnyte,   1130
That I troste to make myne excuse
Of what charge so ever ye ley ageyne me:
For of my bokis parte ye shalle se,
Whiche in your recorddis I know wele be enrolde:
And so Occupacioun your regester me tolde.

126

Forthwithe she commaundid I shuld take my place:
Caliope poyntid me where I shuld sit:
Wythe that Occupacioun presid in a pace:
Be myrry, she sayd, be not aferde a whit,
Your discharge here under myne arme is it: 1140
So then commaundid she was upon this
To shew her boke: and she sayde, here it is.

THE QUENE OF FAME. TO OCCUPACIOUN.

127

Yowre boke of remembraunce we wille now that ye rede,
If any recorddis in nowmbyr can be fownde
What Skelton hathe compilyd and wryttyn in dede,
Rehersinge by order and what is the grownde:
Let se now for hym how ye kan expownde,
For in owre courte ye wote wele his name kan not ryse
Bot if he wright oftener than onys or twyse.

CAPITULUM UNDECIMUM

POETA SKELTON.

128

WITHE that of the boke losond were the claspis: 1150
The margent was illumynid alle withe golden raillis
And byse: enpycturid with gressoppis and waspis,
With butterfliys and freshe pokok taylis,
Enflorid with flowris and slymy snaylis,
Envyvid picturis wele towchid and quikly:
It wold have made a man hole that had be ryght sikkly

129

To beholde how it was garnnysshid and bownde,
Encoverde over with gold of tissew fyne:
The claspis and bullyons were worthe a thowsand pownde:
With balassis and charbunclis the borders did shyne: 1160
Withe aurum musicum every other lyne
Was wryttyn: and so she did her spede,
Occupacioun / immediatly to rede.

Occupacioun redithe and expowndithe sum parte of
Skeltons bokis and baladis with ditis of plesure
in asmoche as it were to longe a proces to reherse
alle by name that he hathe compilyd. &c.

130

Of youre orator and poete laureate
Of England his workkis here they begyn:
In primis The Boke of Honorows Astate:
Item The Boke How Men Shuld Fle Syn:
Item Roialle Demenaunce, worshyp to wyn:
Item The Boke to Speke Wele, or be stille:
Item To Lerne Yow to Dye, when ye wille.

1170

131

Of Vertu also, the sovereyne enterlude:
The Boke of the Rosiar: Prynce Arturis Creacioune:
The Fals Faythe That Now Gothe, which daily is reneude:
Item his Dialoggis of Imagynacioune:
Item Automedon, Of Lovys Meditacioune:
Item New Gramer, in Englyshe compilyd:
Item Bowche of Courte, where Drede was begylid.

132

His comedy, Achademios callid by name:
Of Tullis Familiars the Translacioun:
Item Goode Avysemente, that braynles dothe blame:
The Recule Ageyne Gagwyne, of the Frenshe nacioun:
Item The Popingay, that hathe in commendacioun
Ladis and jantylwomen, soche as deservid:
And soche as be counterfettis, they be reservid:

1180

133

And of Sovereynte, a nobille pamphelet:
And of Magnyfycence, a notabille matter,
How Counterfet Countenaunce of the new get,
With Crafty Conveyaunce dothe smater and flater,
And Clokid Collucyoun is browght in to clatter
With Courtly Abusyoun: who pryntithe it wele in mynde,
Moche dowbilnes of the worlde there in he may fynde.

1190

Honor est benefactive operacionis signum: Aristotiles. [*Rhet.* 1.5]

Diverte a malo, et fac bonum: Pso. [33.15]

Nobilis est ille quem nobilitat sua virtus: Cassianus.
Proximus ille deo qui scit racione tacere: Cato. [*Dist.* 1.3]
Mors ultima linea rerum: Horat. [*Ep.* 1.16.79]

Virtuti omnia parent: Salust. [*Cat.* 2.7]

Nusquam tuta fides: Virgilius. [*Eneid.* 4.373]

Res est solliciti plena timoris amor: Ovid. [*Her.* 1.12]
Si [volet] usus quem penes, &c: Horace. [*Ars.* 71]

Non est timor dei ante oculos eorum: Psalmo. [13.3]

Concedat laurea Lingue: Tullius. [*Off.* 1.22.77]

Fac cum consilio & in eternum non peccabis: Salomon. [Ecclus. 7.40]

Non mihi sit modulo rustica papilio: Vates.

Dominare in virtute tua: Pso. [65.7]

Magnificavit eum in conspectu regum: Sapienc. [Ecclus. 45.3].

Fugere pudor, verumque, fidesque: In quorum subiere locum fraudesque, dolique, insidieque, et vis et amor sceleratus habendi: Ovid. [*Met.* 1.130]

134

Of Mannerly Mastres Margery Mylke and Ale:
To her he wrate many maters of myrthe,
Yit thowthe I say it, there by lyith a tale,
For Margery wynshid and breke her hinder girthe:
Lor, how she made moche of her jantyl birthe!
With gingirly, go gingirly, her tayle was made of hay:
Go she never so gingirly, her honeste is gone away.

Filia Babilonis misera: Psalmo. [136.8]

135

Hard to make owght of that is nakid nowght:
This fustian mastres and this giggishe gase,   1200
Wonder is to wright what wrenchis she wrowght
To face owght her foly with a mydsomer mase:
With pitche she patchid / her pitcher shuld not crase:
It may wele ryme, bot shrewdly it dothe acorde
To pyke owte honeste of soche a potshorde.

De nihilo nihil fit: Aristotiles.

La plus displeysant pleiser puent.

Patet per versus:

HINC PUER HIC NATUS: VIR CONJUGIS HINC SPOLIATUS
JURE THORI: EST FOETUS DELI DE SANGUINE CRETUS:
HINC MAGIS EXTOLLO QUOD ERIT PUER ALTER APOLLO:
SI QUERIS QUALIS: MERETRIX CASTISSIMA TALIS.
          Et relis et ralis, et reliqualis: 1210
          A goode herynge of theis olde talis:
          Fynde no mo soche fro Wanflete to Walis.

Nota.

Et reliqua omelia de diversis tractatibus.

136

Of My Ladys Grace at the contemplacyoun,
Owte of Frenshe vers in to Englyshe prose,
Of Mannys Lyf the Peregrynacioun
He did translate, enterprete, and disclose:
The Traytyse of Tryumphis / of the Rede Rose,
Where in many stories ar brevely contaynnid,
That unrememberd longe tyme remaynnid.

Apostolus: Non habemus hic civitatem manentem, sed futuram perquerimus. [Heb. 13.14]

Notat bellum Cornubiense quod in campestribus et in patencioribus vastisque solitudinibus prope Grenewiche gestum est.

137

The Duke of Yorkis creauncer when Skelton was,   1220
Now Henry the .VIII. / kynge of Englande,
A traytyse he devysid and browght it to pas,
Callid Speculum Principis, to bere in his hande,
There in to rede and to understande
Alle the demenor of pryncely astate,
To be owre kynge / of God preordinate.

Erudimini qui judicatis
terram: Pso. [2.10]

138

Also The Tunnynge of Elinor Rummyng:
With Colyn Clowte, John Ive, withe Joforthe Jak:
To make soche trifels it askithe sum konyng:
In honest myrthe parde / requyrithe no lak: 1230
The whight aperythe the better for the blak:
And after conveyaunce as the world gose,
It is no foly to use the Walshemannys hose.

Quis stabit mecum
adversus operantes
iniquitatem? Pso.
[93.16]

Arrident melius seria
picta jocis: In fabulis
Isopi.

139

The umblis of venysoun, the botell of wyne
To fayre Mastres Anne that shulde have be sent,
He wrate therof many a praty line,
Where it becam and whither it went,
And how that it was wantonly spent:
The Balade also of the Mustarde Tarte:
Soche problemys to paynte it longithe to his arte.   1240

Implentur veteris
Bacchi pinguisque
ferine: Virgilius.
[Eneid. 1.215]

Aut prodesse volunt
aut delectare poete:
Horace. [Ars. 333]

140

Of one Adame Alle-a-Knave, late dede and gone,
Dormiat in pace / lyke a dormows,
He wrate an epitaphe for his grave stone,
With worddis devowte and sentence agerdows,
For he was ever ageyne Goddis hows:
Alle his delight was to brawle and to barke
Ageyne Holy Chyrche, the preste and the clarke.

Adam, Adam, ubi es?
Genesis. [3.9]

Respondet: Ubi nulla
requies, ubi nullus
ordo, sed sempiternus
horror inhabitat: Job.
[10.22]

141

Of Phyllype Sparow the lamentabille fate,

Etenim passer invenit
sibi domum: Psalmo.
[83.4]
The dolefulle destiny and the carefulle chaunce,
Devysid by Skelton after the funeralle rate: 1250
Yit sum there be there with that take grevaunce,
And grudge there at with frownnyng countenaunce:
Bot what of that? Hard is to plese alle men:
Who list amende it, let hym set to his pen:

    For the gyse now a daiys
    Of sum jangelyng jaiys
    Is to discommende
    That they kan not amende,
    Thowthe they wold spende
    Alle the wittis they have::   1260

    What ayle them to deprave
    Phyllype Sparows grave?
    His dirige, her commendacioun
    Kan be no derogacioun,
    Bot myrthe and consolacioun
    Made by protestacioun
    No man to myscontente
    Withe Phyllyppis enteremente.

    Alas that goodely mayd
    Why shuld she be afrayd,   1270
    Why shuld she take shame
    That her goodely name,
    Honorably reporttid,
    Shulde be set and sortid,
    To be matriculate
    Withe ladys of astate?

    I conjure the, Phyllype Sparow,
    By Hercules that helle did harow,
    And with a venomows arow
    Slew of the Epidawris   1280
    One of the Centawris,
    Or Onocentawris,
    Or Hippocentawris:

By whos myght and maine
An hart was slayne
With hornnis twayne
Of glitteryng golde:
And the appils of golde
Of Hesperides withe holde,
And withe a dragon kepte   1290
That never more slepte,
By marcialle strengthe
He wan at lengthe:

And slew Gerione
Withe thre bodys in one:
Withe myghtty corage
Adaunttid the rage
Of a lyon savage:
Of Diomedis stabylle
He browght owte a rabylle   1300
Of coursers and rownsis
Wit lepis and bownsis:

And wythe myghtty luggynge,
Wrastelynge and tuggynge,
He plukkid the bulle
By the hornnid skulle,
And offerde to Cornucopia,
And so forthe, per cetera:

Also by Hecates bowre
In Plutos gastly towre: 1310

By the ugly Eumenides
That never have rest nor ese:

By that venemows serpente
That in helle is never brente,
In Lerna the Grekis fen
That was engenderde then:

By Chemeras flamys
And alle the dedely namys
Of infernalle posty
Where sowllis fry and rosty: 1320

By the Stigialle flode
And the stremys wode
Of Cochitos botumles welle:

By the feryman of helle,
Caron with his berde hore,
That rowyth with a rude ore,
And with his frownsid fortop,
Gydithe his bote with a prop:

I conjure Phyllype and calle
In the name of Kynge Saul,   1330
Primo regum expres:
He bad the Phitones
To witche craft her to dres,
And by her abusyouns
And damnabille illusiouns
Of marvelows conclusiouns,
And by her supersticiouns
Of wonderfulle condiciouns
She raysid up in that stede
Samuell that was dede: 1340

Bot wheither it were so,
He were idem in numero
The selfe same Samuell,
How be it to Saul he did telle
The Phillistinnis shuld hym askry,
And the nexte day he shulde dy:
I wille my selfe discharge
To letterde men at large:

Bot Phillipe I conjure the
Now by theis namys thre: 1350
Dyana in the woddis grene:
Luna that so bryght dothe shene:
Proserpina in helle:
That thow shortly telle
And shew now unto me
What the cause may be
Of this perplexyte!

INFERIAS PHILLIPPE TUAS SCROUPE PULCHRA JOHANNA
INSTANTER PECIIT: CUR NOSTRI CARMINIS ILLAM
NUNC PUDET? EST SERO: MINOR EST INFAMIA VERO.   1360 Phillipe awnswerithe.

    Then soche that have disdaynid
    And of this warke complaynid
    I pray God they be paynid
    No wurse than is contaynid
    In versis two or thre
    That folow as ye may se:

LURIDE CUR LIVOR VOLUCRIS PIA FUNERA DAMNAS?
TALIA TE RAPIANT RAPIUNT QUE FATA VOLUCREM:
EST TAMEN INVIDIA MORS TIBI CONTINUA.

142

The Grontyng and the Groynnynge of the Gronnyng Swyne: 1370
Also The Murnnynge of the Mapely Rote:
How The Grene Coverlet Sufferde Grete Pyne,
When the flye net was set / for to catche a cote,
Strake one withe a birdbolt to the harte rote:
Also A Devowte Prayer to Moyses Hornnis,
Metrifyde merely, medelyd withe scornnis.

Porcus se ingurgitat ceno, et luto se immergit: Guarinus Veronens. [Reuchlin, *Vocabularius Breviloquus*]

Et sicut opertorium mutabis eos, et mutabuntur: Pso. [101.27]

Exaltabuntur cornua justi: Psalmo. [74.11]

143

Of pajauntis that were plaiyd in Joyows Garde:
He wrate Of a Muse thorow a Mud Walle,
How a do kam trippyng in at the rerewarde:
Bot Lorde, how the parker was wrothe withe alle!   1380
And Of Castell Aungell the Fenestralle,
Glittryng and glistryng and gloriowsly glasid:
It made sum mens ien dasild and dasid.

Tanquam parieti inclinato et macerie depulse: Psalmo. [61.4]

Militat omnis amans, et habet sua castra Cupido: Ovid. [*Amores* 1.9.1]

144

The Repete of the Recule of Rosamundis Bowre:
Of his plesant payne there and his glad distres,
In plantynge and plukkynge a proper jeloffer flowre:

Introduxit me in cubiculum suum: Cant. [1.3]

Bot how it was / sum were to recheles,
Not withstandinge / it is remedeles:

What myght she say, what myght he do there to?
Thowthe Jak sayd nay, yet Mok there lost her sho.   1390

145

How Than Lyke a Man He Wan the Barbican,
Withe a sawte of solace at the longe laste:
The colour dedely, swarte, blo and wan,
Of Exione, his limbis dede and past,
The cheke and the nek bot a shorte caste:

In Fortunis favor ever to endure,
No man lyvynge, he saithe, kan be sure.

146

How Dame Mynerve fyrste fownde the olyve tre, *she red*
And plantid it there where never before was none: *unshred*
An hynde unhurt / hit by casuelte, *not bled*   1400
Recoverde when the foster was gone: *and sped*

The harttis of the herde began for to grone, *and fled*
The hownddis began to yerne and to quest: *and dred*
With litille besynes standithe moche rest. *in bed*

147

His Epitomis of the Myllar and His Joly Make,
How her ble was bryght as blossome on the spray:
A wanton wenche, and wele kowde bake a cake,
The myllar was lothe to be owte of the way:
Bot yit for all that, be as be may,

Wheither he rode to Swaffhamm or to Some,   1410
The millar dorste not leve his wif at home.

148

Wythe Wofully Arayd and Shamefully Betrayde,
Of his makyng / devowte meditaciouns:
Vexilla Regis he devysid to be displayde,

With Sacris Solempniis, and other contemplaciouns,
That in them comprisid / consideraciouns:
Thus passithe he the tyme bothe nyght and day,
Sum tyme with sadnes, sum tyme withe play.

149

Thowthe Galiene and Diascorides
Withe Ipocras and Master Avycen   1420
By ther phisik dothe many a man ese:
And thowthe Albumasar kan the enforme and ken
What constellaciouns ar goode or bad for men:
Yit when the rayne raynithe and the gose wynkkith,
Lytille wotithe the goslyng what the gose thynkithe.

*Honora medicum:
propter necessitatem
creavit eum altissimus.
&c.* [Ecclus. 38.1]

*Superiores constella-
ciones influunt in
corpora subjecta et
disposita.* &c.

Nota.

150

He is not wise ageyne the streme that stryvithe:
Dun is in the myre, Dame, reche me my spurre:
Nedis most he ryn that the develle dryvithe:
When the stede is stolyn, spar the stabyl durre:
A jantylle hownde shuld never play the kurre: 1430
It is sone aspiyd where the thorne prikkithe,
And wele wotithe the cat whos berde she likkithe.

*Spectatum admissi
risum teneatis, amici:
Horace.* [*Ars.* 5]

Nota.

151

Wyth Marion Clarion, Sol, Lucerne,
Graund Ivir: of this Frenshe proverbe olde,
How men were wonte for to discerne
By Candelmas Day what wedder shuld holde:
Bot Marion Clarion was caught with a cold colde,
And all overcast with clowddis unkynde:
This goodely floure with stormmis was untwynde.

*Lumen ad revelacio-
nem gentium:* [Luc.
2.32]

anglice,
a kokkolde

152

This jeloffer jantyl, this rose, this lylly flowr,   1440
This primerose pereles, this proper vyolet,
This columbyne clere and fresshest of colour,
This delycate daisy, this strawbery prately set,

*Velut rosa vel lilium, O
pulcherrima mulierum.
&c. Cantat ecclesia.*

With froward frostis alas, was alle to-fret:
Bot who may have a more ungraciows lif
Than a chyldis birde, and a knavis wif?

Thynke what ye wille
Of this wanton bille:
By Mary Gipsy
Quod scripsi scripsi: 1450

Notate verba, signata misteria: Gregori.

Uxor tua sicut vitis
Habetis in custodiam:
Custodite sicut scitis
Secundum Lucam. &c.

153

Of the Bone Homs of Ashrige beside Barkamstede,
That goodely place to Skelton moost kynde,
Where the Sank Roialle is, Crystis blode so rede,
Where upon he metrifyde after his mynde:
A plesanter place than Ashrige is / hard were to fynde,
As Skelton rehersithe withe worddis few and playne   1460
In his distincyon made on versis twayne:

Nota penuriam aque nam canes ibi hauriunt ex puteo altissimo.

FRAXINUS IN CLIVO FRONDETQUE VIRET SINE RIVO:
NON EST SUB DIVO SIMILIS SINE FLUMINE VIVO.

154

Stultorum infinitus est numerus. &c. [Eccles. 1.15]

The nacioun of folys he left not behynde:
Item Apollo that Whirllid up His Chayre,
That made sum to snurre and snuffe in the wynde:

Factum est cum apollo esset Corinthi: Actus Apostolorum [19.1]

It made them to skip, to stampe, and to stare,
Whiche if they be happy / have cause to beware
In rymynge and raylynge withe hym for to melle,

Stimulos sub pectore vertit Apollo: Virgilius. [Eneid. 6.101]

For drede that he lerne them ther A.B.C. to spelle.   1470

POETA SKELTON.

155

Withe that I stode up half sodenly afraiyd:
Suppleyng to Fame, I besowght her grace,
And that it wold plese her, fulle tenderly I praiyd
Owte of her bokis Apollo to rase:
Nay Sir, she sayd: what so in this place
Of oure nobille courte is onys spokyn owte,
It most nedes after ryn alle the worlde aboute.

Fama repleta malis
pernicibus evolat alis.
&c.

156

God wote theis wordis made me fulle sad,
And when that I sawe it wold no better be,
Bot that my peticioun wold not be had,   1480
What shuld I do bot take it in gre?
For by Juppiter and his higthe mageste,
I did what I kowde to scrape owte the scrollis,
Apollo to race owte of her ragman rollis.

Ego quidem sum
Pauli, ego Apollo:
[I] Corinthios. [1.12]

157

Now here of it erkith me longer to wright:
To Occupacioun I wille agayne resorte,
Whiche redde on stille as it kam to her sight,
Rendrynge my devisis I made in disporte
Of the Mayden of Kent Callid Counforte:
Of Lovers Testamenttis, and of ther wanton willis,   1490
And How Iollas Lovid Goodely Phillis:

Malo me Galatea petit
lasciva puella: Vir-
gilius. [Bucol. 3.64]

Nec si muneribus certes
concedat Iollas: [Vir-
gilius] 2. Bucol. [57]

158

Diodorus Siculus of my translacioun,
Owte of freshe Latine into owre Englyshe playne,
Recountynge commoditis of many a straunge nacioun:
Who redithe it onys wold rede it agayne:
Sex volummys engrosid together it dothe contayne:
Bot when of The Laurelle she made rehersalle,
Alle orators and poetis, with other grete and smalle,

Mille hominum spe-
cies, et rerum discolor
usus: [Percius. 5.52]

159

Millia millium et decies
millies centena millia.
&c. Apocalipsis.
[Dan. 7.10]

Vite senatum laureati
possident: Ecclesiastica
canit. [Hymnus in
festo SS. Petri et Pauli
ad Vesperas]

A thowsand thowsand, I trow to my dome,
Triumpha, triumpha! they criyde alle abowte: 1500
Of trumpettis and clariounis the noyce went to Rome:
The starry heven, me thowght, shoke with the showte:
The grownde gronid and trembild, the noyce was so stowte:
The Quene of Fame commaundid / shett fast the boke,
And there withe sodenly owte of my dreme I woke.

160

My mynde of the grete din was sumdele amasid:
I wypid myne ien for to make them clere:
Then to the heven sperycal upward I gasid,
Where I saw Janus with his dowbill chere
Makynge his almanak for the new yere: 1510
He turnnyd his tirrikis, his volvell ran faste:
Goode luk this new yere! The olde yere is paste!

Vates.

Mens tibi sit consulta petis: sic consule menti:
Emula sit Jani, retro speculetur et ante.

SKELTONIS ALLOQUITUR LIBRUM SUUM

ITE BRITANNORUM LUX O RADIOSA, BRITANNUM
CARMINA NOSTRA PIUM VESTRUM CELEBRATE CATULLUM!
    DICITE SKELTONIS VESTER ADONIS ERAT:
    DICITE SKELTONIS VESTER HOMERUS ERAT.
BARBARA CUM LACIO PARITER IAM CURRITE VERSU,
ET LICET EST VERBO PARS MAXIMA TEXTA BRITANNO, 1520
    NON MAGIS INCOMPTA NOSTRA THALYA PATET,
    EST MAGIS INCULTA NEC MEA CALIOPE.
NEC VOS PENITEAT LIVORIS TELA SUBIRE,
NEC VOS PENITEAT RABIEM TOLERARE CANINAM:
    NAM MARO DISSIMILES NON TULIT ILLE MINAS,
    IMMUNIS NEC ENIM MUSA NASONIS ERAT.

LENVOY

Go litille quayre
Demene yow fayre,
Take no dispayre,
Thowthe I yow wrate   1530
After this rate
In Englyshe letter.

So moche the better
Welcum shalle ye
To sum men be:
For Latin warkis
Be goode for clarkis:

Yit now and then
Sum Latin men
May happely loke   1540
Upon youre boke
And so procede
In yow to rede
That so indede
Youre fame may sprede
In lengthe and brede.
Bot then I drede
Ye shalle have nede
Yow for to spede
To harnnes bryght   1550
By force of myght

Ageyne envy
And obloquy:
And wote ye why?

Not for to fyght
Ageyne dispyght,
Nor to derayne
Batayle agayne
Scornfulle disdayne,
Nor for to chyde   1560
Nor for to hyde
Yow cowardly:

Bot kurteisly
That I have pende
For to deffende
Under the banner
Of alle goode manner,
Under proteccioun
Of sad correccioun,
Withe toleracioun   1570
And supportacioun
Of reformacioun
If they kan spy
Circumspectly
Any worde defacid
That myght be racid:

Els ye shalle pray
Them that ye may
Contynew stille
Withe ther goode wille.   1580

Ad Serenissimam Majestatem Regiam, pariter cum Domino
Cardinali, Legato a latere honorificatissimo, &c.

LAUTRE ENVOY

Perge, liber, celebrem pronus regem venerare   1581
Henricum Octavum, resonans sua premia laudis.
Cardineum dominum pariter venerando salutes,
Legatum a latere, et fiat memor ipse precare
Prebende, quam promisit mihi credere quondam,
Meque suum referas pignus sperare salutis.
Inter spemque metum.

    Twene hope and drede
    My lif I lede   Smalle sekernes.
    Bot of my spede   1590

    How be it I rede
    Bothe worde and dede   In nobilnes.
    Shuld be agrede
    Or els. &c.

ADMONET SKELTONIS OMNES ARBORES DARE LOCUM   1596a
VIRIDI LAURO JUXTA GENUS SUUM

Fraxinus in silvis, altis in montibus ornus,
Populus in fluviis, abies, patulissima fagus,
Lenta salix, platanus, pinguis ficulnea ficus,
Glandifera et quercus, pirus, esculus, ardua pinus,   1600
Balsamum exudans, oleaster, oliva Minerve,
Juniperus, buxus, lentiscus cuspide lenta,
Botrigera et domino vitis gratissima Baccho,
Ilex et sterilis labrusca perosa colonis,
Mollibus exudans fragrancia thura Sabeis
Thus, redolens Arabis pariter notissima mirrha,
Et vos, O corili fragiles, humilesque mirice,
Et vos, O cedri redolentes, vos quoque mirti,
Arboris omne genus viridi concedite lauro!

Prenes en gre. The Laurelle.   1609a

EN PARLAMENT A PARIS

Justice est morte,   1610
Et veryte sommielle:
Droit et raison
Sont alez aux pardons.

Les deux premiers
Nul ne les resuelle,
Et les derniers
Sount corrumpus par dons.

OWTE OF FRENSHE IN TO LATYN

Abstulit atra dies Astream: cana fides sed
   Sompno pressa jacet: jus iter arripuit,
Et secum racio proficiscens limite longo: 1620
   Nemo duas primas evigilare parat:
Atque duo postrema absunt, et munera tantum
   Impediunt, nequiunt quod remeare domum.

OWTE OF LATYNE IN TO ENGLYSHE

Justyce now is dede:
Trowthe withe a drowsy hede
As hevy as the lede
Is layd downe to slepe,
And takithe no kepe:

And ryght is over the fallows,
Gone to seke hallows   1630
Withe reson to gither,
No man can telle whither.

No man wille undertake
The fyrste twayne to wake:

And the twayne last
Be withe holde so fast
Withe mony, as men sayne,
They can not com agayne.

A grant tort
Foy dort.　　　　　　　　　　1640

Textual Notes

In preparing the text, the editor has silently expanded abbreviations according to the spelling and word-division of *A*. Original *u*, *v*, *i*, and *j* are modernized. Capitalization is modern. Punctuation is editorial, but based on *A*, using the comma, *virga*, colon, and period. As explained in the introduction, the spelling of those parts of the text taken from *B* and *C* follows the spelling of *A*.

The textual notes describe the makeup of the text, and provide a record of variants that seem significant. The editions of Dyce (*D*), and Scattergood (*S*) are fully collated. Readings from Hammond (*Hd*) and Henderson (*Hn*) are recorded selectively. Modifications that restore the forms of *A* to passages derived from *B* and *C* are attributed to [*A*]. *C* is a reprint of *B*, its authority limited to the missing passages it supplies and to the corrections it makes; similarly, *D* and, more especially, *S*, are reprints of *B*. Therefore, unless otherwise indicated, a variant attributed to *B* will also be found in *C*, *D*, and *S*. Except for some variants that seem to reveal the influence of MS copy on *C*, accidental variants from *C* are not recorded.

Title] *B* only.

Title, 11. solacyons] *B*; solacyous *S*. It seems better on grounds of syntax and editorial principle not to emend, although *solacyous* occurs elsewhere in Skelton, including *Laurel*, 683. (Its use in the title of *STC* 22604, *Dyvers Balettys and Dyties Solacyous devysyd by Master Skelton Laureat*, however, probably derives from *B*'s title: see Kinsman, *HLQ* 16:203–10, who identifies the printer as John Rastell, and suggests that reading *The Laurel* encouraged him to publish work by Skelton ca. 1526–29.) *Solacyons* > L *solacium*, *-a*, means things that soothe, comfort, and relieve. *OED* gives a use by Caxton (1483), defined as "rejoicing"; Skelton's use could mean "occasions of joy." That the word is rare does not mean that Skelton did not use it here, in parallel with *allectyves*.

Prefatory verses] *B* only.

PROLOGUS] [*A*]. Cf. *Bowge of Courte*, *STC* 22597, Sig. A4, "Thus endeth the prologue"; also *C*, Sig. D6v, "The Prolgue to the Bouge / of Courte."

Stanza 1, heading. POETA SKELTON] [*A*]; Skelton Poeta. *B*; no heading *AC*. *B*'s woodcut (Hodnett 2058) illustrates this heading; the heading is not a caption to the cut.

4. orbicular] *ACDS*; orbucular *B*.

6. plenarly] *ADS*; plenary *B*.

23. fylt] *AB*; sylt *CDS*. Long *s* and *f* are often indistinguishable in this MS, because the cross-stroke of the *f*, formed by the first stroke of the next letter, may not completely cross the downstroke of the *f*. This happens in *fond* (741) and *exemplify* (854), where the letter is obviously an *f*; but the same form represents *s* in *diffuse* (111) and *dissuasyve* (151). In 137, the same form represents *f* in *Wherefor* and *s* in *rasid*. In *fylt/sylt*, the upstroke of the *y* crosses the downstroke of *f/s* (though this is hard to see at first), and so *B*'s *fylt* (meaning "filth" or "mud") is probably correct. *C*, followed by *D* and *S*, prefers the alliteration on *s*. Cf. notes to 77, 149. The spelling *-t* for *-th* appears occasionally in *B*: *wit/wiht* for *with* (358, 455, 680, 733, 1302); *dryvit* for *dryvith* (1428). Like other unusual *B* spellings, these could be Skelton's; *fylt* in *A* is another example.

23. moose] *ABCD*; wose *S*. Edwards, 26, proposed this emendation because "myry wose," "wosy myre," and "sylt & fatte wose" are phrases appearing in Skelton's *Diodorus*. Yet *moose* ("moss," i.e., marshy ground, as in the place-name Bidston Moss) is a well-attested word that describes exactly the terrain of the Forest of Galtres. There is no need to emend.

26. telle now where] *AD*; tell where *B*.

27. foster] *A*; forster *B*. that so wele] *B* (well); that so *A*.

28. proces] *A*; purpose *B*.

30. fille] *A*; fell *B*. The change of *i* to *e* is characteristic of *B*.

35. not wele telle] *AD*; not tell *B*.

36. avysid] *A*; advysed *B*.

38. wonderly] *A*; wondersly *B*.

43. Withe in it] *AD*; within that *B*. *B* has misread *yt* as *y^t* in his copy.

47. immortalle] *AC*; inmortall *B*.

47–49. gloss] *A* only. See commentary.

49a. CAPITULUM PRIMUM] *A*, where it appears in the outer margin of f. 209, opposite stanza 8, 52–54.

51. Renowmmyd] *A*; Renownyd *B*.

53. Scyence] *AB*; sciences *C*.

54. lene] *AB*; lenen *CD*; leven *S*. *C* provides a rhyme on the weak second syllable. *S*'s emendation, like that of *mose* to *wose*, 23, is against the authority of the independent witnesses *AB*. *Lene* is not a mistake. It is either a weak rhyme (the second rhyme of the stanza, needing three words, gives Skelton trouble elsewhere), or, more likely, it is evidence of the loss of intervocalic *v* in the other two words (Dobson, 2:965).

56. beseke] *A*; beseche *B*.

58. yave me in] *A*; gave me a *B*.

60. his tyme he] *AD*; he his tyme *B*.

66. enbissy] *A*; embesy *B*.

68. they were the] *ACDS*; the were they *B*.

70. grete lak] *AB*; a lacke *C*.

73. thensugerd] *A*; the sugred *B*.

74. Elyconys] *ACDS*; elycoms *B*.

77. syttynge] *BCDS*, *f/s* equivocal in *A* (see note to 23); fyttynge *HdHn*.

78. avysid] *A*; advysid *B*.

79. Is for that] *A*; Is that *B*.

82. Better] *ACD*; Bete *B*.

83. pullishe] *AD*; publisshe *B*.

85. And if hym] *A*; And if so hym *B*.

88. corde] *A*; accorde *B*.

90. hunderd] *A*; hundreth *B*; hundred *C*.

96. For that he enveiyd: yit wrate] *A*; For certayne envectyfys: yet wrote] *B*.

97. on] *AB*; upon *CD*.

98. byde] *A*; abyde *B*.

101. parabols] *A*; paroblis *BS*; parables *C*; parablis *D*. *D* is certainly correct to emend *o* to *a*; See Intro., p. 21.

106. that be] *A*; ther be *B*.

107. conjecture] *ACDS*; convecture *B*.

113. benygne] *AC*; benynge *B*. *A* always spells this word *benygne* (728, 880, 918), even *benyngne* (213), in the French manner. As the rhyme *benygne/thynge* (728, 730) shows, the spelling reflects Skelton's conservative spelling habits (cf. *repungnaunce, B,* 211), not his pronunciation, represented by *B*'s spelling. Dobson (2:1007) says that forms like *benyng* and *condyng* "appear to be distinctively Scottish" in the 15–16C.

117. have that] *AD*; have the *B*.

119. immortalle] *AC*; inmortall *B*.

120. slawthfulle] *A*; slowthfull *B*; sloughtfull *C*.

126. for that he] *B*; for he *A*.

131. Whiche yave] *A*; That gave *B*.

134. goode my] *A*; my good *B*.

140. sclaunderde] *A*; slaundred *B*; sklaundred *C*. A good example of MS influence, possibly from *A*, upon *C*.

141. opposelle] *A*; apposelle *B*. Another *o/a* error in *B*.

142. avauntage] *ACDS*; avanuntage *B*.

143. debarrid] *AD*; barrid *B*.

149. it is syttynge] *A*, *f/s* equivocal; it sittyng *B* (siteyng) *CDS*; it fitting *Hn*.

151. honor] *AC*; onour *B*.

161. Sithe thowthe] *A*; For though *B*.

164. Where he] *A*; Where in he *B*.

171. yit a grete parte] *A*; a grete parte yet *B*.

178. ye wold] *A*; ye wyll *B*.

180. ofte tyme ye] *A*; oft ye do *B*.

181. For reporte] *B*; Report *A*.

184. kit] *A*; pyke *B*.

185. ther] *ACD*; the *B*.

188. liddurns] *A*; lidderous *B*; lidderons *CDS*.

189. and sum] *A*; some *B*.

196. ryde they and ryn they] *A*; they ryde and rinne *B*.

197. shalle ye] *A*; ye shall *B*.

200. a mummyng] *AD*; mummynge *B*.

201. be set owte] *ACD*; be out *B*.

204. shalle] *A*; wyll *B*.

207. fynde wele] *A*; well fynde *B*.

208. Twishe] *ACD*; Twyse *B*.

209. syt upon] *A*; syt hym upon *B*.

211. repugnaunce] *ACS*; repungnaunce *BD*.

213. benyngne] *A*; benynge *B*; benign *C*.

215. beseke] *A*; beseche *B*. recorde] *A*; good recorde *B*.

227. jurisdiccioun] *A*; jurydiccyon *B*; jurisdiction *C*.

235. whiche] *A*; that *B*.

237. the vew] *A*; a vewe *B*.

239. dare put] *A*; wyll put *B*.

242. now spede yow] *B* (you); now spede *A*.

245. bararag brag] *A*; bararag *B*.

245a. CAPITULUM SECUNDUM] [*A*].

245b. POETA SKELTON] [*A*]; Skelton Poeta *B*.

246–720] *BC* only.

263. Drive] *This ed.*; drove *B*. Since *boryalle wynddis* is the antecedent of *That*, the present tense is needed, in parallel with *blow* and *cast*.

272. melodiowsly] *C* (melodiously); meledyously *BDS*.

285. com] *B* (come); came *C*.

289. yalowe] *B*; yolowe *C*.

295. murnnynge] [*A*]; murmynge *B*; murnynge *CDS*. *B*'s *m* for *n* probably indicates *nn* in the copy. Cf. notes to 375, 1345, 1371.

298. have yow lovyd] *This ed.*; lovyd you have *B*. *B*'s inversion, confusing syntactically, tuneless rhythmically, looks like one of the compositor's reversals of proper word order.

302. his] *B*; this *CD*.

303. immortalle] [*A*]*C*; inmortall *B*.

314. gresse] *CDS*; gras *B*.

326. Declamacyouns] *CDS*; declynacyons *B*.

328. Iconomicar] *DS*; Icononucar *B*.

331. Sallust] *C*; salusty *B*. According to *D*, *B*'s reading "is meant for the Latin genitive." This seems unlikely.

335. flotis] *CDSHn*; droppes *BHd*. See Intro., pp. 28–30.

337–43, stanza 49] *C* only.

340. satirrar] *This ed.*; satirray *CDS*. Cf. *Iconomicar* (328), *historiar* (329), *comicar* (353). makithe men] *This ed.*; men makythe *CDS*. The emendation makes the second half-line iambic, a characteristic of Skelton's rhythm.

341. that no man dothe refuse] *This ed.*; the pleasant god of wyne *CDS*. *C*'s compositor, in some confusion as he fitted the missing stanza into his text, set up the refrain of the preceding stanza, ruining the rhyme scheme. Some attempt at restoring the missing phrase is necessary.

345. mengithe] *B* (mengith); mengleth *C*.

349. flotis] *DS*; droppes *BCHd*. So at 356, 363, 370, 377, 384.

353. comicar] *CDS*; conucar *B*.

358. wit] *B*; with *CDS*. *B*'s *wit* for *with*, retained here and at 680 and 1302, may be Skelton's own variant spelling. According to *OED*, *wit* is a northern form.

366. Cursius] *CDS*; cursus *B*.

375. frownnyd] [*A*]; frowmyd *B*; frownyd *DS*.

388. Chawser] [*A*]; Chaucer *B*. Also at 413a, 421. See note to 1095.

389. enneude] [*A*]; a meude *B*; ennewed *CDS*.

395. rubis] *CDS*; rubie *B*. taberdys] *CHd* (taberdes); tabers *B*. *OED* does not record *B*'s *tabers*. *C*'s reading, then, is probably a correction, not one of his normalized spellings.

399a. CAPITULUM TERTIUM] [*A*].

404. ye encrese] *CDS*; encrese *B*.

406. welny] *B*; welnere *C*.

406a. POETA SKELTON. TO MASTER GOWER.] *C* only.

407–13, stanza 59] *C* only.

413a. MASTER CHAWSER. TO SKELTON.] *B* (Mayster); Maister Chaucher Lawreat poete to Skelton. *C*. *D* dismisses *C*'s heading because, "it contradicts what our author has just told us: see v. 397" (textual note). In fact, apart from the misspelling of *Chaucer*, it may be genuine. If it is, then it will be the earlier form of the heading, and in that case the MS copy intermittently used by *C* was probably *A*. See Intro., p. 29.

420. appoyntid] *This ed.*; poynted *B*. Although otherwise acceptable, the aphetic form seems defective rhythmically.

420a. POETA SKELTON. TO MASTER CHAWSER.] [*A*]; Poeta Skelton answeryth. *B*.

430. welny] *B*; welnere *C*.

432. prothonotory] *This ed.*; prothanatory *BDS*; protonotory *C*.

434a. POETA SKELTON. TO MASTER LYDGATE.] [*A*]; Poeta Skelton answeryth. *B*.

443. to fore] *B*. before *C*.

446. me so sore] *CD*; me sore *B*.

455. Withe] *CDS* (with); wiht *B*. *Wiht* here and at 733 is not necessarily an error. The spelling is recorded in *OED*, which suggests that, like *wit*, it is a northern form. Because *B* tends to reverse letters and words, however, the form is not retained.

460. Engalarid] *CHdHn*: Engolerid *B*.

462. worlde] *CD*; worde *B*. *Word* and *wordly*, common 16C. spellings for *world* and *worldly*, are probably compositor's spellings in *B*. *Worlde* and *worldly*, as at 1477 and 543, are more likely to have been the forms of *B*'s copy.

470. enhachid] *This ed.*; entachid *B*.

472. another] [*A*]*DS*; a nother *B*; an other *C*. These examples of word division are typical. *B* has *a nother* 6 times, a characteristic of the shop, *an other* once. *C* always uses *an other* (7 cases). *A* has the word only once, but undivided, and *A* divides less than the printed texts, and always consistently.

473. rokky walle] *CD*; wall *B*.

476a. CAPITULUM QUARTUM] [*A*].

486. worldly] *CD*; wordly *B*.

490. hunderde] [*A*]; hundreth *B*; hundred *C*.

491. place] *This ed.*; palace *B*. As with 340, the rhythm requires the emendation. Cf. 1475.

492. Pursevaunttis] *This ed.*; of pursevantis *B*. The redundant *of* in *B* is due to anticipation of the word in the next lines.

503. charter] *B*; chart *C*.

504. quarter] *B*; quart *C*.

511. came to flater] *CDS*; come to flater *B*.

516. alle the tyme] *This ed.*; all tyme *B*.

542. Ye] *CDS*; The *B*.

545. that ever] *B*; so ever *C*.

553. Caspian] *CDS*; Gaspian *B*.

553a. CAPITULUM QUINTUM] [*A*].

553b. POETA SKELTON. TO OCCUPACIOUN.] [*A*]; Skelton poeta answeryth *B*.

598, gloss. Cacosyntheton] *This ed.*; Cacosinthicon *BCD*; *S* omits. *C* prints the gloss over the Latin verses. *D* emended to *cacosyntheton* in his textual note.

601. SALIUNCA] *CDS*; salimica *B*.

607. haskarddis] *CDS*; hastardis *BHd*. *Hastarddis* also occurs in Skelton's "Upon the Dolorous Dethe . . . of the . . . Erle of Northumberland" (1489), in both *C* and the MS version (BL MS Royal 18.D.II, ff. 165–166v.). Both *D* and *S* follow *C*, emending the word in *Laurel*, but not in *Northumberland*. *OED* does not list *hastard*, but describes *haskerd* as of obscure origin, possibly northern. The earliest use cited is by Caxton, 1491. Skelton's use predates this. The double error in *Laurel* and *Northumberland* is understandable if the word was new, also because *k* is very easily misread as *t* in 15–16C. cursive hands. Nonetheless, it is possible that *hastard* is correct. See commentary.

636. that] *CDS*; tha *B*.

641. Dasyng dotrellis after] *This ed.*; Dasyng after dotrellis *B*. The *B* version does not make sense. *Dasyng after* is not idiomatic, and if it were, why should the wounded be gazing stupidly (*dasyng*) at stupid people (*dotrellis*)? Surely the wounded, because of their severe injuries, *are* the *dotrellis*, reduced ever after to gazing stupidly about them like drooling drunkards? *Dasyng dotrellis therafter* would be even better.

643a. CAPITULUM SEXTUM] [*A*].

649. aventure] *This ed.*; aventuris *B*. Neither *OED* nor *MED* shows the plural of this noun used with a singular sense.

662. This line is in *C* only.

670–71, gloss] *BC*.

672–75, gloss] *BC*. Nota] *C* only. *B* "has a contraction which I cannot decipher" (*D*).

672. kancor] *B* (cancour); rancour *CHdHn*. A crux, arising from the close similarity of initial *k* and *r*. *B*'s *cancour* reflects the compositor's preference for *c* spellings. Skelton certainly preferred *k*, e.g., *enkankerd* (*Northumberland*, 142).

678. frutis and] *CDS*; frutis *B*.

680. Wit] *B*; with *CDS*.

681. Testalis] *CDS*; testalus *B*.

699. Trions] *CDS*; troons *B*.

705. and verse] *B*; and in verse *C*.

706a. CAPITULUM SEPTIMUM] [*A*].

712. covenabill] [*A*]; convenable *B*; covenably *C*. cf. 821. contryvyd] *CDS*; contyruyd *B*.

713a. POETA SKELTON. TO OCCUPACIOUN.] [*A*]; Poeta Skelton answeryth. *B*.

716. worldly] *CD*; worldly *B*.

720a. OCCUPACIOUN. TO SKELTON.] *B*. *A* omits.

721-1135] *ABC*.

724. myne] *A*; my *B*.

725. losond] *A*; losyd *B*.

727a. POETA SKELTON. TO SKELTON.] *A*; Poeta Skelton answeryth. *B*.

728. benygne] *AC*; benynge *B*. See note to 113.

733. withe] *ACDS*; wiht *B*.

736. God] *AC*; Gog *B*. A text based on *B* should retain *Gog*, which is a well-attested form.

737. by] *ACS*; be *B*. the effecte] *A*; theffect *B*.

739. yone] *B*; yonder *A*.

741. owght fals mesuris] *A*; fals mesuris out *B*.

741a-b. *Interpolata . . . adversarium*] *BC*.

744. OPPETIT] *A*; opetit *BC*; *appetit DS*. See commentary.

745-46. Gloss] *BC*.

747-48. Gloss] *A*, where it is opposite 744-45. *D* reads "Wryght," transcribing a bracketlike mark as W.

751a-b. .17.4.7.2.17.5.18. / .18.19.1.19.8.5.12.] *A* (marginal correction) *BC*; .17.4.7.2.17.5.18.10.10 / .18.19.1.8.19.5.12.10.10. *A* (crossed out).

755. it is to stop up his sight] *A*; it were to stande in his lyght *B*.

761. stir men to brawlyng] *A*; set men a feightynge *B*. and syt] *ACDS*; and set *B*.

765a. CAPITULUM OCTAVUM] *A*.

766. went forthe in] *B*; went in *A*.

767. Turnnyd] *A*; Turnyng *B*. by a] *ACDS*; by *B*.

768. in to] *A*; to *B*.

771. a bevy] *AC*; above *B*; a beve *DS*.

793. yeve] *A*; geve *B*. worke] *A*; warke *B*. Also at 811, 1104.

794. enbrawder] *A*; enbrowder *B*.

795. the glutton] *A*; ther glowtonn *B*.

799. a hu] *A*; an hew *B*.

800. whyght, blak, purpulle] *AD*; whyte / purpill *B*.

803. surfullinge] *A*; surffillyng *B*.

804. bothe birddis and bowris] *A*; byrdis in bowris *B*.

807. avysemente] *A*; advysemente *B*.

818. humanyte] *A*; umanyte *B*.

821b. POETA SKELTON.] *AD*; Poeta Skelton answeryth. *BCS*.

822. thonk] *A*; thanke *B*.

828a-b. CAPITULUM . . . COMMENDACIONE] *A*. This heading is original, not added, implying that it was decided to include these headings while *A* was being written. The scribe (possibly Skelton) by inadvertence wrote *Ca^{ni}tulum ix^{ni}* for *Capitulum ix^{ni}*. The correcting hand, probably the same writer using a makeshift pen, crossed out the whole heading, and rewrote it correctly.

829. masid] *A*; amasid *B*.

830. bestad / driven] *A*; be stad and driven *B*.

831. tempestuows] *AD*; tempeous *B*; tempestous *CS*.

832. troste] *A*; trust *B*. counforte] *A*; comforte *B*.

833. kyttithe] *A*; kuttyth *B*; cutteth *C*.

835. beseke] *AB*; beseche *C*.

837. lawly] *A*; lowly *B*.

838. reconusaunce] *ADS*; recounsaunce *B*; reconisaunce *C*.

852. Thamar] *AS*; Thamer *BCD*.

860. parfight] *A*; profight *B*; parfite *C*; perfight *DS*.

863a. TO MY LADY ELISABETHE] *A*; To my lady elisabeth howarde *B*.

866. vertew and] *B* (vertu); vertew *A*.

871. Creisseyda] *A*; creisseid *B*. Polycene] *A*; polexene *BDS*; Polyxene *C*.

877a. TO MY LADY MYRRYEL] *A*; To my lady mirriell howarde *B*.

879. do her] *AD*; to do you *BCS*.

880. Benygne] *AC*; Beninge *B*.

883. Enbuddid blossome withe] *A*; The enbuddid blossoms of *B*.

884. The lylly whight] *A*; with lillis whyte *B*.

887. how she] *B*; she *A*.

891a. TO MY LADY DAKERS] *A*; To my lady anne dakers of the sowth *B*.

898. counfort] *A*; comforte *B*.

899. Penolope] *A*; penolepe *B*.

901. surmountynge] *ACDS*; surmewntynge *B*.

905. conforte] *A*; comforte *B*.

906. mageran] *A*; margerain *B*. Also at 914, 922.

907. goodlihode] *A*; goodly hede *B*; goodlyhede *DS*. Also at 915.

908. Enbrawderd] *A*; Enbrowdred *B*.

909. maydenhode] *AB*; maydenhede *CDS*.

917. maydenhode] *A*; maydenhede *B*. Also at 925.

918. Benygne] *AC*; benynge *B*.

923. goodlyhode] *A*; goodlyhede *B*.

935. iwus] *ADS*; iwys *B*; I wys *C*. Cf. the rhyme *thus / iwus / us* (*Bowge of Courte*, 338).

949. Lodestar] *A*; Lede sterre *BD*; Lode sterre *C* Lodesterre *S*.

953. vertuys] *A*; vertuows *BS*; vertues *CD*.

953a. MASTRES] *A*; maystres *B*. Also at 972a, 1003a, 1037, 1045, 1055a. HASSET] *A*; blenner haiset *B*.

962. Trost] *A*; Trust *B*.

967. The Courte of Fame] *A*; Inmortall fame *B*. Immortall fame *C*.

968. Mastres] *A*; mistres *B*; maistres *C*. Hasset] *A*; haiset *B*.

985. her] *A*; your *B*.

988. Star] *A*; sterre *B*.

993. I make yow sure] *B* (you); I yow assure *A*.

996. selfe] *B*; sefhe *A*.

1021. the fayre] *A*; fayre *B*.

1028. than] *A*; that *B*.

1030. Margarete] *B*; Marget *A*. the mydsomer] *A*; This midsomer *B*.

1041. benygnyte] *AC* (benignite); benyngnyte *B*.

1055a. ISBELL] *A*; Isabell *B*.

1064. maydenly] *A*; womanly *B*.

1066. mene] *A*; menes *B*.

1077. shew yow] *B* (you); shew *A*.

1080. passithe] *AC* (passeth); passis *B*.

1082. ye] *A*; you *B*.

1086a. CAPITULUM DECIMUM] [*A*].

1086b. POETA SKELTON.] *A*; Skelton Poeta. *B*.

1091. of glas] *ACDS*; with glas *B*.

1095. Chawser] *A*; Chawcer *B*.

1096. kurteisly me] *A*; me curteisly *B*.

1100. thos that they ware] *A*; other besyde *B*. counterfettis] *A*; counterfete *B*.

1111. hawtely and yave] *A*; hawtly and gave *B*.

1112. not a worde amonge them then] *A*; amonge them no worde then *B*.

1113. to me wold] *A*; wolde to me *B*.

1115. us] *ACDS*; hus *B*. *Hus* is probably correct, and a text based on *B* should preserve it. *OED* thinks it is probably a northern form.

1118. higthe] *A*; hy *B*.

1119. thorow] *AD*; by the *BS*.

1120. promocioun] *A*; triumphe *B*.

1121a. POETA SKELTON.] *A*; Skelton poeta *B*.

1122. higthe] *A*; high *B*.

1126. To alle that to] *ACDS*; To all tho that *B*.

1127. hastyve] *AB*; hasty *C*.

1129. for me to] *A*; for to *B*.

1131. troste] *A*; trust *B*.

1132. ageyne] *A*; ageinst *B*.

1136–1640] *BC* only.

1143. boke] *CDS*; bokes *B*.

1149a. CAPITULUM UNDECIMUM] [*A*].

1149b. POETA SKELTON.] [*A*]; Skelton Poeta. *B*.

1163. immediatly] *CS*; inmediatly *B*.

1164–1513, glosses] *B* only.

1170. to Dye] *CDS*; do dye *B*.

1175. Automedon] *S*, adopting emendation from *D*, textual note; antomedon *B*.

1177. Bowche] *B*; Bouge *C*.

1185–1254, stanzas 133–141] Interpolated 1522–23. See Intro., pp. 34–36.

1192. Mannerly Mastres Margery] *CD* (manerly maistres Margery); manerly margery maystres *B*.

1194. I] *CDS*; ye *B*.

1196. Lor] *BD*; Lorde *CS*.

1200. giggishe] *C* (giggisshe); giggisse *B*.

1212a. *reliqua*] *CDS*; relequa *B*.

1214. Frenshe vers in to] *This ed.*; frenshe into *B*. This line has only eight syllables, and the rhythm stumbles after *Frenshe*, suggesting that the text is corrupt. The emendation attempts to balance the line in rhythm, sound, and sense.

1253. hard is] *This ed.*; hard it is *B*. Cf. 112, 1199.

1255–1369] These lines are interpolated from *Phyllyp Sparowe*, 1268–1382, where they form the "adicyon made by maister Skelton."

1277. the,] *CDS*; ye *B*.

1283. Hippocentawris] *DS*; hippocentaurus *B*.

1302. Wit] *B*; With *CDS*.

1309. bowre] *CD*; powre *BS*. Cf. *Phyllyp Sparowe*, 1322.

1313. that venemows] *B*; the venemows *CDS*.

1345. Phillistinnis] *C* (Philistinis) *DS*; Phillistimis *B*.

1357. perplexyte] *C* (perplexite) *DS*; proplexyte *B*.

1359. PECIIT] *B*; *petiit DS*. I have preserved the spelling *c* for this consonant here and elsewhere. Although it gives a strange appearance to some words, it is standard in *B*, and frequent in *C*.

1364. than is] *CDS*; and is *B*.

1370. and the Groynnynge of the Gronnyng] *C* (and the groining of the groning) *DS*; a groynninge gronnyng *B*.

1371. Murnnynge] *C* (Mournyng) *DS*; murmyng *B*.

1376. scornnis] *C* (scornes) *DS*; stormis *B*.

1389, gloss. Prov.] Corrected by *D*, textual note; Cant. *B*.

1394. Exione] *B*: Ereone *C*. his limbis] *HnS*; her lambis *BD*; her lambe is *C*. *B*'s reading puzzled *C*'s compositor. *D* and *Hd* say they can make no sense of the line. *Hn* suggested that *Exione* is Ixion, not Hesione, and that the line refers to his sufferings on the wheel. He emended to *limbis*. *OED* does not record this spelling before 1547, but it would be characteristic of Skelton to use a new, rather pedantic spelling. This would explain the compositor's difficulties. *Hn*'s emendation is supported by the spelling *Exion* in *Diodorus* (1:374/30, 34), and by the mention of Fortune in the next line, connected with Ixion through their common iconographical association with the wheel. See commentary.

1398-1404, italics] *DS*.

1405, gloss. Matt.] Corrected by *D*, textual note; Isaias *B*.

1410. Swaffhamm] *DS*; Swasshamm *B*.

1411, gloss. Deut.] Corrected by *D*, textual note; Pso. *B*.

1415. Solempniis] *B*; solemniis *D*.

1422, gloss. constellaciones] *D*; laciones *B*.

1426-32, gloss. Spectatum . . . amici] Corrected by *D*, textual note; Spectatum admisse risus teneatur amor *B*. "Is the barbarous alteration of this line only a mistake of the printer?" (*D*).

1428-29] These lines are reversed in *B*.

1428. dryvithe] *C* (dryveth) *DS*; dryvit *B*.

1433-39, gloss. Luc.] Corrected by *D*, textual note; pso. Clxxv. *B*.

1437, gloss. *anglice*, a kokkolde] *B* (cokwold) only, printed as part of the text.

1442-43] These lines are reversed in *BC*.

1447-54, gloss. Notate verba, signata misteria] *D*, who regularizes i/y (mysteria); Notat ⟨.⟩ verba signate misteria *B*.

1459. were] *CDS*; where *B*.

1461. distincyon] *B*; Distichon *CDS*.

1462. FRAXINUS] *DS*; fraximus *B*. CLIVO] *CDS*; clino *B*. RIVO] *CDS*; viro *B*.

1466. snurre] *CDS*; surt *B*; snurt *Hd*.

1487. redde] *CDS*; rede *B*.

1492–96, gloss. Percius] Corrected by *D*, textual note; Horace *B*.

1499, gloss. canit] *This ed.*; Cavit *B*.

1505. dreme] *B*; slepe *C*.

1513. *Mens*] *CDS*; meus *B*.

1514a. ALLOQUITUR] *CDS*; alloquium *BHd*.

1573. they] *CDS*; thy *B*.

1580a–96. *Ad Serenissimam . . . Or els. &c.*] *C* only.

1596a–1609. ADMONET . . . lauro!] *C* prints as a separate poem, Sig. Y5.

1597. ornus] *CDS*; orni *B*.

1609a. *Prenes en gre. The Laurelle.*] *C*; Prennees Engre *B*.

1609b–38. EN PARLAMENT . . . com agayne.] *BC*. *C* prints as a separate poem, Sig. X8.

1639–40. *A grant tort . . . dort.*] *B* only.

Commentary

Title page] Almost certainly Skelton's own composition, probably written for *B*. Spelling as in *B*.

4. GARLANDE OR CHAPELET] This domestic, local celebration should not be confused with Skelton's academic laureation which had taken place from three to seven years earlier (Nelson, 40ff.). There was nothing bizarre about Skelton's garlanding; garlands were a common feature of English festivity. "At the Feasts in the Halls of the City of London, the Stewards doe ware garlands of laurel: In some places in the Countrey they hang up Festival Garlands, and on May-day adorn the May-poles with them: . . . as to Nuptial, and Honorary, I can say little: But Funeral Garlands for young Maydens, are still in use, and dedicated to the Church, hanging over the grave . . . . Memorandum: Sir John Gower [the poet] hath a costly Monument in St. Mary Overy's church, where he lies along in his scarlet Gowne: his head is encircled with a kind of chaplet of silver. At about every inch 1/2 length of gold is an interposition of a quarter-foile argent: I have not seen anywhere the like" (Aubrey, 191). Skelton's chaplet, like Gower's, was a sign of his poethood; but in the countess's donation of it, and his response, there is also an element of courtship, however stylized, also illuminated by a sentence in the same passage from Aubrey: "At Newton, in Malmesbury-hundred, is an ancient Custome (still observed) of a Mayd to give a Ghirland to a young man of that parish."

10. Sheryfhotton Castell] The castle ruins are to be seen in the village of Sheriff Hutton, about twelve miles northeast of York. The castle belonged to the Nevilles until Edward IV granted the manor to his brother Richard, Duke of Gloucester. (In the parish church of St. Helen and the Holy Cross there is an alabaster tomb of a boy, said to be Richard's son Edward, Prince of Wales.) In 1485, after Bosworth, castle and manor passed to the crown. Thomas Howard, Earl of Surrey, lived there from 1489–99 as Lieutenant of the North (Tucker, *ELN* 4:254–59). By 1618 the castle was in decay (*VCH, Yorkshire North Riding*, 2:174). Leland visited it: "I markid yn the fore front of the first area of the castelle self 3. great and high toures, of the which the gate house was the midle. In the secunde area ther be a 5. or 6. toures, and the stately staire up to the haul is very magnificent, and so is the haul it self, and al the residew of the house: in so much that I saw no house in the north so like a princely logginges. . . . There is a park by the castel. This castel was wel maintainid, by reason that the late Duke of Northfolk lay ther x. yers" (Leland, 1:65).

10. Foreste of Galtres] Extended from the gates of York twenty miles north-west to Aldborough, and fifteen miles due north to Crayke Hill. "Forest" does not mean continuous woodland, but a tract of land reserved for royal hunting, administered under forest law. In 1316, the forest covered 100,000 acres, including sixty townships. It was disforested under Charles II (*VCH*: *Yorkshire*, 1:501ff.). "From Shirhuten to York vij. miles, al in the forest of Galtres, whereof 4. miles or more was low medowes and morisch ground ful of carres, the residew by better ground but not very high. . . . I saw very little wood yn this quarter of the forest" (Leland, 1:65–66).

11. solacyons] From Latin *solacium, -a*, things that soothe, comfort, and relieve. See textual note.

12. allectyves] Things having power to allure. In the *Dialogue of Comfort*, More uses this unusual word three times in two pages, and nowhere else, once in the phrase "delectable allectives." It may be that More, writing in 1529, had recently read Skelton's title page (More, *Works*, 12:201).

Prefatory verses]

> As long as the everlasting stars shine in eternal day,
> As long as the seas shall swell, our laurel will flourish.
> Thence shall our renowned name be relayed to the stars,
> And everywhere Skelton will be commemorated, another Adonis.

Like all Skelton's Latin verses, these lines would trigger references in the mind of a learned contemporary. *Mansura sidera* would remind him of Virgil's *mansuram urbem* (*Aeneid* 3.86), *aequora tument* of Ovid, *Ex Ponto* 1.3.54, and *sidera fulgent*, perhaps, of Horace, *Odes* 2.16.4: *neque certa fulgent sidera natus*.

1–7] The time of this horoscope is from 7:00–7:30 P.M. on 8 May 1495. The ruling planet is Mars, the rising sign Scorpio (appendix 4, fig. 1).

9. the sommer floure] "As for man, his days are as grass: as a flower of the field, so he flourisheth" (Psalm 102:15).

17–18. I lent me to a stumpe / Of an oke] "Ye shall be as an oak whose leaf fadeth" (Isaiah 1:30), and, even more pertinent to the theme of this poem, "There shall be no memory of him: he shall be broken like an unfruitful tree" (Job 24:20).

22–28.] The marshy setting is proper to the Scorpian native (Intro., p. 60). On the seasonal significance of the hunt, see Intro., pp. 51–52.

22. friththy forest] Not a pleonasm (Edwards, 26), because a medieval forest was an enclosed game preserve, not necessarily wooded.

23. moose] See textual note.

24. belluynge] "When they be in rut, that is to say in their love, they sing in their language that in England hunters call bellowing as a man doth that loveth paramour" (*MG*, 23–24).

26. hynde calf] "And the first year that they be calved they be called a Calf" (*MG*, 29).

27. Faire falle . . . hownde] "Good luck befall the huntsman that can set his hound on so well!"

30–35] "This amounts to saying that he does not know whether his dream is a *somnium animale, naturale,* or *coeleste*" (A. C. Spearing, *Medieval Dream Poetry,* 213). See Spearing on poetic dream lore, 8ff.

47–49. gloss] "The goddess no less heaved the aegis which she carried on her breast." I owe the restoration of this hexameter to Professor George Goold. It is based on Ovid, *Metamorphoses* 2.752–55:

> Vertit ad hanc torvi dea bellica luminus orbem
> et tanto penitus traxit suspiria motu,
> ut pariter pectus positamque in pectore forti
> aegida concuteret.

("The warlike goddess now turned bright, angry eyes upon her, and, greatly perturbed, drew sighs so profound that her bosom and the aegis that lay on her bosom shook together.")

48. Dame Pallas] Represents wisdom and learning, a figure based both on the Greek goddess and the biblical figure of Wisdom. As a character in the narrative, she is also a noblewoman of great dignity, who has her parallel in the second half of the vision in the countess of Surrey.

49. Quene of Fame] Skelton's immediate source for the Queen is Chaucer, *The House of Fame,* but Skelton's Queen is not described in the grotesque allegorical terms of Chaucer's. To judge from her words, from Pallas's calling her "sister" (134), and Skelton's brief description (482–87), as well as the woodcut in *B,* she is a Venus-like figure. Her debate with Pallas is a motif in the tradition of the psychomachia, and reminiscent of other Pallas/Venus confrontations. See Seznec, *Survival of the Pagan Gods,* 108–10.

51. Renowmmyd lady . . . heven] Pallas as Wisdom has her proper place beyond the sphere of the fixed stars of Ptolemaic astronomy, in the heaven of heavens. "I was set up from everlasting, or ever the earth was. . . . When he prepared the heavens, I was there" (Prov. 8:23, 27).

51–54] On the rhyme *heven / Sevene / lene,* see textual note.

53. Madame Regent] As goddess of learning, Pallas is the patroness of the educational curriculum, and the seven liberal arts form the pillars of her "house": "Wisdom hath builded her house, she hath hewn out her seven pillars" (Prov. 9:1). Martianus Capella, *De Nuptis,* provides late Roman authority for associating Pallas with the liberal arts, for he says that "Pallas . . . unveiled her seven-rayed crown," probably an allegory of the arts (trans. W. A. Stahl and Richard Johnson, 2:20).

63. Laureate Tryumphe] By 1495, Skelton had been laureated by three universities: Oxford (?1488); Louvain (?1492); and Cambridge (1493). See Nelson, 40ff., 61–63.

73. thensugerd pocioune] *Sugared,* translating Latin *mellea,* was a favourite word of Lydgate's. In Skelton's youth, sugar was still an expensive, honey-like syrup (Hammond, 416).

74. Elyconys wel] Hippocrene on Mount Helicon, made by a blow of Pegasus's hoof, sacred to the Muses. Caxton, who knew Skelton well, wrote of him in 1490, "I suppose he hath dronken of Elycons well" (*Prologues*, 109).

77. syttynge] See textual note.

93. Ovyde] He was banished to Tomis on the Black Sea, A.D. 8. His offence was a poem and an indiscretion; which and what is not known.

95. Juvenalle] He was in Egypt, ca. 93, but whether he was banished there by Domitian for satirizing a dancer (Satire 7.90–92) is now doubted.

100–105. A poete . . . dust] Perhaps an example of the satirical or political animal fable with no particular meaning, perhaps topical. On a similar passage, see Kinsman, *PQ* 29:61–64.

106–8] "Yet various people with busy minds would like to gather from an obscure passage like this a meaning with some relish to it."

123. Cato] Besides his extant work, *De re rustica*, Cato the Censor wrote a collection of aphorisms; Skelton, however, probably means Dionysus Cato, the supposed author of the *Disticha Catonis* (3d century A.D.), a famous collection of maxims, each consisting of two hexameters, the whole arranged in four books. It was a favorite school text in the Middle Ages and later. Salter and Edwards have traced Skelton's use of it in his *Speculum Principis* (*Diodorus*, 2:423–24).

136. poynte wele that clause] *poynte* can mean "to punctuate," or "to mark words for singing," as in a psalter. There is also a noun *point*, a musical note. Pallas means either, "Interpret, explain, that remark very carefully," or, ironically, "Sing that properly," "Put that to music."

149. syttynge] See textual note.

151–54] "Whose written dissuasion provoked Demosthenes to prepare his own clever persuasion, from which Aeschines could find no escape." Demosthenes' response was so effective that Aeschines left Athens.

155. so famowsly is brutyd] "Is noised abroad with such fame."

162. Jerome in his preambille] The "preamble" is a letter from St. Jerome to Paulinus, prefixed to the Vulgate Bible, beginning *Frater Ambrosius*, and telling how Aeschines praised Demosthenes' oratory to his own pupils.

176–210] Pallas's speech denounces the English court as well as Fame's, singling out the vices of *maintenance* (193), i.e., interfering in the courts, supporting wrongdoers, and *extortion* (194), or illegal exactions of money. Stanza 30 is a pungent dramatization of the mockery that the educated man suffers from court bullies.

209. Jak-a-thrummys bibille] Cf. *Magnyfycence*, 1427, *Colyn Cloute*, 28–32, 282, *Against Garnesche*, 3.204. "Jacke-a-Thrum" was one of the two preachers who, according to the late fourteenth- or early fifteenth-century anecdote, claimed that "in the bibull' it was said that "an ill drynker is impossibull hevone for to wynne: for God luffus nodur hors nor mare but mere men that in the cuppe con stare" (Kinsman, *John Skelton: Poems*, 185). Hammond is probably right to say that Jack-a-thrum's bible is the bottom of an ale-cup.

(Dyce supplied the original reference.) There is a similar joke in Northern Ireland today: "His religion's at the bottom of his Guinness glass."

235. Eolus] Ruler of the winds, and Fame's trumpeter in *House of Fame*, 1571. In this and in other details Fame's call to judgment has eschatological overtones. Cf. "For the trumpet will sound," 1 Corinthians 15:52.

270. A murmur of mynstrallis] Cf. *The Boke of St. Albans*, Sig. F6, "The Compaynys of beestys and fowlys": "A Doctryne of doctoris," "a Melody of Harpers," "a Discrecion of Prestis," &c.

272–73. Orpheus . . . Amphion] Typical figures, representing the power of music. The lyre of Orpheus made beasts, trees, and rocks follow him, and Amphion's lyre made the walls of Thebes to rise (Ovid *Metamorphoses* 6.176ff., 11.1–2).

273. musis of Archady] Poet-singers of Arcadia, not necessarily pastoral poets, as a later poet would mean, but fit company for Orpheus and Amphion. Skelton probably had Virgil, *Eclogues* 10.31–33 in mind: "tamen cantabitis, Arcades inquit, / montibus haec vestris, soli cantare periti / Arcades" ("You O Arcadians," he said, "will sing this song to your mountains: Arcadians alone are expert in song").

274. Whos hevenly armony was so passynge sure] "Whose unearthly music was perfectly tuned." Skelton's insistence upon this detail should alert the reader to the presence of constructional "music" in *The Laurel*, an otherworld narrative, and it links Skelton with the Pythagorean theorizing of musicians at Henry VII's court, among them his friend William Cornyshe, Jr. (Hollander, *The Untuning of the Sky*, 98, based on John Stevens, *Music and Letters* 32:29–37). Perfect tuning is impossible in this world, although the "sweet" music of the adjustable temperament instruments (e.g., voice and violin) can approximate or intimate it.

277–78. noone so grete a tre / Bot that he daunsid] Cf. Isaiah 55:12: "et omnia ligna regionis plaudent manu" ("and all the trees of the field shall clap their hands"). The trees dance because the music, being heavenly and perfectly tuned, is of creative power. Its biblical parallel or type is the Song of the Angels, the *Gloria in Excelsis Deo*, first heard at the Creation (Job 38:7: "When the morning stars sang together, and all the Sons of God shouted for joy."), and again at the Incarnation, the second Creation (Luke 2:13–14).

290. Daphnis] Daphne. The story of Apollo's love for her, and its results, is from *Metamorphoses* 1.452ff.

296. O thowghtfulle harte] A phrase from the opening line of Lydgate's *Life of Our Lady* (Dyce).

300. the tre as he did take] Imitated from *Met.* 1.553–54:

> Hanc quoque Phoebus amat positaque in stipite dextra
> sentit adhuc trepidare novo sub cortice pectus

("Her also Phoebus loves and, his hand placed on the trunk, feels the heart still quivering under the fresh bark").

302. his exclamacyoun] *Exclamatio*, a figure prescribed by Geoffrey de Vinsauf "when for grief or some other cause we cry out" (*De arte versificandi* 2.2.17).

310-15. Sithe I contryvid . . . represse!] Closely imitated from *Met.* 1.521-24:

> Inventum medicina meum est, opiferque per orbem
> dicor, et herbarum subiecta potentia nobis.
> ei mihi, quod nullis amor est sanabilis herbis
> nec prosunt domino, quae prosunt omnibus, artes!

("Medicine is my discovery; throughout the world I am called the help-bearer, and the power of herbs is mine. Alas, that no herb cures love, and that arts that help everyone else are no use to their master!")

323-85. a grete nowmbyr folowyd] This jolly procession of writers, some holding their best-known books, represents the great company of the poets as well as Fame's sometimes whimsical judgments. Apart from the best-known Latin *auctores*, there are some representative Greeks (Theocritus, Hesiod, Homer), and some moderns (Boccaccio, Petrarch, Poggio, Gaguin). Some are mentioned whose names only survive, their works lost or surviving in fragments: Ennius, author of the *Annales*, Lucilius, a satirist, and Pisander, whose name survives because, in Macrobius's *Saturnalia*, Virgil is said to have plagiarized him. Of the authors whose works survive, most were well-known in medieval times, including some not much read now: Lucan, Statius, Sallust, Quintilian (the *Declamations* are no longer thought his), Macrobius, and Boethius. Persius, very difficult to read, was a popular school text, as were the six *Elegies*, ca. 600, attributed to Maximian. Some of Skelton's authors, however, were rare or virtually nonexistent in medieval libraries: Plautus, Propertius, and Valerius Maximus. See R. M. Wilson, "The Contents of the Mediaeval Library," and M. D. Knowles, "The Survival of the Classics" in *The English Library before 1700*, ed. F. Wormald and C. E. Wright, 85-111.

324. poetis laureat] Learned writers. In this period, *poet* was used indifferently of writers in poetry and prose.

326. Quintiliane] Born in Spain, ca. A.D. 35, died at Rome before A.D. 100: the great orator and teacher, praised by Martial, 2.90, as "the glory of the Roman gown." His single extant work is the *Institutio Oratoria*; the *Declamationes Quintilianeae* are thought not to be his.

327. Theocritus] The "bucolycal relacyouns" are the Idylls of Theocritus, a 3d-century B.C. Greek pastoral poet.

328. Esiodus the Iconomicar,] Hesiod, Greek didactic poet ca. 800 B.C., who wrote on husbandry in his *Works and Days*. Skelton has formed *iconomicar* from L. *oeconomicus*, "pertaining to the management of household affairs," which of course included farming. Dyce quotes Bodleian MS. Digby 147, *Carmen Domini Walteri de Henleye quod vocatur Yconomia sive housbundria*.

331. Sallust] Roman historian, ca. 86 B.C.-35 B.C. Popular in the schools for his *Bellum Catilinae* and *Bellum Iugurthinum*. Another work, the *Historiae*, exists in fragments.

334. Bacchus] Skelton's chief source of knowledge about Bacchus/Dionysus was Diodorus, whom he translated, and from whom he learned that besides inventing wine and husbandry Dionysus "delyted in the morall enseignementis of the Muses, studyously enbesyed the wandrynge wytte of men to withdrawe fro waverynge inconstaunce and to brynge it unto some one establisshid studye of fructuous assuraunce": also that he traveled with musicians, minstrels, and satyr poets (Skelton, *Diodorus* 1:353–54).

335. flotis] This unusual word could mean "floating matter," i.e., scum or grease on a liquid or, more poetically, a "head" on a liquid, its froth, or the liquid itself. *OED* gives an example from Caxton meaning "waves": "waves and flotes of the see." Skelton's "flotis" are the equivalent of Keats's "beaded bubbles winking at the brim."

337. Lucan withe Stacius] Lucan, A.D. 39–65, wrote the *Pharsalia*, an epic poem on the Civil Wars; Statius, A.D. 45–96, was another epic poet, known for his *Thebaid* and the incomplete *Achilleid*. Skelton seems not to have known the *Silvae*, lost from the 6th until the 15th century.

338. Percius] Persius, the satirist, A.D. 34–62, a very difficult author, much read in the medieval schools.

340. satirrar] See textual note.

341. See textual note.

344. Titus Lyvius] Livy, 59 B.C.–A.D. 17, historian. Scribes arranged his history of Rome into "decades."

347. Enyus] Ennius, 239–169 B.C. His *Annales*, now lost, were an epic history of Rome.

351. Aulus Gelius] Aulus Gellius, ca. A.D. 130–180, an encyclopedic writer whose *Noctes Atticae* was much enjoyed in medieval times.

352. Orace also withe his new poetry] "New poetry" is puzzling. Has Skelton confused the *Ars Poetica* with Geoffrey de Vinsauf's *Nova Poetria*? It seems an unlikely mistake. Dyce quotes Warton, *History of English Poetry* (ed. 1824), 3:178: "Horace's *Art* is frequently mentioned under this title."

359. Boyce] Boethius, prolific Christian statesman and author, brutally put to death by Theodoric the Ostrogoth, 524; one of the most influential of Western European writers. His *De consolatione philosophiae* remained popular into modern times. "The last of the Roman philosophers, and the first of the scholastic theologians" (H. F. Stewart, ed., *Boethius*, x).

360. Maxymiane] The "mad ditiis" refers to the volume of six elegies, ca. 600, attributed to one Maximianus, and in particular to Elegy 5, which narrates a love adventure between the old poet and a young girl.

365. John Bochas] Boccaccio, carrying his *Genealogia deorum, De claribus mulieribus*, and *De casibus virorum illustrium*.

366. Quintus Cursius] Quintus Curtius, a first-century Latin writer, author of *De rebus gestis Alexandri Magni*.

367. Macrobius] His commentary on Cicero's *Somnium Scipionis* was one of the best known prose works in Latin in the Middle Ages.

372. Poggeus] Poggio Bracciolini, the Florentine humanist, 1380–1459; his "mad tales" are the *Facetiae*, very popular.

374. Gagwyne] Robert Gaguin, 1433–1501, head of the Maturin Fathers. As ambassador to Henry VII, he relieved his frustration by insulting Henry. Skelton joined in the chorus of reply; his "Recule ageyne Gagwyne" is lost. See Nelson, 54, Edwards, 43–45.

380. Lucilius and Valerius, Maximus by name] Lucilius was a second-century satirist, whose work survives in fragments. Valerius, "Maximus by name" to distinguish him from Valerius Flaccus, was a first-century author of a book of exemplary anecdotes for school use, *De factis dictisque memorabilibus libri IX*.

381. Vincencius] Vincent of Beauvais, thirteenth-century encyclopedist, author of the immense *Speculum majus*.

383. Propercius and Pisandros] Propertius, first-century B.C. elegiac poet; Pisander, a Greek poet mentioned by Macrobius, *Saturnalia* 5.2, where a guest accuses Virgil of plagiarizing most of *Aeneid* 2 from him. His own work is lost.

387–91] Gower, Chaucer, and Lydgate are presented as the founders of English poetry, a view that became commonplace in the fifteenth and sixteenth centuries.

397. Thei wantid no thynge bot the laurelle] "Skelton's vanity is painfully obvious here" (Hammond). Not necessarily. Skelton is making a factual distinction between himself and his predecessors, not, like himself, academically trained in literature. Skelton was a new phenomenon, a man of letters, the bulk and range of whose output was unprecedented in England. Only a small portion of it survives. See Nelson, 56–57.

405. brutyd Britons of Brutus Albion] A pun on *brutyd/Brutus*. According to medieval historiography stemming from Geoffrey of Monmouth's *Historia regum Britanniae*, Britain was founded by Brutus, a descendant of Aeneas; hence the Britons are "bruted" in two senses, being both famous and begotten by Brutus.

414–20. Stanza 60] The syntax of this stanza's even-numbered lines is reversed, probably in tribute to Chaucer's syntactical mastery.

428–34. Stanza 62] Fish, 231, thinks that Skelton here parodies Lydgate's style. As the reader will see, this is not so. All three poets are given elaborate language, and each has a specific message to deliver: Gower, that Skelton deserves a place in the poets' college; Chaucer, that they will bring him to the Queen of Fame; and Lydgate, that he is to be "prothonotary" of Fame's court.

432. prothonotory] As we shortly learn (522), Fame already has a registrar in Dame Occupacioun. Skelton was perhaps thinking of a more elevated position, analogous to that of the Protonotaries Apostolical, a college of prelates charged with registering papal acts, making and keeping records of beatification, and directing the canonization of saints (*OED*, s.v. "protonotary").

443. Under the forme] This does not mean "for the sake of ceremony" (Fish, 232), but "as was proper." *OED* defines this phrase as "according to the correct way of doing something." The ironic modern reading arises from contemporary uses of *form*, e.g., "for the form's sake."

459. a palace] The palace of Fame is analogous to interiors found in Flemish art of the fifteenth century. The turrets, towers, halls, bowers, and vaulted roofs, are Gothic. The furnishings, of tapestries, carpets, and "Cloths of Arras," are those of a great house of Skelton's period. The bejeweled and oriental splendour of the decor, however, so unreal and fantastic to a modern reader, is purely symbolic, and based upon the description of the New Jerusalem, Revelation 21:10-27. Like the trumpet of Eolus, the palace of Fame has eschatological overtones. Like Lydgate and the Van Eyck brothers, Skelton made in art something that the Church aimed at in the greater churches, but did not actually realize in forms larger than the reliquary and shrine— although we should not underestimate the Church's achievement: it took twenty-six wagons to remove the treasures of the shrine of St. Thomas of Canterbury after the suppression under Henry VIII.

466-67. With turkis . . . rownde] Cf. Revelation 21:19-20: "And the foundations of the wall of the city were garnished with all manner of precious stones. The first foundation was jasper; the second, sapphire; the third, a chalcedony; the fourth, an emerald; the fifth, sardonyx; the sixth, sardius; the seventh, chrysolyte; the eighth, beryl; the ninth, a topaz; the tenth, a chrysopasus; the eleventh, a jacinth; the twelfth, an amethyst."

468. oliphauntis tethe] i.e., true ivory as opposed to the ivory of the walrus described in 472 as "whalis bone" (Dyce).

475. clothis of Arace] rich tapestry fabrics named from the town of manufacture, Arras in Artois.

484. clothe of astate] canopy.

485. oryent perlys of garnate] "The allusion here may be to Granada, at this time the centre of the European jewel-trade . . . Caxton renders *vin dosoye et de garnate* as 'wyn of oseye and of Garnade' " (Hammond).

493-97] Most of these names are familiar; Poyle, however, is Apulia, and "the Mayne Lande" is Germany (l'Allemagne).

509. Ay, as goode as thow! Ay, faythe, and no better!] Two speakers are exchanging insults.

513-14. Dertmowthe . . . portis] Dartmouth and Plymouth are seaports in Devonshire, Portsmouth in Hampshire. The five ports are the Cinque Ports: Dover, Sandwich, Romney, Hastings, and Hythe.

539. courte of aray] None of the editors comments on this phrase, but what is a court of array? *OED*, s.v. "array," sb. 7, defines an array as "the order of impanelling a jury." Is this then a jury court?

540-46] The metaphor of shipwreck and safe harbour was commonplace. Cf. *Colyn Cloute*, 1251 *ad fin.*, and see Curtius, *European Literature and the Latin Middle Ages*, 128-30. Occupacioun's words of kindly encouragement may be an echo of *Aeneid* 1.390–91, Venus's words to Aeneas: "namque tibi reduces socios classemque relatam / nuntio et in tutum versis Aquilonibus actam" ("For I bring you news of friends restored, your fleet recovered, brought to safe harbor by changing winds.")

553. the hyllis Caspian] In classical times the *Mons Caspius* was a part of the Taurus range. Occupacioun's prophetic trope recalls Anchises' prophecy, *Aeneid* 6.756ff., where *Caspia regna* ("Caspian realms") are among the lands *extra sidera*, beyond the path of the stars, which Augustus's empire will absorb (795, 798).

585. Caldy] Chaldea. The gates represent the history of national states, with the implication that though nations rise and fall, human nature and the life of ambition have not changed.

590. lybbarde] The heraldic beast of the English royal arms.

595. he shoke forthe this writynge] "The leopard has an upraised paw resting on a scroll bearing the inscription" (Hammond).

596–601. FORMIDANDA . . . ROSETO] "Beyond my comprehension" (Dyce). "The despair of editors" (Scattergood). The gloss means "Something badly put together on purpose," "an intentional jumble." In 597 Dyce recognized an imitation of Juvenal, *Satires* 8.129: "nec per conventus nec cuncta per oppida curvis / unguibus ire parat nummos raptura Celaeno" ("if in your circuit through the towns, there is no harpy ready to grab the cash with her hooked talons"): in 601, of Virgil, *Eclogues* 5.16: "Lenta salix quantum pallenti cedit olivae, / puniceis humilis quantum saliunca rosetis" ("As far as the lithe willow yields to the pale olive, / as far as the humble nard yields to the crimson rose-beds"). Skelton's lines are not, like the satire against Roger Statham (742–51), an interpolation, but part of the text. For the poem to be performed, as Winser argues (*Criticism* 19:51ff.), these lines would have to be spoken in English. They would have been incomprehensible in Latin, hardly less so in English. The difficulty is in knowing to whom they are spoken, whose behavior they describe. Hammond's idea that they are about "industry" is based on an elementary mistranslation of *ex industria*. Scattergood believes that since they are spoken by the English leopard, they must be about England. This is sensible. Presumably, too, they are addressed to the English people, those who clamor at the gate for fame and favor. Evidently, they are strongly satiric, describing England, in Juvenal's words, as a harpy snatching money (a reflection on Henry VII's notorious rapacity?). The last line suggests a longing for a new age. Here is a tentative translation: "You endure things excessively fearful, the last lightnings of Jupiter. Envious, she prepares to go to one place after another with her hooked claws, she whom Celaeno will take by means of the moon's money (?). Weapons, plague, mourning, poison, force, deceit: a barbarous country! May the nard yield to the rosary, a despised prickle-bush." The lines are just about incomprehensible, intended to sound like angry, barbarous gibberish.

607. haskarddis] base fellows. See textual note. Although there is a strong case for emending *B*'s *hastardis*, the word's occurrence in *Northumberland*,

24, leaves some doubt whether such a word did not exist, adapted from ME *haster* > OF *hasteur*, ML *hastarius*, a turnspit. It would mean much the same as *haskard*. A turnspit would be a fairly grimy person, and although the origin of *haskard* is obscure, Dyce suggests a relationship to a Scots word *hasky*, meaning dirty or slovenly.

610. blow at the kole] Hammond quotes the phrase "blynkerd blowboll" from "My Darlyng Dere" (Dyce, 1:22–23), and suggests very plausibly that *kole* should be *bole*. "See Colyn Blowbole's Testament for the use of the word *blowbole* to mean 'drunkard': in Barclay's first eclogue Godfrey Gormand 'blows in a bole. . . .' " "Blow at the bole" fits the context better than "blow at the kole," a proverbial phrase (Tilley, C460) meaning to labor in vain. However, cf. *Why Come Ye Nat to Courte?* 84.

612. golde and hole] "precious and perfect" (Hammond). Evidently proverbial. Dyce cites a passage from Heywood illustrating the same use of the phrase to describe hypocrisy: "In words as gold and hole, as men by wit could wish, / She will lie as fast as a dog will lick a dish."

613. powle hatchettis] "soldiers who use pole axes" (Scattergood, citing R. L. Greene in *N & Q* 219:128–30). To judge from its use in "My Darlyng Dere" (28), it meant an ineffectual braggart.

636. Pers Prater] Piers or Peter the chatterbox.

641. Dasyng dotrellis] See textual note.

CAPITULUM SEXTUM] Skelton's garden of poetry is modeled quite closely on Lydgate's garden in *The Churl and the Bird*. A corrupt text of this poem, turning it into an alchemical fable, may underlie the symbolism of Parrot in *Speke, Parrot* (Brownlow, *ELR* 1:3–26).

654. alys ensandid abowte in compas] "sanded pathways all around it." Cf. *The Churl and the Bird*, "Alle the aleis were made playne with sand" (Lydgate, *Minor Poems* 2:470–71).

655. withe singular solas] "in a particularly pleasant manner" (Dyce).

668. a Phenix] "The blessed bird of the sun" (Claudian, *Phoenix*, 7) that has neither mother nor father, but is its own father and its son, dying every thousand years (Claudian) or five hundred (Ovid *Met.* 15.395), and rejuvenating itself from its own ashes. Skelton's bird's fire of olive-wood seems to be his own addition, and probably symbolizes peace. The phoenix, though fabulous, appears regularly in medieval bird-catalogues; cf. *Phyllyp Sparowe*, 513–49, where Skelton interprets the phoenix to mean "that old age / Is turned into corage / Of fresshe youth agayne." In the bestiaries the phoenix symbolizes Christ, but Skelton's phoenix, continually burning, symbolizes the mystery of poetry, ever fresh, and everlasting.

670. Gloss] "a fair olive-tree in the plains." From a passage used as the third lesson at the Matins of the Blessed Virgin.

675. Saby] *Saba*, the city of Arabia famous in classical times for myrrh and frankincense. Cf. Claudian, *Phoenix* 43: "et tumulum texens pretiosa fronde

Sabaeum / componit" ("He builds his pyre, weaving the precious branches of Saba"). See note to 1605–6 below.

681. Phillis and Testalis] girls' names from Virgil, *Eclogues* 2.10, 3.76. *Thestylis* originates with Theocritus, *Idylls* 2, as the name of a maidservant.

685. Dame Flora] The Roman goddess of flowers, whose festival, the Floralia, was celebrated at the end of April and beginning of May, the time of Skelton's vision. It was a rather licentious affair, like the later English Mayday holiday. See Ovid, *Fasti* 5.193–378: "scaena levis decet hanc: non est, mihi credite, non est / illa coturnatas inter habenda deas" ("A wanton stage suits her: believe me, she is not, repeat not, to be listed among the buskined goddesses").

687. Cintheus] Apollo, so named from his birthplace, Mt. Cynthus.

688. Iopas] The Carthaginian poet who sings before Dido and Aeneas at the banquet, *Aeneid* 1.740–46:

> cithara crinitus Iopas
> personat aurata, docuit quem maximus Atlas.
> hic canit errantem lunam solisque labores,
> unde hominum genus et pecudes, unde imber et ignes,
> Arcturum pluviasque Hyadas geminosque Triones;
> quid tantum Oceano properent se tinguere soles
> hiberni, vel quae tardis mora noctibus obstet.

("Long-haired Iopas, whom great Atlas taught, sounds his gilded lyre. He sings of the wandering moon and the labors of the sun; whence came the race of men, and beasts, whence rain and fire; of Arcturus and the rainy Hyades, and the twin bears; why the suns of winter hasten so to dip themselves in the ocean, and what delay stays the slow nights.")

689. poemis] According to *OED*, this word was "apparently not in use till about the middle of the 16th C.," and its "sense was previously, from the 14th C., expressed by *poesy*." The dictionary's first example of *poem* is from Elyot's *Dictionary* (1548). The word is not in *MED*. Skelton's uses of *poem*, however, here and elsewhere (e.g. *Northumberland*, 8; *Diodorus*, 1:358) suggest familiarity and habit.

694. Of fyre elementar] i.e., of the elemental fire supposed to form a sphere just within the moon's orbit.

695–99. that pole artike . . . aspy] *pole artike*: the celestial north pole, here the pole star; *the tayle of Ursa*: the tail of the Little Bear; *Pliades*: the Pleiades; *the two Trions*: Virgil's *geminosque Triones*, the Great and Little Bears.

697. Pliades] Composing no doubt from memory, Skelton has mistaken the Pleiades, the daughters of Atlas, for the Hyades ("the Rainers"), a group in Taurus, called by the Romans the Little Pigs, and associated with damp and rainy weather. The alliteration *Pliades/prechid* shows that Skelton, not an editor, made the mistake.

731. I ne force . . . discuryd] "That I do not care although it be discovered, shewn" (Dyce). "That I care very much if it be disclosed" (Hammond). Dyce seems to be right.

733. I am not ladyn . . . lumpis] A hyperbaton, "I am not laden with lumps of liddrons," i.e. "I am not weighed down by gangs of rascals."

741a–751. *Interpolata . . . CODRO*] "An interpolated satire against the poet's adversary, which requires an industrious interpreter. At first a sort of cheap groom, secondly a kind of slave. Gnat-catching, while he turns his little eye sidelong, look, he snatches, seizes, grabs winged flies. Whatever Maia favors, or whatever Jupiter favors; whatever cold things Saturn favors, or the Sun, Mars, Venus, or the cold Moon: if you put it in words or commit it to writing, immediately his bowels sweat with hidden guilt, and he falls into a passion; goading, he urges on this one and that; he stirs up quarrels. Yet the fires he lights are vain. His lips move silently. 'May Codrus burst his guts!' "

742. TRESSIS AGASONIS] Cf. Persius, *Satires* 5.76: "Hic Dama est non tressis agaso" ("This Dama is a slave not worth threepence"). DAVI:] *Davus* is a slave's name in the plays of Plautus and Terence.

743. AUCUPIUM CULICUS] *Culex* ("Gnat"), a mock-heroic poem attributed to the young Virgil, was the subject of allegorical interpretation because it seems to contain some personal allusion—a tradition maintained by Spenser, whose translation, "Virgils Gnat," dedicated to Leicester, also harbors personal allegory. In Skelton's very obscure satire, therefore, the opponent's gnat-catching may well be a scoffing allusion to his attempts at unriddling Skelton's poetry.

744. OPPETIT] Unnecessarily emended by Dyce to *appetit*. The word is a little flourish of Skeltonic learning; it often occurs in MSS as a variant of *appetere* (*Thesaurus Linguae Latinae*, s.v. "oppeto").

745–46. Gloss] The seven metals are mercury (associated here with Maia, standing in for her son Hermes or Mercury); sulphur (Jupiter); lead (Saturn); gold (Sun); iron (Mars); copper (Venus); and silver (Moon). Whether this passage signals the presence of alchemical symbolism elsewhere in *The Laurel* is hard to say. For other evidence of Skelton's interest in alchemy and his poetic use of alchemical mythology and symbolism, see Brownlow, *ELR* 1:12–16.

748. TACITA . . . CULPA] from Juvenal, *Satires* 1.167 (Dyce).

751. LABRA . . . TACITUS] from Persius 5.184 (Dyce). RUMPANTUR . . . CODRO.] from Virgil, *Eclogues* 7.26: "invidia rumpantur ut ilia Codro" ("that Codrus's guts may burst with envy") (Dyce). Codrus is the name of a contemptible poet, the butt of Thyrsis and Corydon in their singing match.

751a–b. The number code] Based on the Latin alphabet; the vowels are 1–5, the consonants 1–23 (if one includes *y*), yielding the name *Rogerus Stathum* (first worked out by Henry Bradley, "Two Puzzles in Skelton," *Academy*, 1 August 1896). Stathum is unidentified. Edwards, 236–38, thought him the husband of Gertrude Statham, waiting-woman to the countess, and the recipient of a lyric. The number code may also be a signal of the presence of numerical composition elsewhere in the poem. Stathum must have envied Skelton's learning because of its aura of magical and occult power, a feeling this mysterious satire and code would encourage. Skelton sometimes used satire as if it might have more than verbal power, an approach traceable, like his bardic, prophetic view of poetry in general, mainly to classical sources. Yet his classical learning may only have provided authority for an idea he originally acquired from native traditions, Welsh or Scots as well as English. The bardic view of poetry lasted into this century in the west of Ireland. See Tomás Ó Crohan, *The Islandman* (ed. 1951), 86: "I knew that if the poet had anything against me, he would make a satire on me that would be very unpleasant. . . ."

784-86. For yit of women . . . to bralle] These lines, similar in expression to the description of *The Popingay* (1182-84), refer to a poem written for the countess. See note to 1182.

787-807] Like ladies making vestments for a modern cathedral, the Countess and her women set to work. "Sewing, lacemaking, weaving, embroidery, are the various occupations; some work on 'samplers' (*l.* 789) or braid lace (*l.* 789), and some set themselves to weave in the *stool*, a stretcher or tambour-frame mounted on legs for the worker's convenience. In *l.* 791 are enumerated some of the necessary appliances, the *slaiys*, sleys or weavers' reeds, the heddles or cords sustaining the warp on the loom. Tuly or tewly silk, mentioned in *l.* 798, is dark red; the *botum* or bottom of *l.* 799 is a skein of thread, or the clew on which to wind a skein. The tavels of *l.* 791 are bobbins on which silk for the shuttle is wound" (Hammond). This "graceful picture" (Hammond), like the portrayal of Jane Scrope in *Phyllyp Sparowe*, shows a Skelton who is sensitive to, and observant of, the details of a feminine ambience.

819. after ther degre] in order of precedence.

823. sharpe my pen] lit., cut a new nib; fig., stir up my faculties.

828a, b] "Capitulum the ninth, of heroical commendation." The number nine here symbolizes the art of poetry. Dyce's attempt to identify the eleven ladies whom Skelton commends was vitiated by a wrong dating of the poem. Tucker (*RQ* 22:333-45), with a correct date and more accurate biographical information, has more success.

829-35. AS a maryner . . . my gyde] Skelton's fiction, reflected in the poems themselves, is that *Poeta Skelton* composes his poems extempore in a sustained fit of inspiration. The poems' form, however, shows that they were carefully conceived as a set. The formal intricacy of the set casts strong doubt upon Tucker's hypothesis that the set was assembled from poems written individually over a period of years. This is hardly possible.

831. Of . . . aswage] A syntactical inversion. The mariner is driven to hope the wind "of that," i.e., the "stormmy rage," will abate.

835a. TO THE RIGHT NOBILLE COUNTES OF SURREY] Not Elizabeth née Stafford, wife of Thomas Howard II, earl of Surrey and 3d duke of Norfolk (Dyce, et al.), but Elizabeth née Tylney, first wife of Thomas I, earl of

Surrey and later (after Flodden Field, 1513), 2d duke of Norfolk. She died in 1497. Her poem is a four-stanza ballade in rhyme royal, a courtly form and meter befitting a great lady.

843–46. Lyke to Argyva . . . makithe] Skelton's chief figure of praise in these poems is a comparison between his subject and ladies from mythology, history, and the Bible. His chief source is Boccacio, *De claris mulieribus*, although he also draws from classical and native sources, including Chaucer and Lydgate. His praise of the countess begins with two exemplars of wifely beauty and virtue: Argia, "a happy sight to her contemporaries because of her marvellous beauty, and she left to posterity an untainted and noble record of conjugal love" (*DCM*, trans. Guido A. Guarino, cap. 27); and Rebecca, wife of Isaac.

850. Pamphila] Skelton next compares the countess to a lady famous for mastery of domestic arts. Pamphila "was the first to pick cotton from plants and cleanse it of residual matter with the comb . . . she put it on the distaff and showed how to make thread from it and how to weave it" (*DCM*, cap. 42).

852. Thamar] Thamyris, the next lady, was an artist, "a fine painter . . . she was the daughter of the painter Micon, ... She had such marvellous talent that she scorned the duties of women and practised her father's art" (*DCM*, cap. 54). Called Thamyris by Boccaccio and Skelton, this lady's proper name is Timarete.

857–60. Dame Thamaris . . . memory] Since Hammond wrote that "Queen Tomyris and Agrippina seem extraordinary selections from classical story to compare with English noblewomen," readers have suspected Skelton of irony, but without cause. These are perhaps the two most important of Skelton's comparisons, because they are examples of women who defended their lands or families against tyranny. Thamyris, Queen of Scythia, who defeated and killed Cyrus, the invader of her country, "is famous for splendid nobility" (*DCM*, cap. 47), and Elizabeth I was later compared to her (Hammond). Agrippina here is not, as Hammond thought, the mother of Nero, but the wife of Germanicus, who died of self-starvation in defiance of Tiberius: "She was very famous because with relentless purpose she resisted the perfidy of that most proud emperor" (*DCM*, cap. 88). These comparisons undoubtedly reflect the situation of the countess after the accession of Henry VII. Her father-in-law was killed fighting for Richard III at Bosworth, and her husband was imprisoned in the Tower.

863a. TO MY LADY ELISABETHE] Lady Elizabeth Howard, the countess's daughter by Thomas Howard. She married Sir Thomas Boleyn about 1500, and became the mother of Mary and Anne Boleyn, hence grandmother to Elizabeth I (Tucker). Elizabeth receives a two-stanza ballade and three ladies to compare herself with, exactly half the tribute to her mother, and as the elder daughter she follows her mother in due order.

865. Aryna] Irene, an artist, "daughter and pupil of Cratinus the painter . . . . This Irene had unusual talent, and her skill was worthy of remembrance" (*DCM*, cap. 57).

871. Goodely Creisseyda] The point of comparison between Cressida and Elizabeth Howard is that both are beautiful girls on the verge of maturity. This Cressida has not yet met Troilus, let alone betrayed him; but she is very beautiful. On the tone of this and other comparisons, debatable since Hammond, Edwards, and Fish raised the question of irony, see appendix 6.

871. Polycene] Polyxena, daughter of King Priam, "of such radiant beauty that she was able to inflame with love the harsh breast of Achilles" (*DCM*, cap. 31).

877a. TO MY LADY MYRRYEL] Lady Muriel Howard, the countess's younger daughter. She married John Grey, Viscount Lisle, some time before 1500. After his death (1504), she married Thomas Knyvett, apparently for love: the young couple married without license of the king, for which Thomas Knyvett had to pay Henry VII 400 marks (Tucker). Skelton gives her a two-stanza ballade, and just one lady.

882. luste] a synonym for "pleasure" in the pleonastic series "plesure, delight, and luste," without sexual innuendo.

885. Cydippes] Cydippe, with whom the youth Acontius fell in love in the temple of Diana. He threw her an apple wrapped in a "bill" which read, "I swear by the sanctuary of Diana to marry Acontius," and Cydippe, not thinking, read it aloud (Ovid *Heroides* 20).

891a. TO MY LADY DAKERS] Lady Anne Dacre of the South was the countess's daughter by a previous marriage to Humphrey Bourchier (d. 1471). She married Thomas Fenys, Lord Dacre, in 1492. As the countess's daughter, Lady Anne receives a two-stanza ballade. Her precedence in the Howard family is indicated by the position of her poem, but as eldest daughter and a married lady, she receives four ladies.

892. Zeuxes] Zeuxis, a famous Greek painter, ca. 424–380 B.C. He painted a portrait of Helen of Troy for the city of Croton.

894. Apelles] Another famous Greek painter of the fourth century B.C. He was the only painter Alexander the Great would allow to paint his picture.

897. Prynces of yowthe] "Princess of youth," also quoted in *Bowge of Courte* (253), is the opening of a three-part English chanson of the fifteenth century. For a transcription see Manfred Bukofzer, *Music and Letters* 19:119.

899. Penolope] Penelope, wife of Ulysses, "a woman of untarnished honor and inviolate chastity, and a holy and eternal example for women" (*DCM*, cap. 38).

901. Dyanyra] Deianira, daughter of King Oenus of Aetolia, "a virgin of such striking beauty that Hercules and Achelous fought to take her to wife" (*DCM*, cap. 22). The explicit point of comparison between Lady Anne and Deianira, as in the previous example of Helen, is beauty. It would be a serious misreading to think that Lady Anne was being taxed with Helen's inconstancy or Deianira's accident-proneness. As with other married ladies in the group, however, the husband seems to be reflected in the comparisons: Was Lord Dacre absent and unfaithful to his beautiful wife?

905a. TO MASTRES MARGERY WENTWORTHE] Margery Wentworth was the daughter of Sir Henry Wentworth and his wife Anne Say, the countess's half sister. She was the countess's niece. Tucker surmises that she married John Seymour on 22 October 1494, but this seems too early. She became the grandmother of Edward VI through her daughter Jane Seymour, Henry VIII's third queen; and her son Edward was duke of Somerset and Lord Protector. She comes first in precedence among the waiting-women, for whom Skelton uses more popular, less exalted measures than rhyme royal as well as more simple diction and syntax.

906. mageran] marjoram. Marjoram gentle is "of the best sort of Marjerane" (Gerard, *Herball*, quoted by Dyce). "Not only does this provide a pun with the lady's name, but the properties of the herb, its prettiness and its usefulness, also match her virtues" (Scattergood).

925a. TO MASTRES MARGARETE TYLNNEY] Margaret Tylney was married to Sir Philip Tylney, later Surrey's treasurer in the Scottish campaign of 1513. She was sister-in-law to Surrey's second wife, also a Tylney, and Edwards (235) identifies her as a sister-in-law to Jane Scrope, the mistress of *Phyllyp Sparowe*, who married Margaret's brother, Thomas Brews, about 1508.

933-34. Machareus . . . Canace] Machareus and Canace were the children of King Eolus, and the story of their incestuous love is told by Ovid, *Heroides* 11, by Gower, *Confessio Amantis*, 3.143, and Lydgate, *Falls of Princes*, 1. 6833. The last version, one of Lydgate's best passages, was probably in Skelton's mind. Lydgate blames the father for "too rigorous," "too vengeable" treatment of the pair. The explicit point of comparison, though, is that like Machareus in relation to Canace, so Skelton will do his utmost to see that Margaret Tylney's name is included with the others, "wryttyn with gold." One is bound to wonder whether Margaret Tylney knew the story of Canace. If she did not, someone would certainly tell her. On this, and the next allusion to Phaedra, see appendix 6.

935. iwus] See textual note. As Hammond points out, this word is comparable to German *gewiss*, "certainly," the *i-* being a survival of OE past-participial *ge-*. Modern English speakers mistake *i-* for a personal pronoun, and read the word as an imaginary *I wis*, "I know."

940. Phedra] Phaedra, sister of Ariadne, daughter of Minos, wife of Theseus. In Chaucer, *Legend of Good Women*, 1985-2024, she is also "intentyve and diligent" (Skelton's point of comparison) because she invents the stratagems by which Theseus kills her brother the Minotaur. She supplanted Ariadne in Theseus's affections, and Skelton certainly knew the story of her incestuous love for Hippolytus. Lydgate also handles her story in *Falls of Princes*, 1.2801-84.

953a. TO MASTRES JANE HASSET] Not specifically identified. Tucker suggests that Jane Hasset (Blenner-Haiset, *B*) was wife to Ralph Blennerhasset. She was an elderly widow, who died in 1501, aged ninety-seven.

972. Laodomy] Laodamia, an exemplar of wifely constancy and love. After her husband Protesilaus left for Troy, she kept a statue of him in her

room. After receiving news of his death, she committed suicide in the embrace of his phantom, sent her by Zeus (Ovid, *Heroides* 13; Chaucer, *Legend of Good Women*, 263, who mentions her in a list that includes Canace [cf. 934] of women famed for truth in love). The implication is that she is a widow.

972a. TO MASTRES ISABELL PENNEL] Not definitely identified. Tucker thinks this very young girl might be Isabel Paynell, daughter of John Paynell, member of a family that had dealings with the Howards.

977. rosabel] Skelton's anglicization of the first words of John Dunstable's famous chanson, *O rosa bella, O dolce anima mea*, another musical reference. Cf. 897, and the first line of the ballade, "Go, pytyous hart, rasyd with dedly wo" (Dyce, 1:27), apparently based on the opening of the beautiful fifteenth-century three-part song, "Go hert hurt with adversite" (Reese, *Music in the Middle Ages*, 422).

988. Star of the morow gray] Venus as the morning star.

1003a. TO MASTRES MARGARETE HUSSEY] Unidentified. Tucker thinks she might be the wife of John Hussey, sheriff of Lincolnshire, 1493–94, later controller of the household to Henry VII, and chief butler. He was ennobled in 1529 as Lord Hussey, but was executed for his part in the Pilgrimage of Grace. This man's wife was Margaret, daughter of Sir Simon Blount of Mangotsfield. If she died in 1492, as Tucker believes, then she was not Skelton's "myrry Margarete" in 1495 unless Skelton, moved by some special affection, included her and her poem posthumously. According to one of Tucker's sources she was still alive in 1509 (Tucker, *RQ* 22:339, n.18). Skelton's lady, however, was probably another Margaret Hussey, an unmarried girl (See note to 1021). Margaret is a common name. It is most unlikely that in 1495 Skelton portrayed Merry Margaret to her friends as alive, well, and beautiful if they all knew she was dead.

1004. mydsomer floure] The daisy or marguerite, flower of love and courtesy, "she that is of alle floures flour, / Fulfilled of al vertu and honour" (*Legend of Good Women*, 53–4).

1005. hauke of the towre] According to the *Boke of St. Albans*, in the hierarchy of hawks all birds from the eagle down to the hobby ("that hawke is for a young man") are hawks of the tower, i.e., they stoop to their prey from a great height, and are thus "gentle" or noble birds. In the arrangement of the waiting-women, Margaret Hussey is second in order of precedence, leading the second group of three ladies.

1021. Isyphill] Hypsipyle, Queen of Lemnos, "famous for the devotion she showed toward her father, as well as for her unfortunate exile" (*DCM*, cap. 15). This implies that Margaret is a young woman, unmarried, who has loyally supported her father through times of difficulty, with patience, dignity, and cheerfulness. Her moral qualities inspire intense admiration in Skelton.

1024. Cassander] Cassandra, daughter of Priam. "She possessed the gift of prediction" (*DCM*, cap. 33), but although her predictions were true, she was doomed never to be believed. Hammond, reading *u* for *n*, proposes *Cas-*

sauder, the herb, thus making a pair with *pomaunder*. *A*'s bold capital *C*, though, supports the proper name *Cassander*.

1031a. TO MASTRES GERETRUDE STATHAM] Edwards (31, 236–38) speculates that this lady was the granddaughter of John Anstey of Stow-cum-Quy, Cambridgeshire, who married one Roger Statham in 1482, whom he identifies with the victim of the "interpolated satire" (741–751b). Such identifications are bound to be uncertain, but this one is plausible. He goes on to speculate that Skelton, while a student at Cambridge, fell in love with Gertrude Anstey, and lost her to Roger. By this means he explains the biographical reference to a quarrel in Gertrude's poem, but this is very fanciful romancing. Tucker, however, adopts Edwards's theory and argues, on the basis of it, for a date of 1480 for Gertrude's poem—an uncharacteristic lapse.

1042. Pasiphe] Wife of Minos, mother of the Minotaur; an ingenious invention by Daedalus enabled her to have sexual relations with a bull. See appendix 6.

1055a. TO MASTRES ISBELL KNYGHT] Not identified. Tucker thinks she could be the wife of Leonard Knight, a justice of assize for York and the northern counties in 1492. She is evidently of less exalted social standing than the others, and her poem consists chiefly of assurances that she will not be left out.

1070. Galathea] A very lively country girl who figures in Virgil's *Eclogues*, e.g., 3.64–65. The comparison reflects Isbell's lesser social standing, but also, surely, the fact that she is an unmarried girl?

1090. Master Newton] Evidently the Surrey household included a man for drawing, illuminating, and writing. His tools are a pair of compasses, a lead pencil, a fine brush, and spectacles, a relatively recent invention.

1124–28. Of your bownte . . . the light] "The usual amount of your generosity has often been, and still is, proportionate to everything that accommodates itself to reason—unless hasty confidence, caused by use of force, happens to stand in your light." "Credence" and "maytenaunce of myght" refer to a fifteenth-century practice whereby powerful men sent "credences" with letters, i.e., confidential instructions entrusted to the bearer, often backed up by force.

1163a–d. *Occupacioun . . . compilyd. &c.*] With the exception of works listed in stanzas 133–41, everything in this "bibliography" was written before 1495. As Kinsman says (*Canon*, xii), this list gives disproportionate attention to lighter poems, and sometimes omits, or misrepresents, the more important; but the new dating leads one to modify this view. The list is meant to amuse; it is not intended to be complete, and the only misrepresented work is *Colyn Cloute*. Appendix 3 contains a numbered listing of the works mentioned by Occupacioun.

1166. The Boke of Honorows Astate] Lost. Gloss] "Honor is the sign of work well-performed.'

1167. The Boke How Men Shuld Fle Syn] Lost. Gloss] "Turn away from evil, and do good."

1168. Roialle Demenaunce] Lost. Gloss] "The nobleman is he whom his virtue ennobles." Unidentified. The thought is a commonplace. Cf. Juvenal 8.20: "Nobilitas sola est atque unica virtus."

1169. The Boke to Speke Wele, or be stille] Lost. Probably a translation of Alberto of Brescia, *Tractatus de doctrina dicendi et tacendi* (Nelson, 49). Gloss] Cf. Carleton Brown, *Rel. Lyr. 15C*, no. 181: "Werfor wyse Catoun seyth to old & yong: The fyrst chefe vertu is to kepe owr tong."

1170. Item To Lerne Yow to Dye] Lost. Probably a translation or paraphrase of Gerson, *Ars Moriendi*, an immensely popular work. *STC* lists five translations made between 1490 and 1506 (Kinsman, *Canon*, 31). Gloss] "Death is the line that marks the end of all."

1171. Vertu] A lost play. Gloss] "All things submit to virtue [i.e., to power, to mental and physical capacity]."

1172. The Boke of the Rosiar] Lost. Dyce thought it might be the eight-stanza poem "A Lawde and Prayse Made for Our Sovereigne Lord the Kyng," which he first printed from PRO MS. E.36/228, ff. 67-70; but this is too short and too late.

1172. Prynce Arturis Creacioune] Lost. Prince Arthur, eldest son of Henry VII, was created Prince of Wales and earl of Chester on 1 October 1489. A carol in the form of a prayer for Prince Arthur survives in BL Addit. MS. 5465, ff. 104v-108. The music is by Edmund Turgis. The words could be Skelton's. They reflect his habits of syntax, diction, rhythm, and rhyme.

1173. The Fals Faythe That Now Gothe] Lost. "Gothe," i.e., "Goeth," means "is in fashion." Gloss] "Nowhere is faith secure."

1174. Dialoggis of Imagynacioune] Lost. Edwards, 58, thinks it was a translation of *Imaginacion de Vraye Noblesse*, a French prose work presented to Henry VII in 1496. As Edwards describes it, however, the work does not seem to be a dialogue. It is also too late for this part of the "bibliography."

1175. Automedon] Lost. Perhaps a translation or paraphrase of Ovid, *Ars Amoris*. The name *Automedon* is a periphrasis for Ovid, taken from Geoffrey de Vinsauf, *De Arte Versificandi*, 2.3.50 (ed. Faral, 293): "Similiter et Ovidius: 'Tiphis et Authomedon dicar Amoris ego,' id est 'magister.'" The Ovid quotation is from *Ars*, 1. 8, "I shall be called the Tiphys and the Automedon of love." Skelton's title, then, was "The Meditation of the Master of Love," or "Ovid's meditation." Automedon was Achilles' charioteer, and a master of his craft. Gloss] "Love is a thing filled with anxious fear."

1176. New Gramer] Lost. Presumably a textbook compiled before 1495, suggesting that Skelton was a teacher before he became tutor to Henry, Duke of York, ca. 1497-98. In his forthcoming *John Skelton: Priest as Poet*, Arthur Kinney suggests that he was a tutor to the Howard children. Gloss] "If usage so rules, in the power of which [lies the judgment, the law and standard of speech]."

1177. Bowche of Courte] *The Bowge of Courte*, an allegorical narrative in rhyme royal, first published ca. 1499, and previously dated 1498. On the evidence of this listing it must be earlier than 1495. Tucker (*ELN* 7:168-75) and

Brownlow (*ELN* 22:12–20) argue for a date in the 1480s on the basis of historical and astronomical evidence. Gloss] "Nor is the fear of God before their eyes."

1178. Achademios] A lost comedy. Nelson, 49, 139, and Edwards, 34, 168, suggest that Skelton might have written this play ca. 1488 to fulfill the requirements for the Oxford degree of Poet Laureate.

1179. Tullis Familiars] Lost. Caxton mentions this translation of Cicero's *Epistolae ad Familiares* in his *Boke of Eneydos* (1490): "He hath late translated the epystlys of Tulle . . ." (Nelson, 4). This too may have been an academic exercise. Gloss] "Laurels yield to learning."

1180. Goode Avysemente] Lost. In part at least, a treatise on poetry and poetic inspiration, mentioned in *A Replycacion*, 359ff. (Dyce 1:221). Gloss] "Act advisedly, and thou shalt never do wrong."

1181. Recule Ageyne Gagwyne] Lost. See note to 374.

1182. The Popingay] Lost? This description does not correspond to the poem now known as *Speke, Parrot*, datable 1519–21. Scholars generally assume that Skelton here intentionally misrepresents that poem, in part a prophetic denunciation of Wolsey as Antichrist (Brownlow, *SP* 55:124–39). Yet *The Popingay* appears amongst pre-1495 works; its description is similar to the countess's description of some writings by Skelton about women, and its gloss corresponds to a line about Parrot in *Speke, Parrot*. One concludes, therefore, that *The Popingay* was an earlier version of *Speke, Parrot*. It was a rhyme-royal allegory, written before 1495, spoken by Parrot (the popingay's name, akin to Peterkin), mainly about women, but with satiric passages and in part focused on the interest of its speaker, Parrot. In 1519, Skelton revived this old poem, retaining Parrot and the stanzas about him as well as some of the passages about women, and he redirected it as a satire against Wolsey. In 1523, he was content to have the two versions of the poem confused. Gloss] "Let not a rustic butterfly serve me as model." An untraced dactylic pentameter. Probably the missing gloss to *Speke, Parrot*, 211: "Parrot is no . . . butterfly."

1185. Sovereynte, a nobille pamphelet] Lost. This and the next thirteen works were interpolated ca. 1522–23 (Intro., p. 34). Gloss] "Rule with thy power." Skelton has altered the Psalm verse: "qui dominatur in virtute sua in aeternum" ("who ruleth with his power for ever").

1186. Magnyfycence] An interlude or political morality, generally dated 1516, Skelton's only surviving play. Gloss] "He glorified him in the sight of kings."

1187–91. Gloss] "Modesty, truth, and faith fled, and in their place came tricks, plots, snares, violence, and the wicked love of property."

1192–98. Of Mannerly Mastres Margery . . . gone away] One "Mannerly Margery" poem survives, in a setting for three voices by Skelton's friend William Cornyshe, Jr., Gentleman of the Chapel, later Master of the Children of the Chapel (Dyce, 1:28; John Stevens, *Music and Poetry*, 358). Gloss] "O wretched daughter of Babylon."

1197. With gingirly . . . hay] *Gingerly*, of obscure origin, means "daintily," "elegantly," and was used especially to describe walking or dancing with small steps. *Made of hay* might mean "ticklish" or "well-covered." If the latter, then similar jokes were still current in eighteenth-century Scotland; see *Songs and Poems of Robert Burns* (Oxford, 1968), 2:717, "Bonnie Mary": "The hair of my a——e is grown into my c——t, / And they canna win to, to m—we me."

1199. Gloss] "Nothing is made out of nothing." Proverbial, usually attributed to Aristotle, e.g. by *Dicta notabilia sive illustriores sententiae* (Venice, 1547), 89, with a reference to *De generatione* 1, where one finds, "That which is formed by means of a process must of necessity be formed out of something by something into something" (733b, Loeb ed.). The saying was proverbial by the time of Boethius, who has "Nam nihil ex nihilo exsistere vera sententia est" (*De consolatione* 5.1).

1203–5. With pitche . . . potshorde] Margery tries to mend her broken pitcher, i.e., her *honeste*, with a patch of pitch; but it is already a fragment, a potsherd. Gloss] "The most displeasing can please." Untraced, presumably proverbial. Not "Frenssh of Parys."

1205a–9. *Patet* . . . TALIS] The lines are mysterious. Literally translated, they mean:

As it is revealed in the verses:

Hence a boy was born here: hence a husband was deprived
Of conjugal rights. He is a child of the race of Delos.
Hence I rejoice the more because this boy will be another Apollo.
You ask in what way? By way of a very chaste whore.

Although oracular, the lines must be intended to be understood. The most obvious meaning is that Skelton had a child by Margery. The joke, a broad one, is that the boy will be another Apollo because he is born of Delian, i.e., Apollonian, blood. This is because his father is Skelton the poet.

1210. Et relis . . . reliqualis] A nonsense verse, the equivalent of "&c, &c, &c." Cf. *Ware the Hawke*, 320.

1211–12.] "Such good cheap eating as these old tales is no more to be found in the breadth of Britain."

1212b. *Et reliqua . . . tractatibus*] "And the rest of the sermon comes from various tracts." This is not very good Latin, but Dyce's emendation, *reliquae omeliae*, is unnecessary.

1213. My Ladys Grace] "Grace" does not necessarily identify the lady's rank because it may not be a title, but only the complimentary form of reference used widely of aristocrats in Skelton's time. It might even mean "favor", though this is perhaps unlikely. The lady is unknown, although all possible candidates have been proposed: Lady Margaret Beaufort (Dyce, Pollet, Kinsman); Agnes, duchess of Norfolk (Edwards, Tucker); Elizabeth née Stafford, countess of Surrey (Brie), and Elizabeth, née Tylney, countess of Surrey (Tucker).

1215. Of Mannys Lyf the Peregrynacioun] Lost. The original will have been the *Pèlerinage de la vie humaine* of Guillaume de Guilleville, a very popular work in its time. Gloss] "Here we have no permanent city, but we seek the city that is to come."

1217. Traytyse of Tryumphis / of the Rede Rose] Lost. The gloss indicates that the Cornish rebellion of 1497 was one of its subjects (Edwards, 60), and it therefore supplies a *terminus ad quem* for dating the original *Laurel*. It will have been similar to Bernard André's *Les douzes triomphes de Henry VII* (Nelson, 28, 53–54). Gloss] "He writes of the Cornish war, fought in the open country and exposed, waste, lonely places near Greenwich."

1220. The Duke of Yorkis creauncer] On Skelton's tutorship of Prince Henry, see Edwards, 54–59; also Nelson, 71, 76.

1223. Speculum Principis] "A Mirror for a Prince." A short prose treatise of moral instruction for Prince Henry, dated at Eltham, 28 August 1501, and presented to Henry after his accession, probably on New Year's Day, 1511, as a reminder of his old tutor. In the 18C. the MS was known to be in Lincoln Cathedral; in 1934, F. M. Salter discovered it in the British Museum, and edited it (*Speculum* 9:25–37). Gloss] "Receive instruction, ye who rule the earth."

1227. The Tunnynge of Elinor Rummyng] A poem in Skeltonics on the alewife of the Running Horse alehouse, Leatherhead, Surrey, now dated ca. 1516 (Kinsman, *HLQ* 18:315–27).

1228. Colyn Clowte] A major Skeltonic satire against negligent churchmen in general, against Cardinal Wolsey in particular, written in 1522 (Nelson, 189–90), and here comically misrepresented. Gloss] "Who will stand with me against the doers of wickedness." This gloss belies the description of the poem, for which Skelton originally used it as an epigraph.

1228. John Ive] Lost. John Ive was a Lollard active "in the end of the reign of King Edward the Fourth," mentioned in a heresy trial of 1511 (Dyce).

1228. Joforthe Jak] Lost. "Joforthe" was a drover's cry (Dyce). This and "John Ive" were probably short pieces or "trifels."

1231. Gloss] "Serious things depicted in jest please better." A dactylic pentameter.

1233. to use the Walshemannys hose] Cf. *Colyn Cloute*, 780–81: "To make a Walshman's hose / Of the texte and of the glose." The expression is proverbial; it means to stretch or force the meaning of a text at one's convenience, as Skelton is doing here by describing *Colyn Cloute* as a trifle. A Welshman's hose was reputed a poor fit, and so necessarily very elastic (Dyce, Scattergood).

1234–35. The umblis of venysoun . . . sent] Lost. One poem to Mistress Anne survives, "Womanhod, wanton, ye want" (Dyce, 1:20), probably written ca. 1497–1504 when Skelton was in London. Gloss] "They take their fill of old wine and fat venison."

1239. The Balade . . . of the Mustarde Tarte] Lost. Edwards, 51, illustrates its possible subject by quoting Villon, "Elle alla bien à la moutarde," and an anonymous rondeau: "En trop de lieux brassez moustarde / Vostre mortier ne vault plus rien." See Partridge, *Dict. of Slang and Unconventional English*, s.v. "mustard-pot."

1241. Of one Adame Alle-a-Knave] One of a pair of goliardic epitaphs for parishioners of Diss, Norfolk, where Skelton was rector (Dyce, 1:168). Gloss] " 'Adam, Adam, where art thou?' He replies: 'Where there is no rest, no order, but where everlasting horror dwelleth.' "

1248. Of Phyllype Sparow] Skelton's most famous longer poem, ca. 1505, upon a dead pet sparrow and its mistress, Jane Scrope, a niece of Lord Scrope of Bolton Castle, Wensleydale, Yorkshire. Gloss] "Yea, the sparrow hath found out an house for herself."

1255–1369. This defense of *Phyllyp Sparow* was written soon after the poem, for it describes Jane Scrope as a "goodely mayd" (1269). She married ca. 1508 (Edwards, 113). Skelton probably inserted the defense into *The Laurel* in 1522/23. It is a fine piece of light verse, in which Skelton conjures up from Tartarus Philip's soul to tell him the cause of "this perplexyte," i.e., the attacks on the poem. The conjuration is made in the name of Hercules, a notable traveler to Tartarus and other classical otherworlds, as well as of other creatures associated with Tartarus and death. He also includes the Witch of Endor, the famous biblical example of necromancy.

1256. jangelyng jaiys] Among them Alexander Barclay, who speaks contemptuously of *Phyllyp Sparow* in his *Ship of Fools*, and who also attacked Skelton in the prologue to his *Eclogues*, and in *Eclogue* 4.

1278. that helle did harow] In bringing up the three-headed dog Cerberus from Tartarus; the twelfth labor (eleventh in Diodorus Siculus).

1280–83. Slew . . . Hippocentawris] Hercules killed Chiron the centaur, skilled in medicine, the teacher of Aesculapius, to whom Epidaurus was sacred. Skelton means "slew one of the Epidaurian, or medical, centaurs—or onocentaurs —or hippocentaurs." He could have learned of onocentaurs ("ass-centaurs") and hippocentaurs ("horse-centaurs") from Isidore of Seville (*Etymologia* 2.3.39) or from Reuchlin's *Breviloquus* (Salter/Edwards, *Diodorus*, 2:xlix).

1285. An hart] This was the Arcadian stag, object of Hercules' fourth labor, "whiche was dyvulgate thurgh the universal world for the most famous beste, whos aureate hornes glyteringe as bright as burned golde were valewd of excedynge ryches" (*Diodorus*, 1:378).

1288. appils] The eleventh labor (twelfth in Diodorus). Atlas took the apples from his daughters while Hercules supported the globe for him.

1294. Gerione] The tenth labor, the fetching of Geryon's cattle, "which famously were spoken of, whyche were pastured and had theyr fedynge in Hiberia marchynge toward the grete see Occeane" (*Diodorus*, 1:390).

1298. a lyon] The first labor, the killing of the Nemean lion, "an huge myghty beest, and of excessyf bygnes . . . that . . . must be slayn without all wepen [or] edge tool of forcyble sharpnes" (*Diodorus*, 1:371).

1299. Diomedis stabylle] The eighth labor, to capture the wild, flesh-eating horses of Diomedes that were the terror of Thrace, "whiche horses were excedynge ferre alle other horses in furyous rage & gretenes of stature, wylde of loke, daungerous to meddle wyth . . . they were fedde with mannys flesshe" (*Diodorus*, 1:386).

1305. bulle] Achelous, the river-god, with whom Hercules fought for the hand of Deianira. When he transformed himself into a bull, Hercules broke off his right horn. According to some accounts, e.g., Ovid, *Met.* 9.87, it became the cornucopia.

1309. Hecates bowre] Hecate was the goddess of the witches, and a great favorite with Pluto, which is why her bower was in his tower.

1311. Eumenides] The furies or "kindly ones." Since they hounded their victims incessantly, they had no rest themselves.

1313. serpente] The second labor of Hercules, to kill the Lernaean Hydra, "the venemows water serpente . . . of whose monstruews fashen to make discripcioun it wolde engendir in yow . . . a wonderffulle admyratyve. . . . This serpente had growinge owt of hys body, uggely enstuffid with venemows poison, an hundirde nekkis wyth an hundirde hedis; and as often as any of them by aventur was chopped away, ij grew uppe agayne . . ." (*Diodorus*, 1:372).

1317. Chemeras flamys] This could refer either to Mt. Chimaera, a volcano, or to the fire-breathing monster slain by Bellerophon, a story which some authors thought originated with the volcano.

1321-28] These lines invoke the hateful river-boundary of Tartarus, the Styx, and its ferryman, Charon, as well as one of its tributaries, Cocytus.

1330-40] The story of Saul and the Witch of Endor is in 1 Kings 28 (Vulgate), 1 Samuel 28 (A.V.).

1332. Phitones] Pythoness. The original Pythoness was the divinatory priestess of Apollo at Delphi, but Skelton had biblical authority for his word, for the Vulgate text (1 Kings 28:7) calls her familiar spirit *pytho*: "Est mulier pythonem habens in Endor."

1342. idem in numero] one and the same. Skelton says he will resolve the question whether the apparition was Samuel himself "to letterde men at large," i.e., to learned men at some length.

1351-53] The three names of the goddess Diana, in heaven, in the earth, and in the underworld.

1358-60. INFERIAS . . . VERO] "Philip, the beautiful Jane Scrope begged for your funeral rites. Why is she now ashamed of our song?" "It is too late. The ill-fame is of less consequence than the truth."

1367-69. LURIDE . . . CONTINUA] "Why, pale Envy, do you censure the gracious funeral rites of a bird? May a fate like the bird's overtake you! For you, however, envy is a continual death."

1370. The Grontyng and the Groynnynge of the Gronnyng Swyne] Lost. Skelton was fond of this phrase. Cf. "Ageinst Venemous Tongues," 4, and "Ageinst Garnesche," 2. 2. It is an example of his grasp of English. *Groynnynge*, pres. part. of *groine, groyne* < OF *groignier*, OE *grunnian*, to grumble or complain, is hard to distinguish from *gron(n)ynge*, pres. part. of *grone* < OE *granian*, to groan, sigh, lament. Skelton, however, distinguishes them clearly while playing upon their similarity. Gloss] "The pig swallows down his food, and sinks himself into the mud." Not from Guarino, *Ars diphthongandi*, but Reuchlin's *Breviloquus*, often bound with it, without attribution to Reuchlin (Salter/Edwards, *Diodorus*, 2:xxiv).

1371. The Murnnynge of the Mapely Rote] Lost. Dyce quotes a line of a song in Ravenscroft, *Pammelia* (1609), "Why weepst thou maple roote?" suggesting that it derives from Skelton. Kinsman (*Canon*, 28) quotes R. L. Greene, *Carols*, 318: "Why wepyst thou in an apple-rote?"

1372. How The Grene Coverlet Sufferde Grete Pyne] Lost. A tale of a girl in a green cloak? In the north, to wear green brought very bad luck in love (Child, 2:182). Gloss] "As a vesture [i.e., coverlet] shalt thou change them, and they shall be changed."

1375. A Devowte Prayer to Moyses Hornnis] Lost. Nelson, 50, quotes from de Guilleville's *Pèlerinage* in Lydgate's translation to show that Moses' horns were interpreted allegorically to mean the authoritative punishment of "shrewes" and "folkys Rebel in werchyng." He concludes that Skelton's lost poem was a satire or a moral tract. The curious notion that Moses had horns is based on the Vulgate text of Exodus 34:29: "Cumque descenderet Moyses de monte Sinai . . . cornuta esset facies." It does not sound as though Skelton's poem was serious. Gloss] "The horns of the just shall be lifted up."

1377. pajauntis . . . plaiyd in Joyows Garde] Lost. In Malory (*Works*, ed. Vinaver, 3:1257), this is the name of Lancelot's castle, said to be either Bamborough or Alnwick, both seats of the Percies in Northumberland. Skelton's pageants might have been played at either of those houses. It is possible, too, that his Joyows Garde was a temporary structure erected at court for an entertainment on an Arthurian theme.

1378. Of a Muse thorow a Mud Walle] Lost. Gloss] "as a tottering wall [shall ye be], and as a broken hedge."

1381. Of Castell Aungell the Fenestralle] Lost. The original Castle Sant' Angelo was the papal fortress in Rome, but Skelton is unlikely to have written about its windows. The gloss, "Every lover is a fighter, and Cupid has his own camp," indicates that the work was about love and suggests that Skelton's castle was another pageant-stage at court (Kinsman, *Canon*, 25). Cf. 1391.

1382. Glittryng and glistryng] A pair of nearly identical words from different sources: *to glitter* < ME *glitren* < OE *gliddrian*; and *to glister*, ME *glistren*, cf. MDu *glinsteren*, MLG *glisteren* (*MED*).

1383. dasild and dasid] Another nearly identical pair which Skelton takes pleasure in distinguishing: *to dazzle* is a 15–16C. derivative from *to daze*, to stupefy or bewilder.

1384. The Repete of the Recule of Rosamundis Bowre] Lost. Evidently personal, although the gloss and "bowre" suggest a work based on, or related to, the story of Fair Rosamund, the mistress of Henry II, whom he kept in a labyrinthine "bower." She became a favorite theme for pathetic expostulation. Cf. Daniel, *The Complaynt of Rosamund*, and Drayton, *The Epistle of Rosamond to King Henry the Second*. Gloss] "He brought me into his bedchamber." The original is "Introduxit me rex in cellaria sua."

1389. Gloss] "The mouth of a foolish woman pours forth foolishness." Skelton has changed *fatuorum* to *fatuae*.

1390. Mok . . . sho] Cf. *Colyn Cloute*, 181: "Sho the mockysshe mare," and *Why Come Ye Nat To Courte?* "Mocke hath lost her sho." Evidently proverbial, though not in Tilley or Whiting, the phrase must mean that something has gone wrong.

1391. How Than Lyke a Man He Wan the Barbican] Lost, undoubtedly indecent, with a play on *barbican*: a small round tower in the outerworks of a defended place. Gloss] "Fortune aids the bold." Cicero, who calls it a proverb, has "Fortes Fortuna adiuvat" (*Tusc. Quaest.*, 2.2.11). See also Erasmus, *Adagia* 1.2.45.

1394. Exione] Lost. On the reading *Exione* for *Ixion*, see textual note. On the association of Fortune's wheel with Ixion's wheel, see Patch, *The Goddess Fortuna*, 167.

1396. Gloss] "[O] mind of men, knowing neither fate nor the approaching doom." Skelton has reversed "fati sortisque futurae."

1398. How Dame Mynerve] Lost. See note to 1601. Gloss] "Minerva, inventrix of the olive."

1398-1404. Stanza 146] The italicized words are a puzzle. The first pair make a pun, and all of them more or less fit the sense of the stanza, but to no apparent purpose.

1402. Gloss] "And the herds of stags gather in dusty flight."

1405. Epitomis of the Myllar and His Joly Make] Lost. Gloss] "Two women milling in the bakehouse: one is taken, the other left behind." Mistakenly attributed to Isaiah in *B*.

1411. Gloss] "Fear shall devastate him in the streets, panic at home." Mistakenly attributed to the Psalms. An adaptation of the Vulgate text, "Foris vastabit eos gladius, et intus pavor."

1412. Wofully Arayd] A poem beginning with these words survives in two musical settings, one by Skelton's friend William Cornyshe, Jr., the other by the remarkable John Browne, in BL MS. Additional 5465 (the "Fayrfax" MS), ff. 63v-67, 73v-77. John Stevens, *Music and Poetry*, 369-70, prints this text. BL MS. Harleian 4012, f. 109 has another text, printed by Carleton Brown, *Religious Lyrics of the Fifteenth Century*, no. 103. Dyce found a text written in a 16C. hand on a leaf of a copy of pseudo-Boethius, *De disciplina scholastica* (Deventer, 1496), then in the collection of Richard Heber. It included two stanzas not in Addit. 5465, and ended "Explicit quod Skelton." Dyce accepted this ascription on the basis of the appearance of "Wofully

Arayd" in *The Laurel*, and printed a conflated text from Heber and Addit. 5465. The ascription is not now accepted (Brown, 326; Kinsman, *Canon*, 32–33) because the poem occurs in a MS thought too early for Skelton (Brie, *Englische Studien* 37:22–25), and is written in a tradition "which seems too early for Skelton" (Brown, 326), because the Harley text is preceded and followed by assurances of pardon to the devout reader. The denial of the poem to Skelton, however, is unduly hasty. He was an orthodox, even pious pre-Reformation Catholic; the poem bears the marks of his rhythm and diction, and it appears in a MS, Addit. 5465, which contains one other known lyric by him, and probably contains more. Like all poems of its kind, it is based on Lamentations 1:12: "O vos omnes qui transitis per viam, attendite et videte si est dolor sicut dolor meus." Its literary model is a well-known Latin poem by Philippe de Grève, Chancellor of Paris, *Homo vide quid pro te patior* (Brown, *Religious Lyrics*, 267). Skelton's poem has a devotional purpose, and the promise of pardon to the readers of the Harley textt would not have surprised him at all. Brie's belief that the Harley text is too early is based on a mistakenly late dating of the beginning of Skelton's career, now known to have been under way ca. 1482–83.

1412. Shamefully Betrayde] Surely not a separate title, as Kinsman (*Canon*, 31) thinks, but a paraphrase of the first stanza of "Wofully Arayd," where the word "betrayde" appears. Pollet, 260, thinks these words are the second line of Skelton's lost poem, but this is an unduly literal reading.

1414. Vexilla Regis] Lost; evidently a translation or praphrase of the great passion hymn, *Vexilla regis prodeunt*, of Venantius Fortunatus, sung at vespers in Passiontide, and formerly as a processional on Good Friday. Pollet, 260, is mistaken in thinking this piece must have been a pageant; he has misunderstood Skelton's punning boast that "the banners of the king appear" or "are displayed" (L. *prodeunt*) in the English of his translation as well as in the Latin original. Dyce identified the poem with one published by Kele in his *Christmas Carolles* (ca. 1550; *STC* 5204.5), which uses "Vexilla regis prodeunt" as a refrain. This is a version of a poem that appears in other texts, including Towneley Play XXVI (Brown, *Religious Lyrics*, 325). It too is an appeal from the cross. It has no mark of Skelton's distinctive style and rhythm, and the ascription is no longer accepted. Gordon, *John Skelton*, 115–18, however, defends it.

1412–15. Sacris Solempniis] Lost. A translation or paraphrase of St. Thomas Aquinas's hymn *Sacris solemniis juncta sint gaudia*, sung at matins of Corpus Christi. Skelton used the second and third lines as "antiphons" in the "Commendations" of *Phyllyp Sparowe* (1062, 1115).

1419–20. Galiene . . . Avycen] Medical authorities. Galen (ca. A.D. 130–200), Dioscorides Pedancius (2d C.), and Hippocrates (ca. 460–357 B.C.) were Greeks; Avicenna (980–1037) was an Arab. Gloss] "Honor the physician: for the need thou hast of him hath the most high ordained him."

1422. Albumasar] Abu Ma 'Sar, Arab astronomer/astrologer, 805–85, whose *De magnis coniunctionibus* was familiar to Skelton. Gloss] "The stars above exercise influence upon beings subject to their powers. &c." Unidentified.

1426–32. Gloss] "Admitted to a viewing, friends, can you help laughing?" The gloss indicates that this explosion of proverbs had a meaning for Skelton's audience lost to us. To judge from the marginal *nota*, the stanza's last two lines were especially gratifying.

1433. Marion Clarion] Lost. *Clarion* is from F *clair*, bright.

1434–39. Graund Ivir . . . untwynde] We are probably meant to refer Marion's story to two kinds of proverb, about old age and winter, and about weather. An example of the first kind would be "Il n'a pas besoin de grand hiver," meaning that someone is weak or unfortunate (Le Roux de Lincy, *Livre des proverbes*, 1:67). Here it suggests that an old man, himself a hard winter, is no use to Marion. The second group of proverbs is about the war of light and dark at Candlemas, and they are not limited to France. See Aubrey, 223: "There is a general tradition in the most parts of Europe, that inferreth the coldness of succeeding winter from the shining of the Sun upon Candlemasday, according to the proverbial distich,

> Si sol splendescat Maria purificatione,
> Major est glacius post festum quam fuit ante.

There are English versions in Tilley (C52) and Whiting (C30). De Lincy, 1:63, has a French version: "selon les ancients le dit, / Si le soleil clair luit / A la chandeleur, vous croirez / Qu'encor un hiver vous aurez." Apparently, "Marion Clarion" was a story told allusively in proverbs about a beautiful girl married to an old man, who, deciding to bring some warmth into her life, let her light shine prematurely. As the proverbs say, sun at Candlemas means more winter, and so Marion caught a cold, and "This goodely flowre with stormmis was untwynde." Marion should have waited for her winter to end naturally, i.e., for the old man to die. For the image of the broken flower, see Ovid, *Met.* 10.737–38.

1433–39. Gloss] "A light for the enlightenment of the peoples," better known in the A.V. text: "A light to lighten the gentiles." From the Song of Simeon, spoken over the Christ-child at his presentation in the temple. It is the antiphon at the Mass of the Presentation of Christ in the Temple, which is also the Feast of the Purification of the Blessed Virgin. It is sung at Compline (Evensong in the Church of England). By quoting it, Skelton reminds us of another Mary, another old man, and another child irregularly conceived.

1440. Gloss] "As a rose or as a lily, thou fairest among women, &c., sings the Church." Based on Ecclesiasticus 50:8: "quasi flos rosarum . . . et quasi lilia." The English reader will remember Song of Songs 2:1: "I am the rose of Sharon, the lily of the valleys" ("Ego flos campi et lilium convalium"). "O pulcherrima mulierum" is from Canticles 5:9, &c. All these expressions are used of the Blessed Virgin. Cf. also Ecclesiasticus 39:17–19.

1449. Mary Gipsy] St. Mary of Egypt (2 April). Her legend, very popular, and analogous to that of Mary Magdalen, said that she was an Egyptian runaway who became a prostitute in Alexandria. Aged twenty-eight, she joined (for business reasons) a band of pilgrims to the Holy Land, was converted by a miracle, and lived thenceforth a life of strict austerity in the desert beyond the Jordan. This narrative is based on a more prosaic account of a naked female solitary whom St. Cyriacus found in the desert beyond Jordan, who told him she had been a singer and actress, and that her name was Mary (Butler, 2:14–16). Skelton swears by this St. Mary because his theme is a girl who is to be pitied and forgiven, and who was also very beautiful.

1450–54.] "What I have written, I have written. As a vine you have your wife in your keeping: keep her as you know how, according to Luke. &c." Gloss] See textual note. Dyce's reading means, "Note the words: sealed mysteries." *B*'s text means either "Note the words; recognize the mysteries" or "Familiar words. Recognize the mysteries." If the correct text is "Notata verba, signata mysteria," it means, "The words are familiar, but the mysteries they contain are concealed." Unfortunately I have not traced the source, although the general idea is a common one. Cf. Ambrose, *Cain and Abel* 1.4.13: "quam profunda latent mysteriorum secreta in litteris" ("What hidden depths of things beyond our knowledge are concealed in writing!"). Skelton's mosaic of scriptural references must conceal the mystery of his "bille": Pilate's words, John 19:22 ("What I have written I have written"); Psalm 128:3 ("Thy wife shall be as the fruitful vine upon the walls of thy house"), and Luke 1:13 ("Thy wife Elisabeth shall bear thee a son").

1455. Of the Bone Homs of Ashrige] This poem might be merely the distich following stanza 153, but it was probably a longer piece. The Bonhommes were an English order of regular priests under the Augustinian rule, similar to canons regular. Their monks were called brethren, their superiors rectors, and their monasteries colleges. Edmund, earl of Cornwall, founded the College of the Precious Blood in 1283, endowing it for seven priests. In 1376, the Black Prince increased the endowment, and the number of brethren rose to twenty. At the suppression (6 November 1539), there was a rector and sixteen brethren. The income was about £416, rather large for a small house. Always closely connected with the crown and the royal family, it became a residence for Henry VIII's children after the suppression, and Elizabeth I and Edward VI spent their childhood there. The buildings, still standing in 1575, were destroyed at the beginning of the nineteenth century. James Wyatt built a house on the site (1814), the property of Earl Brownlow. A peculiarity of Ashridge, mentioned in Skelton's note, and the theme of his distich, was its lack of water: dogs, latterly horses, drew water from a deep well (*VCH, Buckinghamshire*, 1:386–89; *Hertfordshire*, 2:210). Skelton's warm tribute to the college indicates that he enjoyed a special relationship with the Bonhommes; perhaps he was educated there. He was still quite a young man when he wrote this stanza.

1457. Sank Roialle] The Precious Blood. This relic is said to have been found in a vase enclosed in a lead box inscribe *Jesu Christi Sanguis*, which is traceable to Mantua as early as 553 (*NCE*). A second phial was dug up in a hospice garden there in 1048. In 1267, Edmund, Earl of Cornwall, bought a phial of the relic from the Count of Holland. He gave one third of the substance to the Cistercian Abbey of Hailes, and granted the remainder to the College of the Bonhommes at its dedication in 1286 as The College of the Precious

Blood. The Holy Blood of Hailes became a famous object of pilgrimage. At the suppression, it was burnt at Paul's Cross, and pronounced to be "no blood, but honey clarified and coloured with saffron." Whatever it was, it was very old in 1539, and the chemistry of the Crown commissioners was certainly not sophisticated enough to identify it. In addition to the original at Mantua, there were portions of the relic at Bruges and Weingarten as well as Ashridge and Hailes (Adair, *Pilgrims' Way*, 93-94; *NCE*, s.v. "Precious Blood, III").

1461. distincyon] ME *distinccioun* translating ML *diffinitio*; a statement or definition (*MED*). C emends to *distichon*, which is plausible but unnecessary.

1462-63. FRAXINUS . . . VIVO] "Without a stream, the ash tree on the little hill (i.e., Ashridge) flourishes and puts forth leaves: there is none like it under the open sky without running water." Gloss] "Mark the scarcity of water, so that dogs there draw it from a very deep well."

1464. The nacioun of folys] Lost. Gloss] "The number of fools is infinite." In appendix 3 this and the next title are counted as one work, which they seem to be.

1465. Apollo that Whirllid up His Chayre] Lost. This line is the first of the couplet with which Chaucer's *Squire's Tale* breaks off. Several poets used it to begin poems, e.g., the author of *The Flower and the Leaf*. Gloss] "It came to pass while Apollo was at Corinth." "Apollo plies the spurs under the breast."

1477. Gloss] Unidentified. Evidently a proverb based on *Aeneid* 4.180: "Rumor swollen with mischief flies on swift wings."

1482. Gloss] "I am of Paul, I of Apollo."

1485. Gloss] "Galathea, playful girl, throws an apple at me." Skelton uses the same gloss on *Speke, Parrot*, 257.

1489. Of the Mayden of Kent Callid Counforte] Lost.

1490. Of Lovers Testamenttis] Lost.

1491. How Iollas Lovid Goodely Phillis] Lost. Probably pastorals based on Virgil, *Eclogues* 3.78. Gloss] "Nor, if you compete with gifts, will Iollas give in."

1492-96. Diodorus Siculus . . . contayne] Four and a half books out of the six are preserved in Corpus Christi College, Cambridge, MS. 357, ed. Salter and Edwards (1956). Gloss] "A thousand kinds of men, and diverse the ways of their lives."

1499. Gloss] "Thousands of thousands, and ten thousand times a hundred thousand. &c." " 'Laurel-crowned they take their seats in the assembly of heaven,' sings the Church."

1513-14. *Mens . . . et ante*] "You ask what well-considered meaning this might have for you? Then give your mind some consideration (i.e., "have some regard to your mind," *consule menti*): let her be like Janus; he looks before and after." The second line is from Geoffrey de Vinsauf, *Poetria*

Nova, 281: "Aemula sis Jani: retro speculeris et ante" (Faral, 205). *Vates* refers either to Skelton himself or, as Edwards thought (*Diodorus*, 2:xxxvii) to Geoffrey, whose name, in that case, Skelton had forgotten. This does not seem likely.

1514a–1526. SKELTONIS . . . NASONIS ERAT] "Skelton addresses his book: Go, radiant light of the Britons; celebrate, our songs, your dutiful British Catullus! Say Skelton was your Adonis, say Skelton was your Homer. Uncouth [though you are], run now abreast with the Latin line; and though the greatest part is woven of British speech, our Thalia does not appear too slovenly, nor too disheveled my Calliope. Nor let it grieve you to suffer the weapons of envy; nor let it grieve you to endure the rage of the dog. For certainly, Virgil himself bore threats not unlike; nor was the muse of Ovid exempt." This Latin envoy, so much more assertive than the more modest, self-deprecating English one that follows, says the kind of thing Skelton judges proper to a poet placing himself in the tradition of Latin literature. Its theme is the language of *The Laurel*, and it records Skelton's conviction that through the medium of work like his, his language and nation were moving towards parity with, "running abreast with," Latin. This very early adumbration of English imperialism is a prophetic, even oracular statement, made in Latin because that is the language in which such statements have already been made, in particular by Virgil and Ovid, the two poets mentioned. The modern English reader probably ought not to treat the English translation as equivalent to the Latin, for Skelton has used Latin to say something that had not been said, and could not be said, in English in his time.

1517. ADONIS] See Introduction, pp. 87–88.

1518. HOMERUS] Skelton, who had not read Homer, uses the name symbolically to mean a national, originating poet.

1526a. LENVOY] The theme of this English envoy, addressed to English readers, but hoping for some Latined ones, recalls the theme of Fame's debate with Pallas: he who writes seriously will encounter opposition.

1580a–87. *Ad Serenissimam . . . metum*] "To the King's most serene majesty, equally with the Lord Cardinal, most greatly honoured legate *a latere*, &c. The Other Envoy: Go, book, lowly reverence the famous King, Henry the Eighth, resonating his rewards for praise. Equally, and with the same reverence, you should salute the Lord Cardinal, legate *a latere*, and pray him remember the prebend he once promised to consign to me; and you will restore me to hope for the token of his favour. Between hope and dread." There seems to be some irony in this address, reminding king and cardinal of obligations, the one to reward poets who praise him, the other to keep a promise. Latin *pignus*, token, can also mean pledge, mortgage, or pawn. There is some implication that the cardinal's promise was a pledge made in return for something.

1580b. *Legato a latere*] Papal legate.

1585. Prebende] A benefice or living supplied from the revenues of a cathedral or collegiate church. Skelton also reminds Wolsey of his promise of a prebendary's hood, an "ammas gray," in the Envoy to the poem about the duke of Albany, written in late 1523 (Dyce, 2:84).

1591. Smalle sekernes] The placing of this line and of 1595 is the same as the arrangement of 960 and 967 in *A*, and must reproduce Skelton's MS.

1596a–1609] "SKELTON ADMONISHES EVERY TREE TO YIELD PLACE TO THE GREEN LAUREL, IN KEEPING WITH ITS NATURE. Ash tree of the woods, rowan of the mountains, poplar of rivers, fir, wide-spreading beech, pliant willow, plane, juicy fig-bearing fig tree and acorn-bearing oak, pear, Jupiter-oak, lofty pine, sweating balsam, wild olive, and olive of Minerva, juniper, box, mastic with the tough points, grape-bearing vine so acceptable to Lord Bacchus, holm-oak and useless wild vine, hateful to husbandmen, frankincense yielding perfumes for unmanly Sabaeans, likewise the famous myrrh perfuming the Arabs: and you, O weak hazels and humble tamarisks, and you, O fragrant cedars, and you also, myrtles, every kind of tree, yield to the green laurel!"

These hexameters are in *C*, sig. Y5, listed in the table of contents as *Praise of the Palmtre*, and detached from *The Laurel*, where they belong. Although the poem might seem merely an exercise on a commonplace theme, the catalogue of trees (see Curtius, *European Literature and the Latin Middle Ages*, 194–95), assembled from phrases out of the Latin poets, it is also Skelton's last bardic flourish. In commanding the trees to move and give place to the laurel, he is imitating Orpheus (*Metamorphoses* 10.86–143), whose music, after his return from the underworld, draws the trees into a grove. Like Orpheus, Skelton calls up twenty-eight trees. His theme is that among all the varied activities of life in this world, poetry is the most valuable.

1597–98. Fraxinus . . . fagus] Based on Virgil, *Eclogues* 8.65–68.

1600. Glandifera et quercus] Lucretius, *De rerum natura* 5.939. ardua pinus] Claudian, *Phoenix* 32.

1601. Balsamum exudans] Cf. Virgil, *Georgics* 2.118–19: "sudantia ligno balsamque." oliva Minerve] In her contest with Poseidon for the city of Athens, Athena (or Minerva) gave the city the olive, the gift most useful to mankind, associated with her ever after. Skelton wrote a poem on the theme, mentioned at 1398 of *The Laurel*, and glossed from Virgil, *Georgics* 1.18–19: "oleaeque Minerva inventrix."

1605. thura Sabeis] *Georgics* 1.57. Also cf. 2.117: "solis est turea virga Sabeis" ("to the Sabaeans alone belongs the frankincense branch").

1607. O corili fragiles] *Metamorphoses* 10.93. humilesque mirice] Virgil, *Eclogues* 4.2.

1609a. *Prenes en gre. The Laurelle*] These words follow the hexameters in *C*. *B* has only the first three words. This little instruction might refer to (1) all laurels, (2) the laurel of the hexameters, or (2) *The Laurel*. (3) is most likely, in which case the period after *gre* is merely ornamental, and the sentence is Skelton's last, characteristic commendation of his poem to his reader: "Take in good part" or "Accept favourably *The Laurel*."

1609a. EN PARLAMENT A PARIS] Printed separately by *C*, sig. X8. "These lines bear very little relation to the rest of the poem. They are simply three versions of the conventional 'abuses of the age', a popular topic in medieval protest verse" (Scattergood). It is unlikely that this little composition is meant to stand alone. As a final coda to *The Laurel*, this poem tallies with "that undercurrent of rancour and hostility towards the Government which emerges so clearly in the critical passages of [*The Laurel*]" (Pollet, 145).

1639–40. *A grant . . . dort*] "To our great hurt, faith sleeps."

Additional notes

352. Orace also withe his new poetry] Horace's *Ars*, often called the *Poetria*, was frequently bound with Geoffrey's *Poetria Nova* in the Middle Ages. See Marjorie Curry Woods, "Classical Examples and References in Medieval Lectures on Poetic Composition," Allegorica 10 (1989): 10, n.3.

380. Valerius, Maximus by name] In his forthcoming article, "Skelton's *Speculum Principis* and Valerius Maximus," David Carlson shows that Skelton drew upon Valerius for *exempla* in the *Speculum*. According to Professor Carlson, Valerius was popular in the late Middle Ages, twenty editions having been published in Europe before 1500.

1509. Janus] There is an image of Janus as beginning and ending, old age and youth (Intro., pp. 56–58, 61) in *Les Belles Heures de Duc de Berry*, reproduced in Phillipa Tristram, *Figures of Life and Death in Medieval English Literature* (London: Paul Elek, 1976), Pl. 13.

Appendixes

1. *The Division of* The Laurel *into* Capitula

Three headings indicating the division of *The Laurel* into *capitula* survive in MS *A*: *capitula* I, VIII, and IX. The first was written into the outer margin of f. 209, next to stanza 8, after the MS was finished, in a lighter ink and with a different pen. The second was written on f. 215, in fairly narrow space between stanzas 107 and 108, after the stanzas themselves, but with the same ink and pen. In both cases one can tell that the divisions indicated by these headings preceded the headings themselves, and were not afterthoughts. This is because although there was no space left for the headings, there was space left for a distinctive, probably rubricated, initial that was never supplied, but that would have marked a break in the text. The third heading was written concurrently with the preceding and following text. It occupies the wide upper margin of f. 217, over stanza 117, and is in the writer's most expansive style, with a large, flourishing capital *C* that signals the importance of this ninth *capitulum*, containing the ladies' poems. In writing *capitulum* the scribe erred, and this mistake was later corrected with the same pen and ink used to add the first heading. From this one infers that the scribe began to add the headings as he wrote the MS, perhaps beginning with number 8, and that he put in the earlier ones when he was correcting his work.

Although this scribe also began stanza 117 with a guide-letter in lieu of a decorative capital, he did not indent the first lines of the stanza properly to leave room for it. Instead, he indented the whole stanza to make room for the decoration of the countess's poem that follows, and he allows the huge initial *A* that begins that poem to encroach upon the resulting space. This shows how important he thought the countess's poem was, but it also shows that he did not really expect that the decorated initial would ever be added, and that he was beginning to think that his own very decorative calligraphy was enough. If this is so—and he certainly left too little space for the initial—then the spaces and their guide-letters accompanying the two previous headings are purely conventional, and represent wishful thinking. Further evidence of this appears at two places in the last surviving leaves. On f. 223v the first word of Isbell Knyght's poem, *Bot*, has a small guide-letter *b* written inside the scribe's own large capital. On f. 225v the first word of *Poeta Skelton*'s speech to the Queen of Fame, *Right*, has a small, faint *R* which is actually appended to the tail of the huge *R* that begins the word. In this case initial and guide-letter were written simultaneously.

This all suggests holograph, not scribal work. We seem to have a MS which is a fine fair copy made by an author who changed his mind about some of its features as he proceeded. Perhaps he tired a little, and decided he might as well draw his own more elaborate initials as he went along, and not bother about the red ink. His decision to include *capitula* headings may be connected with his abandoning of the plan to include rubricated initials marking the divisions. The divisions themselves, in his mind all along, and no doubt marked in his draft, correspond to the major incidents of the vision and sometimes, though not always, to changes of scene. Hence *capitulum X* should mark the beginning of the scene where *Poeta Skelton* presents his credentials to the Court of Fame. Yet there is no indication of it where one would expect it, at stanza 119. There are three possibilities:

1. The heading was once there, but has been lost because of fire damage to the outer and upper margins of the page. Skelton did not mark the place with space and guide-letter because he had abandoned that feature of his MS.
2. The heading belongs on f. 225v, over stanza 124, where it has also been lost because of damage. The small *R* attached to the large capital *R* is a vestige of his original scheme of marking divisions by ornamental capitals.
3. Either there is no *cap. X* at all, or it began with Occupacioun's reading of her register.

Both (2) and (3) are unlikely because they combine two very important incidents, the ladies' poems and the hearing before Fame, into one division. The most likely is (1), even though no evidence for it now remains in the MS. If, however, we place the heading over stanza 119, a further question arises: was there an eleventh *capitulum* devoted to Occupacioun's reading of her book?

Either a 10- or an 11-*capitulum* scheme is possible. The first works well with the text of 1495, dividing the vision into equal halves of 72 stanzas and providing a final *capitulum* of 33 stanzas, a fitting number. Since ten is the number of completion and reward, it also seems right that the vision should end with a tenth rather than an eleventh *capitulum*. This scheme does not work well for the 1523 text, longer by 9 stanzas. An 11-*capitulum* scheme works for either text. It preserves a 33-stanza final section for both. It also provides a central *capitulum*, and so maintains the principle of centricity, as well as symmetry, so important elsewhere in the vision.

With either scheme the chief difficulty is to locate the missing headings. Here the printed text proves helpful, because although it does not preserve the headings, it uses ornamental initials in a way that evidently reflects the appearance of its MS copy. Some of them indicate divisions in the text, although they do not always come exactly where one would expect them. For instance, the initial corresponding to the heading of *cap*. IX in the MS adorns stanza 116, not 117. Nonetheless, there is an initial at stanza 119, where we have suggested that *cap*. X begins, and it is reassuring that the scenes of Pallas and Fame, of the summons, the palace of Fame, the walled field, and the garden are well marked. Consequently, it is very important that the 1523 text puts an initial at stanza 130, where Occupacioun begins to read, thus suggesting an eleventh *capitulum*. It also uses an unusually large initial at stanza 101 to indicate that the scene with Envyows Rancor should be separated from the scene in the garden of poetry. If one does this, then there will be 5 *capitula* in the second half of the vision, and the garden scene, as *cap*. VI, will be its center, as one would expect.

The evidence of the 1523 quarto, then, combined with that of the MS, supports a division into 11 *capitula*, the garden of poetry occupying the sixth, central place. One curious fact, already mentioned briefly in the introduction, supports this conclusion. If one applies to Skelton's own name the simple number code under which he attacks Roger Stathum (751a, b), the result (9.4.8.13 / 18.10.2.11.19.4.13) adds up to 111. This number provides further explanation of Skelton's fondness for 11; it also expresses the turning of 11 into 12 on which the numerical symbolism of *The Laurel* is based, and it represents the principles of symmetry and centricity governing the form of the vision. It also contains the number 3; three of the *capitula* concern poetry: III, VI, and IX.

In the table of the *capitula* that follows, *caps*. I, VIII, and IX are fixed by the MS. *Caps*. II, VI, VII, X, and XI are arranged by inference supported by the 1523 quarto. The quarto gives no clear guide to the place of *caps*. III, IV, and V. In *cap*. IX, which consists of the ladies' poems, the rhyme-royal stanzas addressed to the countess and her daughters are not included in the stanza count because they are not part of the vision. In the 1495 text, *cap*. XI had 24 stanzas, the whole vision 144.

Prologue   sts. 1–7

Cap. I	Dame Pallas & the Queen of Fame	8–35	28
Cap. II	The Summons & Poets' Procession	36–57	22
Cap. III	The English Poets	58–68	11
Cap. IV	Occupacioun & Fame's Palace	69–79	11
Cap. V	The Walled Field	80–91	12
Cap. VI	The Garden of Poetry	92–100	9
Cap. VII	The Intruder in the Garden	101–107	7
Cap. VIII	The Garland	108–116	9
Cap. IX	The Ladies' Poems	117–118	2
Cap. X	The Hearing	119–127	9
Cap. XI	Occupacioun reads her book	128–160	33
			153

2. Rhyme-Word Test

		1–245, 721–1142 (A)	%	246–720, 1143–1512 (B, C)	%	Totals (A,B,C)	%
	Rhyme words	618		810		1428	
	Nonrhyme words	3594		5233		8827	
Dyce:	RW's emended	8	1.29	10	1.23	18	1.26
	NRW's emended	40	1.1	56	1.1	96	1.1
	Undetected error	6–7		8–9		15	
Scattergood:	RW's emended	9	1.45	9	1.1	18	1.26
	NRW's emended	24	0.7	49	0.9	73	0.8
	Undetected error	28		8–9		37	
Brownlow:	RW's emended	2	0.3	11	1.36	13	0.9
	NRW's emended	10	0.3	71	1.36	81	0.9
	Undetected error	1–2		0		0–1	

Note. The first column gives figures for that part of the text preserved in *A*, the second for the remainder preserved in *B* and *C*, and the third for the whole. In column one, the figures for Dyce and Scattergood describe their treatment of *B*, their copy for that part of the poem; the figures for Brownlow describe his treatment of *A*, his copy. Trivial corrections are excluded from the tally. Their inclusion would not significantly change the proportions of the table, although it would give an inflated estimate of the amount of error present.

3. The Procession of the Poets, and Skelton's Bibliography

1. THE PROCESSION OF THE POETS

      I. "A murmur of mynstrallis"

———

      II.   Amphion, Orpheus,
and other Arcadian muses

———

      III.   Apollo

———

      IV.   The poets

      1. Quintilian
      2. Theocritus
      3. Hesiod
      4. Homer
      5. Cicero
      6. Sallust
      7. Ovid
      8. Lucan
      9. Statius
      10. Persius
      11. Virgil
      12. Juvenal
      13. Titus Livius
      14. Ennius
      15. Aulus Gellius
      16. Horace
      17. Terence
      18. Plautus

      V.   Bacchus

      19. Seneca
      20. Boethius
      21. Maximian
      22. Boccaccio

23. Quintus Curtius
24. Macrobius
25. Poggio
26. Gaguin
27. Plutarch
28. Petrarch
29. Lucilius
30. Valerius Maximus
31. Vincent of Beauvais
32. Propertius
33. Pisandros

34. Gower   35. Chaucer   36. Lydgate

———

2. SKELTON'S BIBLIOGRAPHY

1. The Boke of Honorows Astate
2. The Boke How Men Shuld Fle Syn
3. Roialle Demenaunce
4. The Boke to Speke Wele
5. The Boke To Lerne Yow to Dye
6. Vertu, an Enterlude
7. The Boke of the Rosiar
8. Prynce Arturis Creacioune
9. The Fals Faythe That Now Gothe
10. Dialoggis of Imagynacioune
11. Automedon, Of Lovys Meditacioune
12. New Gramer
13. Bowche of Courte
14. Achademios, a Comedy
15. Tullis Familiars
16. The Boke of Goode Avysemente
17. The Recule Ageyne Gagwyne
18. The Popingay
[19. Sovereynte]
[20. Magnyfycence]
[21. Mannerly Mastres Margery Mylke and Ale]
[22. The Peregrynacioun of Mannys Lyf]
[23. The Traytyse of Tryumphis of the Rede Rose]
[24. Speculum Principis]

[25. The Tunnynge of Elinor Rummyng]
[26. Colyn Clowte]
[27. John Ive]
[28. Joforthe Jak]
[29. The Umblis of Venysoun]
[30. The Balade of the Mustarde Tarte]
[31. Of Adame Alle-a-Knave, an epitaphe]
[32. Phyllype Sparow]
33. The Grontyng and the Groynnynge of the Gronnyng Swyne
34. The Murnnynge of the Mapely Rote
35. How The Grene Coverlet Sufferde Grete Pyne
36. A Devowte Prayer to Moyses Hornnis
37. Pajauntis that were plaiyd in Joyows Garde
38. Of a Muse thorow a Mud Walle
39. The Fenestralle of Castell Aungell
40. The Repete of the Recule of Rosamundis Bowre
41. How Than Lyke a Man He Wan the Barbican
42. Of Exione
43. How Dame Mynerve Fyrste Fownde the Olyve Tre
44. Epitomis of the Myllar and His Joly Make
45. Wofully Arayd
46. *Vexilla Regis*
47. *Sacris Solempniis*
48. Marion Clarion
49. Of the Bone Homs of Ashrige beside Barkamstede
50. Apollo that Whirllid up His Chayre
51. Of the Mayden of Kent Callid Counforte
52. Of Lovers Testamenttis
53. How Iollas Lovid Goodely Phillis
54. Diodorus Siculus
55. The Laurelle

Note. The titles in square brackets were interpolated in 1522–23.

4. Skelton's Astrology

Like virtually everyone in his time, Skelton believed that the stars, especially the two luminaries, sun and moon, and the five wandering stars, the planets, as part of an animated, living universe, in their own character and in relation to each other, influenced life on earth.

Real knowledge of astronomy and astrology had disappeared from Western Europe with the collapse of the Western Empire and the consequent loss of Greek learning. Hellenistic science, including astrology, began to return with the translation of Arabic treatises into Latin in Spain and Sicily in the twelfth and thirteenth centuries. This material was the source of Chaucer's mastery of the subject. In the fifteenth and sixteenth centuries European scholars recovered the Greek originals, and with them the mathematics of celestial mechanics. In Skelton's generation occurred the first developments, in the work of astronomers like Georg Peurbach and his pupil Johann Müller (Regiomontanus) that led to the work of Copernicus, Brahe, Kepler, and Galileo. In Skelton's England, real knowledge of the subject required mastery of Latin, and so astrology was still a learned, even occult study.[1]

Of the astronomical and astrological authorities available to him, Skelton regularly mentions three: Ptolemy, Haly, and Albumasar. Of these, he can hardly have known the work of Ptolemy, "Prince of astronomy" (*Phyllyp Sparowe*, 504), directly, although the mathematics of Ptolemy's *Almagest*, modified by the Arabs, underlies the Alfonsine Tables as well as the *Ephemerides* of Regiomontanus, both of which he will have used. Similarly, the astrological lore of Ptolemy's *Tetrabiblos*, a synthesis of the lore of the ancient world, underlies all subsequent astrological symbolism in the West. Skelton's Haly was Albohazen Haly filii Abenragel (Ali ibn Abi Al-Rajjal), an eleventh-century Cordovan astrologer, author of the immensely influential *Libri de judiciis astrorum*. Albumasar (Abu Ma 'Sar) was a ninth-century astrologer whose writings Skelton certainly knew at first hand, for at the end of *Speculum Principis* he gives a reference to Albumasar's famous treatise, *De magnis coniunctionibus*, Tractate 2, Difference 8, which treats of conjunctions between Mars and Saturn.[2]

Hitherto, commentary on Skelton's astrological stanzas has tended to miss the symbolism entirely, or to interpret it by arbitrary reference to medieval authorities.[3] Yet this is not how such statements work. An astrological statement is, first, a description of time; in fact, in an age when clocks were still notoriously unreliable, celestial observations provided the only accurate record of time. The symbolic import of an astrological statement follows from the nature of the time described. The two are inseparable. Since we no longer measure time by celestial movements, we find this hard to grasp at first. Yet it is true.[4]

Although astrological symbolism, from the time of Ptolemy onwards, is remarkably fixed and unvarying, and although much of it has always been common knowledge, the symbolism itself is merely the raw material for the process of synthesis by which the astrologer interpreted the relationships of the heavenly bodies at a specific time. Therefore, apart from its role in a specific horoscope, or description of time, astrological symbolism has no *specific* meaning at all. The planet Mars is hot and dry, angry and aggressive; but those qualities only become operative or inoperative in relation to a particular horoscope. In the first stanza of *The Laurel*, Skelton says that Mars, being retrograde, has "put up his sword." This is (1) a reference to a celestial event, one of the criteria by which one discovers the time for the horoscope, and (2) a comment upon the planet's behavior and influence. Yet until we know the time, i.e., the whole horoscope, we cannot say anything specific about the meaning of Mars's behavior, who he stands for, and whether his influence is good or bad.

As descriptions of time, Skelton's astrological statements will be found to be neat and precise. Three hitherto unnoticed examples from *Speke, Parrot*, all from the envoys forming the last part of the poem as it now survives, will illustrate the point.

> 1. Lucina she wadythe among the watry floddes,
>   And the cokkes begyn to crowe agayne the day.
>
> (287–88)

These beautifully cadenced lines describe a precise time on a certain day. Nelson discovered (162–63) that Skelton dates this first envoy, according to his private calendar, 30 October 1521. By consulting tables and calculating the ascendant, we find that on that day, just before daybreak, the last of the old moon would be rising, as Skelton says, over the eastern horizon at cockcrow. So, looking east from England (where Skelton was) to France (where Wolsey, the poem's recipient, was), the moon would indeed be "wading among the watery floods."

> 2. Prepayre yow, Parrot, breuely your passage to take,
>   Of Mercury undyr the trynall aspecte. . . .
>
> (324–25)

The date of this envoy is 17 November 1521. A "trinal aspect," a very benign one, is formed when a pair of planets are separated by 120° of the zodiac. At midnight on the seventeenth (halfway through the Renaissance astronomical day, which began at noon), Mercury, at 4° 27' of Sagittarius, was within allowable trine aspect (129°) of the moon at 25° 1' of Cancer. Toward the end of the day the aspect was closer, about 123°. On that day, therefore, Skelton could literally send his poem under the trinal aspect of Mercury, the messenger and god of eloquence and persuasion.

> 3. The skye is clowdy, the coste is nothyng clere;
>   Tytan hathe truste vp hys tressys of fyne golde;
>   Iupyter for Saturne darre make no royall chere.
>
> (390–93)

Skelton only dates this poem, Parrot's complaint, to the year "34" which, as Nelson explains (163), refers to the year in Skelton's private calendar from early November 1521 to early November 1522. The poem's dismal forebodings, then, apply to the larger period of the year, not to a day, a week, or a month. The first line forecasts a winter storm; the second says that the sun has bound up his beams—probably a reference to approaching winter, both real and symbolic. Then the reference to Jupiter tells us that this is no ordinary bad weather; for on 24–25 November 1521, Jupiter entered Capricorn, the house of Saturn, and stayed there until 11 December 1522. During all that time, the royal planet, imprisoned in Saturn's house, would be able to make no "royal cheer." In Parrot's political symbolism, Jupiter and Saturn are Henry VIII and Wolsey, and so the poem says that there is to be no rapid end to the disastrous domination of the king by the cardinal.

The horoscopes that begin *The Laurel* and the *The Bowge of Courte* are also neat and precise. Both yield specific dates. They also share features not explained by their relationships to the dream-narratives that follow, which are very different from each other.

In both horoscopes Mars, retrograde, is the ruler, and the moon is in Scorpio. Both, too, are linked to Skelton's private calendar, which began in early November when the sun, in Skelton's time, was in the middle of Scorpio. In fact, during the twenty-four hours from midnight, 3 November, to 4 November 1488, the year when the calendar began, the moon was successively in conjunction with the sun, Venus, and Mercury in Scorpio. A natural conclusion is that the horoscopes and the calendar must relate to each other through a nativity or birth horoscope that provides their common features.

At first this seems most unlikely. One would prefer to think that Skelton simply made up his horoscopes for literary, rhetorical reasons, and that the connection with the calendar is a coincidence; but an interlinked chain of evidence makes this hypothesis impossible to maintain:

1. Bibliographical evidence, corroborated by evidence from the poem's numerological construction, shows that *The Laurel*, published in 1523, existed in an earlier version.
2. Firm evidence of the Howard ladies' identity and of the Howards' sojourn at Sheriff Hutton proves that the original must be dated 1492–97.
3. The horoscopical date, independently calculated by Tucker and Gingerich and confirmed by the present editor, confirms (1) and (2), and is in turn corroborated by them.

4. If *The Laurel* is dated ca. 1495, then *The Bowge of Courte*, hitherto dated September 1498, but mentioned in the earlier-written part of *The Laurel* "bibliography," must be before ca. 1495.
5. The date of *The Bowge* horoscope is 19 August 1482. This does not force one to date the poem that early. Yet the early date corroborates *The Laurel* evidence, and once again the mutual corroboration is decisive.
6. The earliest datable poem named in the nine interpolated stanzas of 1522–23, "Triumphs of the Red Rose," concerned events of 1497, which is therefore a *terminus ad quem* for the original *Laurel*. It is the same date provided by the death of the countess of Surrey.

We must, then accept the dates of the horoscopes as real, and the horoscopes as meaningful elections (to use the correct astrological term) for the person, a self-projection of Skelton, who narrates each poem; and this means that a nativity *must* underlie them, for as Curry explains, "An election is useless and signifies nothing unless the root of a nativity is known and unless the figure erected for the election corresponds approximately with the horoscope at birth."[5] This being so, we are enabled to postulate a nativity for 2 May 1463. And this in turn enables us (1) to interpret *The Laurel* horoscope as an elective taken for the culmination of the native's life, symbolically communicated in the dream-vision that follows, (2) to explain the iconography of the 1523 edition, and (3) to discover a third elective for the putative end of the native's life, ca. 1 November 1535.

These are impressive results. Yet a difficulty remains. The 1463 nativity, when calculated, proves very dramatic. It is also similar in essentials (Mars and Moon in Scorpio) to that provided by Chaucer for Constance in *The Man of Law's Tale*. So, although the evidence requires us to postulate a factual, hence autobiographical basis for the horoscopes, they also have a literary precedent, and it might also seem that they are "too good to be true."

There are two answers that resolve this difficulty. First, Skelton's horoscopes are extremely specific to a day, and to a time of day, and they relate to a narrative "I" who is, in effect, Skelton himself, and who by this means times his visions. Second, it is very likely that Skelton will not have known the exact time of his birth. He will, therefore, have supplied a precise birth-time by inference from known events of his life and the approximately known time of birth. This has always been a common astrological practice, and the result is a "rectified" horoscope. It is not a mere fiction, because unless there is an approximate time to base it on, there is nothing to rectify. We need only grant

Skelton the knowledge that he was born in the beginning of May 1463, and his horoscope will be a sufficiently accurate indicator, from his point of view, of his birth and fortunes. If it also pays homage to Chaucer, so much the better.

In the following diagrams, the positions of the signs of the zodiac relative to the mundane houses are calculated by the method of Regiomontanus; times and planetary positions are based on the modern tables of Bryant Tuckerman. The differences between the latter and positions derived from the Alfonsine Tables or from the *Ephemerides* of Regiomontanus are generally insignificant for our purposes, and it is easier for the reader to check calculations made from readily available modern tables. Considering that it had so little relation to reality, the Ptolemaic model of celestial movements gave surprisingly accurate results, although it could be very inaccurate in predicting the movements of Mars and Mercury, in the case of the former because of the irregularity of the orbit, of the latter because of the difficulty of making observations with the naked eye. When Alfonsine positions are significant, therefore, they are taken into account.[6]

The older tables also gave a time for the equinoxes that can differ from modern predictions by many hours. In the calculation of the horoscopes, however, this is at most a matter of a couple of minutes of sidereal time. If the horoscopes were to be based upon known, accurate, standard times, this would be important; but since we are discovering approximate times from the horoscopes, it is insignificant.

Although the editor makes no claim to astrological expertise, brief elucidatory comments on the horoscopes are offered, based upon standard material found in all major sources.[7]

1. *THE LAUREL*

> Arrectynge my syght toward the zodiak
> The signnys twelve for to behold afar,
> When Mars retrogradant reversid his bak,
> Lorde of the yere in his orbicular,
> Put up his sworde for he kowde make no war:
> And when Lucyna plenarly did shyne,
> Scorpioune ascenddinge degrees twiys nyne:

Mars, retrograde, and the moon were in conjunction in Scorpio once in Skelton's active lifetime, on 8 May 1495. Scorpio rising 18° indicates a precise time, about 7:00 P.M. on that day of the year. The moon was not exactly full until 10:35 A.M., 9 May at 26° 57′ Scorpio. By then it was no longer conjunct with Mars, and Scorpio, of course, was not rising (see fig. 1).[8]

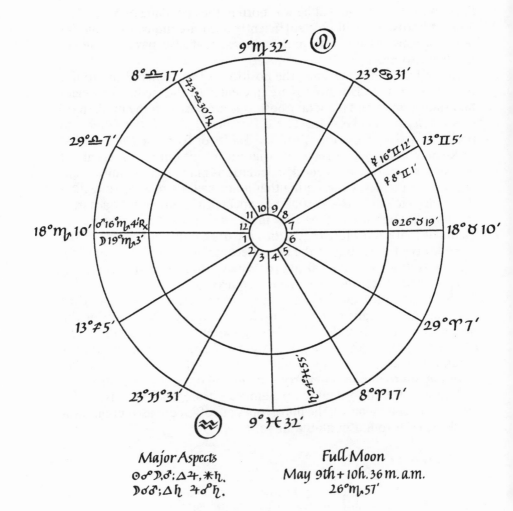

Major Aspects
☉☌♀ ☽.♂; △♃, ✳ ♄.
☽♂♂; △♄ ♃ ♂ ♄.

Full Moon
May 9th + 10h. 36 m. a.m.
26°♏57′

Fig. 1. 7.00 p.m., May 8th, 1495, at Sheriff Hutton, Yorkshire.

This elective horoscope must have a nativity as its basis, to which it corresponds in major features. Mars retrograde was in conjunction with a full moon in Scorpio on 2 May 1463, when Scorpio would again be rising 18° at about 7:25 in the early evening. The moon would then be separating from conjunction with Mars, which was at its closest at 3:00 A.M. If one were to draw the horoscope for 3:00 A.M., Aries would be rising, and so Mars would still be lord of the nativity, Aries being his diurnal house. Nonetheless, since Skelton portrays himself so definitely as a Scorpian in the opening stanzas of *The Laurel*, we should preserve the Scorpian character of the nativity, and so calculate the horoscope for 7:25 P.M., 2 May (see fig. 2).

On the whole, this is an unfortunate nativity, revealing a powerful nature at odds with its surroundings. The retrograde Mars-moon conjunction in Scorpio, Scorpio rising, Mars therefore lord of the nativity, indicates a proud, quarrelsome, fiery disposition that will suffer from the enmity of false friends and powerful people. The sun in Taurus emphasizes the martial tendencies, suggesting pleasure as well as success in strife. On the positive side, Mercury in conjunction with Venus shows musical and poetic gifts, and these allied to the other indications promise a keen wit and a gift for satire. The Scorpian character of the nativity, and the moon's position in the twelfth house also suggest an interest in hermetic or occult subjects. The sun square to Saturn also suggests boastfulness, disfavor, and enmity.

Alfonsine positions give the same result, except that Mercury at 7° 43′ Gemini is no longer in conjunction with Venus or square to Saturn, but trine to Jupiter, promising learning and good sense. This somewhat improves the nativity, but evil aspects predominate, nonetheless. Energy, passion, and intellect are frustrated by quarrels, betrayals, and a difficult temperament. Jupiter's position, evilly aspected to Mars and the moon, virtually stationary in Saturn's diurnal house, Aquarius, is striking: "Jupyter for Saturne darre make no royall chere" (*Speke, Parrot*, 399). The positions of both planets, the greater fortune and infortune, "applying" to a conjunction that will not occur until spring 1464, and evilly aspected with the other planets, focuses the struggle between fortune and ill-fortune in the nativity. The same drama appears in the moon's position. She is separating from conjunction with Mars to form aspects with Jupiter and Saturn. With Jupiter she will enter sextile aspect in Sagittarius, his diurnal house; this is extremely fortunate, promising friends, health, honor, success, preferment, and injury to enemies. With Saturn she enters square aspect, and this is unfortunate, promising fears, anxieties, and loss of reputation. Since she will be in "reception" in Jupiter's house, that aspect is rather stronger, and so the balance tips a little toward the better fortune.

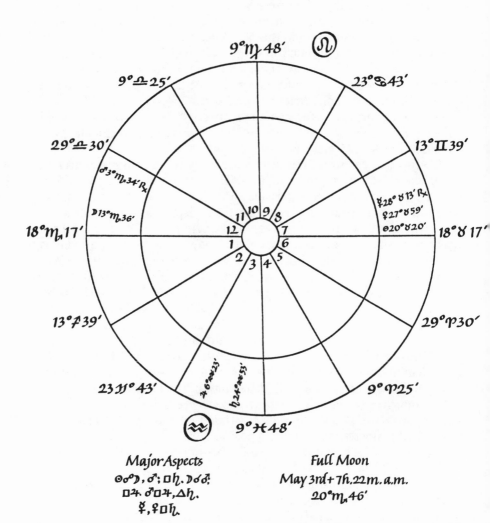

Fig. 2. 7.25 p.m., May 2nd, 1463, at Sheriff Hutton, Yorkshire.

This nativity enables one to see that in the elective horoscope that begins *The Laurel*, a moment of great fortune has arrived. Jupiter is exalted in the tenth house, bringing honor, powerful friends, and success. Saturn, in opposition to Jupiter, and in Jupiter's house, Pisces, is held in check for the time being.

This elective horoscope corresponds to the native's entry into his thirty-third year. As we have seen (pp. 58–60) it is possible, following the constructional and iconographic indications in the poem, to calculate a horoscope for his putative end, which would come, according to the formalized time-scheme of the poem, at seventy-two; and although this ending is no more *in* the poem than the nativity, nonetheless it is part of the conceit of time on which the poem's structure and thought are based. To see this, it is simply necessary to impose the months of the year upon the zodiac, treating the year's circle as a symbol of the life of man, and then to combine that static diagram with the horoscope (see fig. 3).

In the combined diagram, the month of May meets June at a point corresponding to the thirty-third year.[9] This point in the life-zodiac also corresponds to Jupiter's position in the tenth house of the horoscope. May's opposite in the life-year is November, which shares the fourth house with December, and corresponds in the horoscope to the position of Saturn. A complementary horoscope to the May elective, depicting the culmination of life, would therefore delineate the approach of death, and should be cast for some time in November, probably for the birthday, or New Year's Day, of Skelton's private year, November first or second, at about 7:00 A.M. (which will also keep Scorpio in the ascendant). If one makes the calculations for the native's sixty-ninth to seventy-second years, concentrating upon the significators for the purpose, Saturn, Mars, and Jupiter, one finds that throughout the period Saturn and Jupiter are approaching opposition, that in the sixty-ninth year (1531) Saturn occupies the eighth house, of death, and that in 1533, the seventy-first, Saturn shares the eighth house with Mars. If Skelton made these calculations himself, however, as he worked out the ingenious scheme of his poem, he would have found that in 1535, the year of his seventy-second and final birthday according to the scheme, the pattern completed itself (see fig. 4). Jupiter and Saturn are opposed, Jupiter once again in Saturn's house, almost "transiting" Saturn's position in the nativity. This is exceedingly ominous, as is the position of Mars, ruler and significator of the native's fortunes, who is now on the cusp of the house of death, the eighth. And so the three horoscopes complete the pattern, symbolizing an entire life. Needless to say, this is not how an actual astrologer would have gone about the

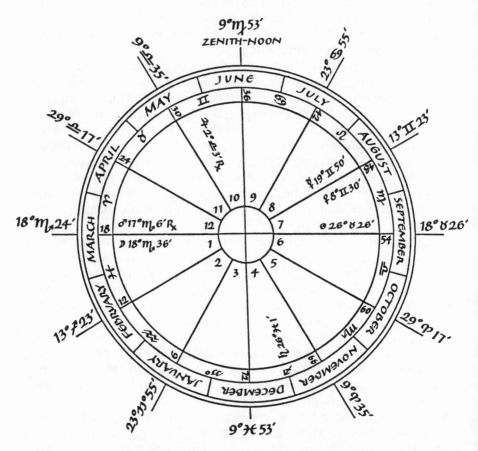

Fig. 3. 7.00 p.m., May 8th, 1495, at Sheriff Hutton, Yorkshire.
In this figure the calculations are based on the
Ephemerides of Regiomontanus.

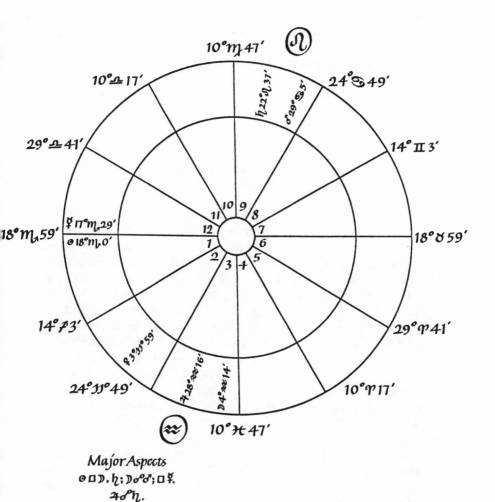

Major Aspects
☉ □ ☽, ♄; ☽ ♂ ♂; □ ☿.
♃ ♂ ♄.

Fig. 4. 7.20 a.m. November 1st, 1535, at Sheriff Hutton, Yorkshire.

prediction of an actual death; it is, rather, the way an ingenious poet framed his vision in the context of a symbolic pattern of life.

2. *THE BOWGE OF COURTE*

> In Autumpne, whan the sonne *in Vyrgyne*
> By radyante hete enryped hath our corne;
> Whan Luna, full of mutabylyte,
> As emperes the dyademe hath worne
> Of our pole artyke, smylynge halfe in scorne
> At our foly and our unstedfastnesse;
> The tyme whan Mars to werre hym dyde dres:

Here the criteria are that the sun is in Virgo (about eight days earlier in Skelton's Julian calendar than now), Mars is approaching the end of a period of retrogression, the moon has just been in the longitude of Alphecca, the brightest star ("the dyademe") of the constellation *Corona Borealis* (5° Scorpio in Skelton's time), and is in unfriendly aspect to Mars. If the moon is "smylynge halfe in scorne" at some time in the evening (since the poem begins with the poet going to bed), then she is probably in her first quarter. One time satisfies all these criteria, about 8:00 P.M., 19 August 1482 (see fig. 5).[10] There is an insignificant difference of about 15′ of arc in the Alfonsine position of the moon, but Mars's position is 5° different at 20° 40′ Aquarius. He is still in the eleventh house, but the moon, although "applying" to square aspect with Mars, will not begin to be within it until about midnight. This does not affect the dating of the dream-vision, which is based upon the retrogression of Mars, and the moon's position in Scorpio.

At eight o'clock in the evening, the moon is in the sky, though beginning to set, and Aries, the diurnal house of Mars, is rising. Mars, then, is ruler and significator, but he is retrograde and in square aspect to the moon in Scorpio, so that his strong, assertive, aggressive character is suppressed, and he is vulnerable to dangerous influence. His position in Aquarius in the eleventh house, which concerns friendships, portends betrayals and hypocritical friends. The moon, being in the first fifteen degrees of Scorpio, is said to be in *via combusta*, which means that no judgment of the outcome should be made (Lilly, 122). Nonetheless, the general character of the horoscope implies that the "querent," represented by Mars, is embarking on a scheme that will turn out badly.

If one moves the time forward toward midnight, required to bring the moon into square aspect to Mars according to the Alfonsine position of the planet, the threats of the eight-o'clock chart are more ex-

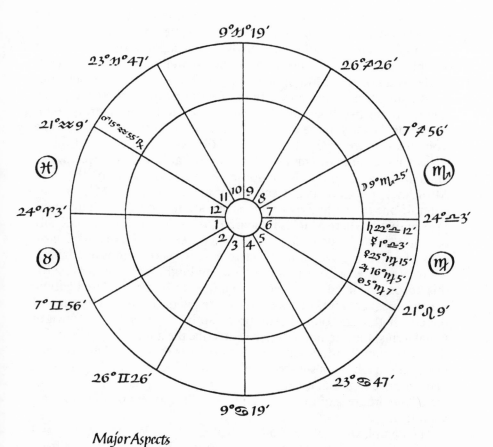

Major Aspects

☉ ✱ ☽; ☽ □ ♂; ✱ ♃
♂ △ ♄

Fig. 5. 8.00 p.m., August 19th, 1482, at Harwich, Suffolk, where the dreamer of <u>The Bowge of Courte</u> falls asleep.

plicit (see fig. 6). Cancer, the house of the moon, is now rising, and so the moon rules, as the description of her as "emperes" suggests that she should. She is "full of mutabylyte," occupying the watery sign Scorpio, and ruling watery Cancer. She is well-dignified, powerful, fickle, and hostile to Mars; and being in the fifth house, which concerns courtships, suits, and affairs of speculation and business, she emerges in the psychodrama of the horoscope as the prefiguring counterpart of the lady in the dream, Dame Saunce-Pere, the Fortune-like woman who owns the ship, *Bowge of Courte*, that Drede sails in. A voyage made under this moon will be unprofitable, perhaps even tragic. Mars in Aquarius in the eighth house, the house of death (on the cusp, Alfonsine), portends death caused by mental anguish. More to the point, if one treats the *Bowge* horoscope as an elective based upon the 1463 nativity, where Mars is in Scorpio, then this position specifically portends death by drowning—and, of course, *The Bowge of Courte* ends when Drede, overcome by terror and despaire, jumps overboard.

From an interpreter's point of view, midnight seems preferable for this horoscope in some respects, even though it seems a late bedtime for the speaker, and the moon is no longer in the sky. (One should remember that although horoscopes can be described and drawn in visual terms, they do not necessarily describe the appearance of a visible sky; they map significant moments of time as they are related to each other and to a human subject.) Both eight o'clock and midnight work, and produce significant results, and it may be that Skelton was thinking of the progress of the horoscope as a plot moving parallel with his narrative.

The complexities of Skelton's astrology, like his cryptograms and riddling Latin, show that he expected some of his readers to gain from his writing, among other things, some of the pleasure a modern person might take in puzzles and conundrums. He must have expected them to work out his astronomy, otherwise the meaning of his astrological stanzas remains hidden. A reader of *The Bowge* might see that Mars retrograde, ill-dignified, ill-aspected to the moon, portends misfortune; but specific information, giving a date, the exact planetary positions, and predictions of betrayal, failure, and death, only emerges from the full horoscope. A similar reader of *The Laurel* would discover an intimation of misfortune in the lines on Mars and the moon, but he would not find it borne out by the poem. Again, only a full horoscope would tell him that good fortune impends for someone whose life has been one of misfortune and enmity.

The interpretation of full horoscopes, unfortunately, rapidly becomes a very complex, subjective process, and not a very profitable one for inhabitants of a universe that excludes planetary influences.

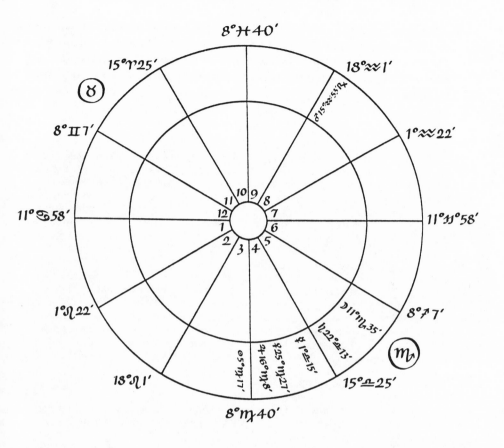

Fig. 6. Midnight, August 19th, 1482, at Harwich, Suffolk.

It will always be a question how deeply Skelton wished to embroil his readers in his own experiences and their occult, or hidden, meanings. He was entirely typical of his age in taking astrology seriously, but he was remarkably original in making the private use of it in his work that he did.

NOTES

1. Keith Thomas makes this last point, in *Religion and the Decline of Magic* (London: Weidenfeld & Nicolson, 1971), 288. His account of the practice of astrology in sixteenth- and seventeenth-century England is excellent, his bibliographical note (283) helpful. Skelton preceded the popularization of astrology described by Thomas, and there is also little sign in his work of the hermetic developments described by Garin, *Astrology in the Renaissance* (London: Routledge & Kegan Paul, 1983). Historians and critics concentrate upon the significance of astrology rather than its content and practice. Francis R. Johnson, *Astronomical Thought in Renaissance England* (Baltimore: Johns Hopkins University Press, 1937), and Thomas R. Kuhn, *The Copernican Revolution* (Cambridge: Harvard University Press, 1957) are indispensable guides to the scientific aspects of the subject, and Shumaker and Heilbron, *John Dee on Astronomy* (Berkeley: University of California Press, 1978) is a corrective to more enthusiastic writings. W. C. Curry, *Chaucer and the Mediaeval Sciences*, 2d ed. (New York: Barnes & Noble, 1960), Johnstone Parr, in his articles and in *Tamburlaine's Malady, and Other Essays on Astrology in Elizabethan Drama* (reprint, Westport, Conn.: Greenwood Press, 1971), and J. C. Eade, *The Forgotten Sky: a Guide to Astrology in English Literature* (Oxford: Clarendon Press, 1984), all show a command of the practicalities of astrology.

2. F. M. Salter, *Speculum* 9 (1934): 36.

3. As for example in A. R. Heiserman, *Skelton and Satire* (Chicago: University of Chicago Press, 1961), 20ff., and John Scott Colley, *Tennessee Studies in Literature* 18 (1973): 19–32.

4. D. S. Landes, *Revolution in Time* (Cambridge: Harvard University Press, Belknap Press, 1983) gives a fascinating account of timekeeping. It seems probable that the unknown medieval genius who invented the verge-and-foliot escapement mechanism (Landes, 67ff.) initiated the process of thought and technical development that would render the Ptolemaic model of the heavens obsolete.

5. Curry, *Chaucer and the Mediaeval Sciences*, 174.

6. Professor Owen Gingerich, of the Center for Astrophysics, very kindly computed the Alfonsine positions for me. Any errors in interpolation are my own.

7. The natures and qualities of the signs, planets, houses, and aspects were common astrological currency. Specific quotation in illustration would be otiose. The difficulty of astrology for the practicing astrologer always lay in synthesizing the elements of the horoscope into a whole, not in knowing the quality of the parts. I have consulted Skelton's Haly (Albohazen Haly), *Libri de iudiciis astrorum*, and Albumasar, *De magnis coniunctionibus*, as well as William Lilly, *Christian Astrology* (London, 1647), the best English synthesis of standard material, ambitious and well-written. The works by Lilly to which Curry refers (*Chaucer and the Mediaeval Sciences*, 337, n.7, n.15, etc.), *An Introduction to Astrology*, and *The Astrologer's Guide*, are nineteenth-century adaptations first published in 1835 under the editorial pseudonym Zadkiel, and are not always reliable guides to Lilly's text. Of modern guides to astrology, of which there are many, most of them worthless to a scholar, the best are the handbooks

of Alan Leo. If one discounts the theosophical element in them, they give an entirely traditional account of the subject.

8. Gingerich and Tucker explain, *HLQ* 32:213–14, that Mars was indeed "Lord of the year" in 1495, a status that depends upon a planet's position relative to the others at the four cardinal points of the year. They also observe, correctly, that the calculations required to ascertain Lordship are tedious and ambiguous, the final judgment inevitably somewhat subjective. Nevertheless, having performed similar calculations for 1463, the putative year of Skelton's nativity, I think Mars was also Lord in that year. In medieval astrology Lordship was important. Mars Lord of the year and well-dignified is very fortunate, in the twelfth or fifth house bringing joy among friends and security from enemies and, in conjunction with the moon at night, rewards (Haly, *Libri de iudiciis*, 259). In the 1495 figure this fortune is offset by retrogression and opposition to the sun. In the nativity, the diminution of fortune is stronger because Mars is "cadent from an angle," i.e., just passed from Libra, an angular or cardinal house, and in square or quartile aspect to Jupiter. Even so, the Lordship considerably mitigates the ill-fortune of the nativity, as does the moon's "application" to Jupiter.

9. For the reader's information, in this figure planetary positions and the cusps of the mundane houses are calculated from the *Ephemerides* of Regiomontanus. As will be seen, the difference between this figure and figure 1, calculated from modern tables, is very slight.

10. Detailed arguments for the dating will be found in Brownlow, *ELN* 22 (1984): 12–20. The present figure is more accurate in the house cusps than that printed in *ELN* (to the author's surprise!). That figure also gave an incorrect position for Saturn. Those details do not affect the date.

5. Skelton's Proverbs and Adages

References are to the collections of Tilley and Whiting. [*] means that Skelton's is the first usage listed in *T* or *W*. [**] means that Skelton's is the only one. The proverbs are arranged in alphabetical order by key word, which is italicized. (In nos. 4 and 8, K = C)

1. Idyl jangelers have bot litille *brayne*. (566)
2. With litille *besynes* standithe moche rest. (1404) *W* B613
3. How men were wonte for to discerne / By *Candelmas* day what wedder shuld holde. (1435–36) Cf. *T* C52: If Candlemass Day be fair and bright, / Winter will have another flight: / If on Candlemass Day it be shower and rain, / Winter is gone and will not come again.
4. From *Karlyle* to Kente. (196) *W* C45
5. Wele wotithe the *cat* whos berde she likkithe. (1432) *T* C140; *W* C108
6. Who may have a more ungraciows lif / Than a *chyldis* birde, and a knavis wif? (1445–46) *T* C320; *W* C206
7. *******Claterars* love no pece. (241) *W* C277
8. To blow at the *kole*. (610) *T* C460

9. Nedis most he ryn that the *develle* dryvithe. (1428) *W* D199; *T* D278

10. To be in the *dumps*. (734) *T* D640

11. *Dun* is in the myre. (1427) *T* D643; *W* D434

12. A slipper holde the tayle is of an *ele*. (501) *T* E60, E61; *W* E45, E48

13. Alle thynge passithe as dothe the sommer *floure*. (9) *W* F305, F317, F327

14. *Fortune* variythe in an howre. (11) *W* F523

15. *Golde* and hole. (612)

16. To seke *hallows*. (1630)

17. Masid as a Marche *hare*. (632) *T* H148; *W* H113, H116

18. He haltithe often that hathe a kyby *hele*. (502)

19. A jantylle *hownde* shuld never play the kurre. (1430)

20. To rede *Jak-a-thrummys* bibille. (209) *W* J1

21. Displese not an hunderd for on *mannys* plesure. (90)

22. *Mok* hath lost her sho. (1390)

23. Better a dum *mowthe* than a braynles skulle. (82)

24. Hard to make owght of that is nakid *nowght*. (1199) *T* N285

25. **When the *rayne* raynithe and the gose wynkkith, / Lytille wotithe the goslyng what the gose thynkithe. (1424–25) *W* R19

26. It may wele *ryme*, bot shrewdly it doth accorde. (1204) *W* R102

27. To styk by the *rybbis*. (638) *T* R101, R30

28. *Ryvers* ryn not tille the sprynge be fulle. (81) ?*T* R141

29. To *speke* fayre before the, and shrewdly behynde. (620) *W* S580

30. When the *stede* is stolyn, spar the stabyl durre. (1429) *T* S838; *W* S697

31. To stryve ageyne the *streme*. (1426) *T* S927; *W* S830

32. There by lyith a *tale*. (1194) *W* T31

33. It is sone aspiyd where the *thorne* prikkithe. (1431) *W* T222

34. **Fro *Wanflete* to Walys. (1212) *W* W8

35. To use the *Walshemannys* hose. (1233) *W* W196

36. The *whight* aperythe the better for the blak. (1231) *W* W231

37. *Not a *worde* then bot mum. (1112) *T* W767

38. *Wordis* be sworddis. (567) *T* W777

39. *Writynge* remaynnythe of recorde. (89)

40. Who *writithe* wisely hathe a grete tresure. (91)

6. The Allusions in the Ladies' Lyrics

Many of Skelton's comparisons in the lyrics to the ladies of *The Laurel* were no doubt as unexpected in 1495 as they are now, and none of them is necessarily as simple as a quick reading suggests.

Dyce noticed the strange comparisons of Margaret Tylney to Canace and Phaedra, and of Gertrude Statham to Pasiphaë; but he saw no irony in either or, if he did, he kept it to himself. He pointed out that Gower had told the story of Machareus and Canace, the incestuous children of King Eolus: "He expresses no horror at their incestuous passion, but remarks on the cruelty of their father. . . . Lydgate relates the story with a somewhat better moral feeling" (2:322–23). On the comparison of Mrs. Statham to Pasiphaë, Dyce commented, "Lest the reader be surprised at finding Skelton compare Mistress Statham to Pasiphaë, I cite the following lines from Feylde's *Contraversye bytwene a Lover and a Jaye* . . . in which she and Taurus are mentioned as examples of true love;

> "Phedra and Theseus
> Progne and Thereus
> *Pasyphe and Taurus*
>   Who lyketh to prove
> Canace and Machareus
> Galathea and Pamphylus
> Was never more dolorous
> *And all for true love.*"

Dyce also quoted a passage from Caxton's *Boke of Eneydos* to the effect that Pasiphaë was a noble and beautiful lady who, being great with child, "was delyvered of a creature that was halfe a man and halfe a bulle."

One suspects Dyce himself of a little irony in these notes. This is not so with E. P. Hammond, who quoted Dyce but remarked, "Feyldes's tone is not certain; nor is Skelton's . . ." (Hammond, 520, note to 1. 910). She also suspected mischief in the comparison of the countess to Queen Tomyris and Agrippina, "extraordinary selections from classical story to compare with English noblewomen" (518, note to 1. 827). Nonetheless, Hammond also produces evidence that the early Renaissance not only included Tomyris among great queens, but also on occasion counted Pasiphaë and Sextus Tarquinius among the great lovers.

Stanley Fish follows Hammond, and adds to the list of suspected comparisons those of Lady Elisabeth Howard to Cressida and of Lady Anne Dacres to Helen and Deianira. "Although these are calculated ambiguities," he writes, "the performance itself is not a calculated insult." This is probably true, otherwise Skelton's stay at Sheriff Hutton, one imagines, would have been sharply curtailed. Fish continues:

Skelton says here in another way what he had said in *Speak, Parrot*. The conventions of fifteenth-century poetry are pleasant but inaccurate . . . the joke is on the mode rather than the Countess for whom he feels an affection that can only be cheapened by conventional conceit . . . the ease with which he twits his friends is a tribute to the intimacy of their society; the laughter behind these lyrics is of the quality that only friends enjoy, or provoke. (Fish, 229–30)

Fish's point is that the idealism of "heroical commendation" (Skelton's name for the mode in which he is writing, 828b) excludes "the intrusions of the real world" (230), and that because there are not enough famous and virtuous ladies to supply comparisons all round, "the poet must arbitrarily falsify even myth to fit it into the artificial mold." So the sophisticated poet makes jokes about his commendatory genre and his subjects, the living ladies who, themselves no paragons—for this is the real world—are expected to join in the laughter. This debunking reading of an old poem and its society removes the foundations of idealism, courtesy, and admiration on which poem and society alike seem to have been based. The thought of Skelton and his patroness laughing over the failings of herself and her ladies, over the inadequacies of her poet's art, and the "intrusions of reality" as she hands him his "coronelle" falsifies the whole scene of mutual gift giving.

Fish's view that *The Laurel* is "one long peal of laughter at the expense of the conventions it pretends to follow" has itself become conventional, being quoted without acknowledgment by David A. Loewenstein: "If Skelton mocks anything by such teasing comparisons, it is the convention of praise itself rather than the ladies" (*Neophilologus* 68: 611–22). A lady who thought herself mocked would not be much comforted by that explanation. If offered by the poet, it would appear cowardly, if by another reader, impertinent.

How then are we to read these comparisons? It is obvious from the examples presented by Dyce and Hammond that the figure of speech comparing a real person to an exemplary figure allowed a medieval or Renaissance poet considerable latitude in the degree of specificity implied. Comparison with Helen of Troy might imply fame, beauty, infidelity, misfortune, or rape. Comparison might be based on any one of these, alone or combined with any or all of the others. We should therefore be attentive to an author's explicit point of comparison, and we should read the comparison in the context of the whole work of which it is part. And of course one must identify the allusion correctly.

Application of these rules simplifies matters. Hammond mistook Agrippina the wife of Germanicus, mentioned in the countess's poem, for Agrippina the mother of Nero. There is no insult in this or the comparison to Queen Tomyris. Both compliment the countess for fortitude and loyalty to her family and husband after the disaster of Bosworth, when her father-in-law was killed and her husband wounded, imprisoned, and attainted.

In the poem to Elisabeth Howard, the point of comparison between her and Cressida is that both are very beautiful girls on the verge of maturity. As the poem says explicitly, this Cressida has not yet met Troilus, let alone betrayed him. Troilus *would* have fallen for Lady Elisabeth *if* he had seen her, but he hasn't. When the poem was first read to its intended audience, laughter and a blush, perhaps would have accompanied the second line of the stanza:

> Goodely Cresseyda, fairar than Polycene,
> For to envyve Pandarus appetite. . . .

(871–72)

Here the tone is mingled in a way that everyone who has experienced a festive occasion in a family will recognize. This compliment—and it is a compliment—is seasoned with a touch of satire, not directed at the girl, but at the world of elderly roués she has the capacity to invigorate. It has a didactic edge to it, too, because it carries a hint of warning about the dangers of beauty. If the Lady Elisabeth showed tendencies to exploit her beauty, this joke would tend to cure her; yet the warning is as affectionate as the rest of the compliment.

In Lady Anne Dacres's poem, the point of comparison between her and Helen and Deianira is, once again, beauty, and Skelton could certainly have claimed that the comparison went no further than that. Who, however, might have challenged him? Lady Anne is married, and since she is also compared to Penelope for her "trouthe," one wonders whether, as in so many of these poems, the lady's male kin and acquaintance are not reflected in the comparison. Helen, Deianira, and Penelope all had difficulty with husbands: was Lord Dacre absent and unfaithful to his beautiful wife? In Lady Elisabeth's poem, the reference to Pandarus implies the behavior of men, presumably men about the household. In Margaret Hussey's poem a male relative hovers in the background again because the comparison of her to Hypsipyle implies loyal support of a father during difficult times (note to 1021). The comparison of Jane Hasset to Laodamia definitely tells us that she is a widow, and it also implies that she misses her husband keenly (note to 972).

In several cases, therefore, we find an implied reference in addition to the explicit point of comparison, and in each case it points to a male relation in the background. So far, however, all the implied references have been socially acceptable, including the slightly monitory joke about Pandarus. This does not seem to be the case when one turns to the two really difficult poems.

In the poem to Margaret Tylney, the point of comparison between her and Canace is that Skelton will make her famous as Machareus made his sister Canace famous; and because Machareus did that by getting her pregnant, a reader's—or an informed listener's—eyebrows are bound to rise. Skelton then compares Mistress Tylney to Phaedra, both ladies being diligent and industrious, Phaedra's diligence (as a reader of Lydgate would have known) having won her a husband, Theseus. The reader whose eyebrows rose at Canace, however, will remember Phaedra's incestuous desire for her stepson, Hippolytus. Yet there is no overt cue for laughter or irony in the poem:

> Wherefor delight
> I have to wright
>
> Of Margaryte
> Perle oryente
> Lodestar of lyght
> Moche relucent:
> Madame Regent
> I may yow calle
> Of vertuys alle

(945–53)

To a modern mind, the absence of an overt cue makes the implied attack, if there is one, all the more cruel, so much so that Skelton would have had to have the countess's protection, even complicity, to get away with it. Yet as J. A. Burrow said, reviewing John Scattergood's edition of Skelton in the *Times Literary Supplement* for 15 April, 1983, Skelton's poems often imply a social world that is very strange to us. This poem may contain neither joke nor attack: it may express sympathy with Margaret Tylney over an escapade for which she received harsh treatment from a father or a husband, or both. If, as is very likely, she and the other adult ladies knew the stories of Canace and Phaedra from Lydgate's *Falls of Princes*, then Skelton's little poem might be meant to convey the poet's and her other friends' sympathy. In that case, the last stanza is Skelton's rehabilitation of her in the temple of fame, and another example of the transformation of suffering into art. This, though speculative, is preferable to the ironic reading, for which there is no justification in the poem except the allusions themselves and which turns a holiday into a rather unpleasant occasion. (Since the allusions themselves are the point at issue, they cannot be used as evidence of irony.)

This leaves the most difficult comparison of all to be explained. Skelton compares Gertrude Statham to Pasiphaë for "benygnyte," saying quite plainly that they had quarreled, but have now made things up. Gertrude, it seems, was one of the ladies who planned his "coronelle," and so now he recompenses her, too, with a poem.

Edwards, 31 and 236–38, identified Gertrude as the wife of Roger Statham, a minor household functionary whom Skelton attacks in the "interpolated satire" (741a–751b). If we adopt this identification, however, then once again we discover that what looks like an attack on the lady is really an implied comment on a male relation, in this case Roger. Why should Skelton single out for praise Gertrude's "benignity" or graciousness? If one turns to Lydgate's account of Pasiphaë, which Skelton knew, one finds two remarkable things. First, Lydgate presents her as a very grand, very beautiful lady who had an unfortunate shortcoming. Second, toward the end of his account he presents —with some relief, one feels—an alternate version of the story:

> But in this matter summe bookis varie
> And affirme how queen Pasiphe
> Of kyng Mynos loved a secretarie
> Called Taurus, in Bochas ye may se. . . .
> (*Falls of Princes*, 1:2696–709)

This version of Pasiphaë's affair with the bull offers exactly the kind of subtlety in allusion that Skelton enjoyed. Having made a very broad joke about Gertrude's dubious sexual tastes, he could then explain, if challenged about the bull, "Not a bull—a secretary!" The laughter would intensify as everyone realized that the joke applied really to Roger, not Gertrude.

Gertrude and Pasiphaë, then, were equally gracious, equally benign, whether to bulls or to secretaries: the poem is far more an attack on the husband than the wife, who may have appreciated the joke. One must not *assume* that this marriage, or any of the marriages mentioned, was either happy or even tolerable for the wife. At least one contemporary, who wrote the gloss to 748, thought that Skelton's portrait of Roger was justified.

The Laurel is almost as much the ladies' poem as it is Skelton's. The making and the presentation of his "coronelle" is a feminine affair, and the only other male present, as far as we know, is another artist, Master Newton. To read the ladies' poems properly, we need to do what Skelton did and take the ladies' point of view. In this respect all the criticism, including recent academic criticism, has been deficient.

Glossary

[*] indicates a word whose appearance in *The Laurel* or whose particular usage in *The Laurel* is earlier than any recorded in *MED* or *OED*.

adj.	adjective
adv.	adverb
ger.	gerund
n.	noun
n.pl.	noun, plural
phr.	phrase
pl.	plural
pp.	past participle
pres.	present
prp.	present participle
sg.	singular
superl.	superlative
v.	verb
v.pret.	verb, preterit
v.pass.	verb, passive

accessary, n. a source of help 523.

advertisement, n. the act of being informed 808.

adyment, n. adamant; of surpassing hardness, impregnable 306.

afforce, v. > OF *efforcier.* to attempt 817.

affyaunsinge, * *prp.* pledging 555.

agerdows, adj. > F *aigre-douce,* sour-sweet 1244.

ale pole, * *n.* ME *ale stake,* pole or post set up as a sign to an ale house 613.

allectyves, n.pl. > L *electuarium,* a sweetened medicine that melts in the mouth, hence things that are very attractive or tempting title page, 11.

amounte, v. elevate in rank, raise the value of 346.

apparently, * *adv.* plainly, "manifestly to the understanding" (*OED*) 170.

arrectynge, * *prp.* > L *arrigere,* to straighten; hence, raising l; offering up 410.

askry, v. > ME *ascrien.* Cf. OF *escrier,* to cry out upon, to shout defiance to, an enemy; to challenge 1345.

assignement, n. appointment or designation to office; bidding, orders 195.

assurdid, * *v.pret.* > OF *assourdre* > L *assurgere,* to arise; confused in OF with *essordre* > *exsurgere,* and so meaning to burst forth, to break out (*OED*) 302.

astatis, n.pl. either "high-ranking people" or "kinds of people" 45.

atteintid, pp. convicted 611.

aurum musicum. mosaic gold, a sulphide of tin used as a pigment in illumination (*OED*) 1161.

avysemente, n. reflection, consideration. with *good*: due consideration 807.

avysid, v.pret. looked about, took note 386; *reflex. as I me avysid*, as I took thought with, bethought myself 36.

axys, n.pl. a form of *access*, current ca. 1400–1700, with stress on first syllable; attack, fit 315.

balassis, n.pl. a kind of ruby 1160.

bale, n. evil, harm. *bote of bale*, deliverance from trouble, relief from sorrow 376.

bararag, n. the sound of a trumpet; Skelton's invention 236.

baratows, adj. > OF barat, strife. quarrelsome; *baratows broisiours*, wounds, bruises caused by quarrels 673.

barbellis, n.pl. Cf. OF *barbel* > LL *barbellus.* a large freshwater fish of the carp family, named from the fleshy appendages at its mouth 661.

barbican, n. outer fortification; specifically a small round tower before the outward gate of a castle or city 1391.

barge, n. seagoing vessel of moderate size with sails 546.

bate, v. bait, set a dog on an animal 27.

bawdias, n.pl. bawdies, dirty people. > ME *baudi*, soiled, dirty 639.

belluynge, prp. call of the male deer in the mating season 24.

benygne, adj. benign, gracious, kindly 728, 880, 918. also *benynge* 213.

besene, pp.adj. dressed 483. *wele besene*, good-looking 1070.

bestad, pp. placed, situated. *hardly bestad*, in great trouble 830.

bet, pp. beaten, inlaid 41.

birdbolt, n. blunt arrow for shooting birds 1374.

birralle, n. precious stone, transparent, pale green to light blue, yellow, or white 467.

ble, n. complexion, coloring 1406.

blinkarddis,* n.pl. one who blinks, has poor sight. *brainles blinkarddis*, stupid people who can't see properly, or drunks 610. See note.

boryalle, adj. northern 261.

bote, n. boot, help. *bote of bale*, deliverance from trouble, relief from sorrow 376.

botum, n. small object about which a ball of thread is wound, a core (*MED*) 799.

bowns, n. a heavy, noisy blow or a loud noise produced by an explosion 624.

bowris, n.pl. inner apartments, private rooms 460.

bracers,* n.pl. aphetic form of *embracers*, habitually corrupt people. > ME *embracen*, to bribe or "fix" a jury (*MED*) 189.

bremis, n.pl. freshwater fish, found in lakes and deep water 661.

brevely, adv. briefly 1086.

broisiours, n.pl. > OF *brisëure.* a wound, bruise; the act of bruising, etc. 673.

broken workis. ? a raised surface of heavy embroidery (Hammond) 801.

brutyd, * *pp.* reported abroad 155. *pp.adj.* famous 405.

bullyons, n.pl. ornamental bosses; on a book, convex ornaments 1159.

burne, pp. adj. burnt. *burne gold,* burnt, i.e., refined gold, hence pure 41. (*burne* is a form of the *pp.* of ME *burnen,* to polish, confused with *pp.* of *brennen,* to burn. Cf. Chaucer, *H. Fame,* 1387, "As burned gold hyt shoon to see.")

burris, n.pl. either knots or knobs in embroidery, or embroidered imitations of burrs 803.

buttuns, n.pl. either a term in embroidery, or embroidered buds, probably rosebuds 803.

byde, v. await, endure 98.

byrnston, n. brimstone, i.e., sulphur 631.

byse, n. blue-gray pigment, close to azure 1152.

calcydony, n. pale white gemstone 587.

captaciouns, * *n.pl.* > L *captationes,* acts of seizing. things which command attention 815.

carollis, n.pl. round dances accompanied by singing; songs in general 705.

carpettis, n.pl. a thick, usually woolen cloth used to cover floors, beds, tables, altars, but mainly for sitting or kneeling 474, 787.

cast, pp. ? formed by pouring into a mold or, more generally, given a particular shape 658.

caste, n. a throw. *a short caste,* fig., "not far" 1395.

castinge, ger. term in embroidery; ? laying out the design 802.

casuelte, n. chance, accident. *by casuelte,* accidentally 1400.

charter, n. a document, signed and sealed, issued by authority 503.

chayre, n. chariot 1465.

claryonar, n. one who blows a charion, a shrill trumpet used in war 233.

clere story, n. a series of windows in the upper part of a nave, choir, or transept wall; here, a similar feature in a secular building 479.

close, adj. enclosed, used of religious orders 305.

cloyster, n. fig., a religious house. *cloyster virgynalle,* order of virgins 305.

colyaunder, n. coriander 1022.

compassid, pp. pondered, considered 13.

conceyte, n. mental powers, the mind 16.

condicyouns, n.pl. personal qualities 615.

confecture, n. a preparation of drugs, preserved fruits, sweets, etc. > ML *confectura* 110.

congruence, n. agreement. *of verey congruence,* as is truly fitting 52.

constru, v. expound 109.

conveyaunce, n. cunning management, sleight of hand 1232.

coragiows, adj. brave, generous; heartening, encouraging 164.

corde, v. aphetic form of *accorde,* to agree 88.

cordialle, n. medicinal drink to stimulate the heart; an exhilarating drink; something comforting 131.

costiows, adj. expensive 570.

cote, n. the coot, water hen 1373.

coundight, n. pipe for conveying water 658.

counteryng, ger. singing in contrapuntal parts 705.

courte rollis, n.pl. court registers 192.

covenabill, adj. appropriate 712, 821.

coverlet, n. counterpane, quilt, altar cloth, cloak, &c. Cf. AF *cuver-lit* (*MED*). ? Used by Skelton figuratively of a girl in a green cloak 1372.

creauncer, n. tutor, guardian 1220.

cribbis, n.pl. wickerwork baskets 640.

cure, n. effort, pains. *busy cure,* solicitous or devoted pains 928.

daggid, adj. either with clothes cut or slashed into points around the hem, or dirty, bemired, "daggled" 630.

dasid, pp.adj. stupefied 734, 1383.

dasild, pp.adj. from *dazzle,* a 15–16C. derivative of *dase,* to stupefy; struck blind 1383.

dastarddis, n.p. worthless wretches, base fellows 190.

dasyng, prp.adj. staring mindlessly 641.

dawkokkis, n.pl. lit., a male jackdaw; fig., a silly person, a noddy 618.

derayne, v. to fight; *derayne batayle,* accept a challenge, prepare for combat 1557.

devil way, adv. phr. orig. an intensifying of *away,* here an interjection of disgust 635.

devyse, n. intent, desire, inclination; possibly plan or project 442.

dirige, n. Mod E *dirge* > L *dirige,* the first word of the antiphon at Matins of the Office of the Dead, hence the name of the whole office 1263.

discharge, n. document of release from accusation or blame 1140.

disclose, v. open up, make known 1216.

discuryd, pp. 14–16C. variant sp. of *discovered* 731.

discust, pp. decided, settled 881.

disgisyd, pp. disgise, dress elaborately, to costume for masques or revels. splendidly arrayed, ornamented 38.

dissuasyve, * *n.* a dissuasive speech 151.

distincyon, n. translates ML *diffinitio*; a definition or assertion 1461.

dome, n. judgment, opinion. *to my dome,* in my opinion 1499.

dotarddis, n.pl. people who *dote,* act foolishly; imbeciles. frequently used with *old* 734.

dotrellis, n.pl. silly, simpleminded people 641.

dredefulle, adj. anxious, afraid 828.

dribbis, * *v. 3 pers.pl.pres.* slaver, dribble 641.

dumpe, * *n.* reverie, fit of abstraction, also of melancholy or depression; heaviness of mind 15. *dumppis, n.pl.* dazed or puzzled state 734.

dysars, n.pl. dice-players (? jesters. See *dysowre*) 608.

dysdaynous, adj. haughty 618.

dysowre, n. ME *disour,* story-teller, minstrel, hence jester 635.

embosid, pp. embose > OF *bois,* woods, used of a hunted animal, to take shelter in the woods, hence to be driven to extremity. In 16th C. a hunting term: "foaming at the mouth" 24.

enbateld, pp. i.e., *embatailled* > *embataillen,* to provide with battlements 570.

enbosid, pp. > OF *embocer.* ornamented in relief; embossed 467.

enbrasid, pp. > OF *enbracier.* arm-in-arm (? or with arms about each other) 393.

enbybid, pp. > L *imbibere,* to suffuse or saturate with a liquid. soaked, wet 682.

encrampisshed,* pp. encrampishen, to contort, make crooked the body. hampered, constricted 16.

enderkkid,* pp.adj. made obscure 108.

enduse, v. bring forward, include 94.

engalarid,* pp. ? galleried (*OED*) 460.

engladdid,* pp. gladdened 536. Not in *OED* or *MED*. *OED* has *gladded* (1568).

engrapid,* pp. covered with grapevines (Skelton's coinage) 656.

engrosid, pp. decorated with imagery (*MED, engrossen, v.* 4) 41. gathered in quantity 335. collected, with the subaudition *very big* 1496.

enhachid,* pp. > F *enhacher.* inlaid, adorned. 40, 470.

enhardid, pp.adj. made hard 306.

enlosengyd,* pp. ornamented with lozenges of alternate colours 469.

enneude, pp. > L *innovare.* revived 389.

enplement, n. assignment to a specific task or office 402. The word arises from a confusion of *emploiment* with *implement,* equipment, furniture. 16–17C. spellings of *implement* as *emploi-, imploi-, impell-* (*OED*) show the confusion.

enrailid,* pp. enclosed as with a railing 656.

ensewynge, prp. following 321.

envawtid,* pp. arched over 476.

enveiyd, v.pret. denounced violently 96.

enverdurid,* pp. made green 666.

epitomis,* n.pl. brief accounts 1405.

extasy, n. trance, inspired state 37.

extorcioun, n. unlawful or violent seizure of money by crown officers 194.

facers, n.pl. swaggerers, bullies 189.

faculte, n. ability, field of knowledge 816.

fallows, n.pl. arable land. *over the fallows,* proverbial, means "gone away" 1629.

fatalle, adj. pertaining to fate. *fatalle persuasioune,* destined inducement 34.

fawte, n. fault 112. The *l* was not pronounced until modern times.

fenestralle, n. window 1381.

flagrant, adj. variant of *fragrant* 671, 978.

florisshinge, ger. blooming, budding; also decoration, e.g., illumination of manuscript letters 802.

florthe, n. floor (14–16C.) 480.

flye net, n. ? net set by a *flier* or birdcatcher, or else a butterfly net 1373.

foisty,* adj. smelly 639.

force, v. to care about. *I ne force,* I don't care 731.

formally, adv. handsomely, in good order, with punning meanings, (1) "beautifully" from L *forma,* a beauty, *formosus,* beautiful, and (2) "firstly" from *forme,* first 686.

forme, adj. > OE *forma,* first, *superl.* of *fore,* before. first 595. *formar, comp. adj.* before, preceding; *whiche hathe the formar date of*, which takes absolute precedence of 842. *formest, superl. adj.* first in position and rank 287, 685.

forme, n. under the forme, according to the correct way, to customary etiquette. Cf. Mod. E *in due form* 443.

fortop, n. forelock 1327.

foster, n. forest officer, huntsman 27, 1401.

frame, * *n.* loom 792.

freshe, adj. vigorous, vivid 329.

fret, pp. richly adorned 485.

fret, pp. eaten up, destroyed. *to-fret*, chewed to pieces 1444.

friththy, * *adj.* > *frith*, a woodland or forest, hence wooded, ? with subaudition *peaceful* > *frith*, peace, as in *frith and grith*, peace and prosperity 22.

froward, adj. severe, inclement 1444.

frownsid, pp.adj. curled or frizzled 1327.

fructuows, adj. edifying 821.

furnnyshe, v. accomplish, complete 92.

fylt, n. 16C. spelling of *filth*; dirt, muck 23.

gabille, n. heavy rope, cable 833.

galle, n. a swelling or blister, esp. in a horse. *rubbid sum on the galle*, chafed some in a sore place 97.

gambawddis, n.pl. > OF *gambade.* gambols 608.

garnate, n. ? Granada, a center of the medieval gem trade (Hammond) 485.

gase, * *n.* a frivolous person, a bubblehead 1200.

get, n. offspring. ? variant of *jet*, fashion. *of the new get*, of the new generation, recently spawned; *of the new jet*, in the latest style 1187.

giggishe, adj. > ME *gig*, a foolish, loose, lively, or wanton young woman 1200.

gingirly, * *adv.* of walking or dancing, with a favorable or neutral sense: neatly, daintily, with small steps 1197.

girnid, v.pret. snarled, showing the teeth in pain, astonishment, etc., pulled a face 265.

gise, n. habit, practice 121.

glint, pp.adj. slippery 572.

glose, v. speak deceitfully, flatter 760.

glum, * *n.* a sullen, frowning look 1111.

glutton, * *n.* ? a kind of needle (Dyce) 795.

gray, n. brock, badger 101.

gre, n. good will. *take it in gre*, accept gracefully, in good part 1481.

gretely, adv. greatly 99.

gronnyng, ger. > ME *gronen*, OE *granian.* sighing, lamentation, groaning 1370.

grope, v. take hold of 832.

grossolitis, n.pl. i.e., *chrysolite*, a sea-green and gold gem 466.

grounde, n. foundation 866. "cloth used as a basis for embroidery or decoration" (*OED*) 41.

groynnynge, ger. > OF *groignier.* grumbling, complaining 1370.

gummys, n.pl. gums: soluble secretions of trees, usually medicinal 675.

gun stone, n. a stone used as cannon or gunshot; cannonball 629.

hailid, pp. dragged or pulled violently 622.

habilymente, n. dress 44. *habilymenttis* 851.

hallows, n.pl. saints. *gone to seke hallows*, proverbial: "over the hills and far away" 1630.

harnnes, n. body armor, personal weapons 1550.

hart, n. male of the red deer. *harttis*, 24, 1402.

haskarddis,* n.pl. base fellows 607.

heddellis,* n.pl. heddles, "small cords through which the warp is passed in a loom after going through the reed" (*OED*) 791.

herber, n. a pleasure garden 652.

higth, higthe, adj. high 50, 1118, 1122.

historiar, n. cf. ME *historier*, narrator 329.

honeste, n. chastity, good moral reputation 1198, 1205.

howris, n.pl. hours. *withe in what howris*, ? when, ? how long 457.

humors, n.pl. bodily fluids 32.

hyght, v. I hyght yow, I assure you 643.

hynde, n. female of the red deer 1400. *hynde calf*, fawn of the red deer, up to a year old 26.

iconomicar,* n. > L *oeconomicus*, concerning the management of household affairs. an authority on husbandry 328.

inbryngis, 3 pers.sg.pres. brings in, adduces. Chiefly Scots and NE 689.

indempnyte, n. security 1130.

inferrid, pp. > L *inferre.* brought forward 141.

intentyve, adj. busy, occupied 942.

jacinctis, n.pl. jacinths, gems of blue and purple, sometimes red 480.

jeloffer, n. Mod.E *gillyflower.* < LL *caryophyllum* (cf. OF *gilofre*), any of several clove-scented flowers, including carnations and pinks 983, 1440.

kancor, n. a spreading ulcer 672.

kardars,* n.pl. card-players 608.

ken, v. teach 825.

kit, v. 15–16C. spelling of *cut* 184.

korage, v. aphetic form of ME *acoragen*, embolden 152.

kownnage. n. coining money 611.

krakkis, n.pl. > OE *cracian*, to crack, ME *craken*, to boast. loud talk, bragging 189.

kuriowsly, adv. with careful art, exquisitely 461, 853.

kurris of kynde. dogs by nature, hence biters, snarlers 619.

kyby, adj. chilblained, chapped, or ulcerated 502.

kylle,* v.pass. to be killed 95.

library, n. memoirs, records 780.

liddurns, n.pl. > ME *ledroun* > OF *larron, ladron.* rogue, rascal 188, 733.

losellis, n.pl. > v. *lose*, hence orig. "lost people"; bums, crooks 188.

lucerne, n. > L. *lucerna*, an oil-lamp. a lamp 1433.

lumpis, n.pl. lots, heaps, gangs 733.

lure, n. enticement, attraction 992.

make, v. to write or compose, esp. in verse 112.

masid, pp. stupefied, confused 266. terrified, bewildered 632.

mastris, n.pl. quarrels, disturbances 383.

matriculate, pp. enrolled, registered 1275.

mayntenans, n. specifically, wrongful or officious interference in others' law suits, esp. by a lord or his followers; more generally, supporting, abetting a wrong (*MED*) 193, 1127.

meddelyd, pp. infused with, accompanied by 295.

melle, v. deal with, meddle with 1469.

meritory, adj. earned, deserved 429.

mesuris, n.pl. a musical term; rhythmical patterns, modes, melodies. *fals mesuris*, badly tuned intervals 741.

mislynge, ger. mizzle, to rain in very fine drops 698.

moose, n. a bog, morass, moor, or marshy place (common in northern place-names) 23.

motyve, n. proposition, argument 114.

mum, n. silence. *not a worde . . . then bot mum*, not a sound 1112.

muse,* n. gap in a fence or hedge through which hunted game passes 1378.

mydsomer mase, n.phr. midsummer madness, a midsummer game 1202.

nept, n. catnip 982.

nowghty, adj. wicked; immoral, unclean 188.

opposelle, n. question put in opposition 141.

orbicular,* n. > L *orbicularis*, circular, or > ML *orbiculis*, dim. of *orbis*, a small orb. Skelton's term combines the *n.* and *adj.* forms. orbit 4.

overthwharte, adj. contrary 307.

owtray, v. overcome 156.

pakkis, n.pl. usually with *naughty*: people of low, worthless character, perhaps because they cheat at cards (*OED, pack, v²*, II.5) or because they belong to a gang or *pack* of rascals (*OED, pack, sb¹*, 3.a) 188.

palle, n. fine, rich cloth 474.

parde, interj. par-dieu, by God, without a doubt 95.

passid, 3 pers.sg.pret. surpassed 159.

pavylioune, n. a tent 38.

pellit, n. a ball, usually of stone, shot as a missile from mangonels and mortars, later a bullet 637.

penselle, n. fine paintbrush for delicate work 1091.

perle oryente, n.phr. lustrous pearl 948.

pevyshe, adj. > L *perversus*, perverse, capricious; hence silly, crazy (*MED, OED*) 266, 626.

pevishnes, n. folly, silliness 637.

piplyng, prp. adj. dim. of *piping, prp.* of *pipe*, to blow gently, used of the wind (*MED*) 676.

plummet, n. a lead pencil 1091.

plumpe, n. a group, crowd, or flock of people 258.

pomaunder, n. a ball of aromatic substances, carried, or worn at the neck or waist, to ward off infection 1023.

pope holy, adj. represents F *papelard*, hypocritical, sanctimonious 612.

porishly,* adv. squintingly, looking through half-shut eyes 626.

porte salu, n. > L *portus salutis*, safe harbor 541.

posterne, n. back, side, or private gate or door 766.

posty, n. i.e., *poustie* > L *potestas*, power, authority 1319.

potshorde, n. fragment of pottery 1205.

poyntid, pp. either: equipped, furnished (aphetic form of *appointed*), or dotted (*pp. point*, to mark with pricks, dots) 473.

prece, n. crowd, throng 455. *put* [oneself, etc.] *in prece*, exert oneself 239, 794.

pretory, n. > L *praetorium*, hall, palace. great hall 477.

preventid, pp. anticipated 428.

probate, n. analysis, working out 368.

problemys, n.pl. enigmatic or oblique poetic statements; riddles 338, 1240.

proces, n. > L *processus*, a setting forth. an orderly, well-arranged narrative or exposition title page, 28, 819.

promotyve, * *adj.* attended by promotion, i.e., elevation in rank or position 116.

proper, adj. commendable, goodly 984.

prothonotary, n. chief clerk or registrar (cf. *Protonotaries Apostolical*, a college of twelve, formerly seven, prelates, who register papal acts, make and keep records of beatification, and direct the canonization of saints [*OED*]) 432.

provysioun, n. foresight, prudence 757.

pryme, n. first division of the day, 6:00–9:00 A.M., or the canonical hour of prime. *or it be pryme*, before it is time to begin 525.

pursevaunttis, n.pl. junior heraldic officers attendant on the heralds 492.

pusaunt, adj. powerful, mighty 50.

pyne, n. affliction, distress 1372.

pynk iyde, * *adj.* having small, narrow, half-closed eyes 626.

pyrlynge, * *prp.* twisting or spinning threads into a cord 796.

quarter, n. the inside of a horse's hoof. *fals quarter*, "a soreness on the inside of the hoofs" (Dyce), hence fig., some private, disabling condition 504.

quest, v. term in hunting: to cry or bark together, used of hounds in the chase 1403.

quikly, adv. vividly; as if alive 1155.

race, v. to erase by scratching out 72, 1484. *2 pers.pl.pret. rasid* 137. *pp. racid* 1576.

ragman rollis, n.phr. a list, catalogue 1484.

raillis, n.pl. ? a linear decorative design enclosing the margins of a manuscript or its binding (cf. *enrailid with rosers*, 656) 1151.

raist, 2 pers.sg.pres. of *race* (q.v.), fig. used to mean to afflict (Scattergood), to hurt. ? an aphetic form of *array* (Dyce) meaning to treat (Hammond) 317.

raunge, n. area of ground over which ranging takes place (hence *ranger*, a forest officer) 25.

rebawddis, n.pl. ribalds; low, dissolute, foul-mouthed people (orig. retainers who performed the lowest offices in royal and baronial households: low-born menials) 607.

reconusance, n. recognizance; acknowledgment of a duty or obligation 838.

recule, n. i.e., F *recueil*, a literary compilation or collection 1384.

redres, n. a formal act of amendment or correction 229.

reflayringe,* prp.adj. from *reflayre*, to spread a scent abroad 977.

regraciatory,* n. thanks 431.

reme, n. kingdom; 14–16C. spelling of *realm* > OF *reaume* 758.

remembraunce, ger. > *remember*, to record, list, narrate, commemorate. hence commemorative faculty 812; commemorative account 845; record 1143.

remorde,* v. rebuke stingingly 86.

repete, n. ? account or recital (the former seems more likely, although *OED*, whose earliest example is dated 1609, calls it a rare usage) 1384.

rerewarde, n. the rear, the back 1379.

revolde, 1 pers.sg.pret. of *revolve*, indicating pronounciation with loss of *v*: turn about or around 664.

rochis, n.pl. small freshwater fish of the carp family 661.

rosary, n. rosebush 979.

rosers, n.p. rosebushes 656.

rowme, n. place, office, position 116.

rownid, 3 pers.pl.pret of *rowne* > ME *runien*, to whisper 250.

rownsis, n.pl. riding horses 1301.

rowthe, adj. rough (northern) 803.

sadly, adv. soberly, seriously 386.

salfe cundight, n. i.e., F *sauf-conduit*, safe-conduct 503.

saumplars,* n.pl. beginners' exercises in embroidery 789.

sawte, n. aphetic form of *assawte*; assault 1392.

scut, n. the short, erect tail of a hare, rabbit, or deer; hence the animal itself, seen running in flight; esp. the hare 632.

seson, n. ? relish, meaning (Scattergood) 108.

slaiys, n.pl. term used in weaving: a tool "used to beat up the weft" (*OED*) 791.

slawthfulle, adj. slothful (northern) 120.

slipper, adj. slippery 501.

smaragdis, n.pl. emeralds 480.

smater, v. to talk ignorantly, to chatter 1188.

snuffe, v. to inhale strongly (in an effort to identify a scent); to express scorn 1466.

snurre, v. > MLG *snurren*, to snort 1466.

solacyons, n.pl. > L *solacium*, a soothing, a comfort, relief or solace   title page, 10.

sophisticatid, pp. adulterated, mixed 110.

stellify, v. to place among the stars, to turn into a star 963.

stole, n. a frame on which to work embroidery or tapestry 790.

straunge, adj. I made it straunge, I held back, pretended not to understand 444.

sufferaunce, n. indulgence 113.

sufferayne, adj. sovereign, supremely excellent 523.

suffir, v. permit 160.

sumdele, n. > OE *sum dael*; somewhat, in part 1506.

superflu, adj. ME and 15–16C. form. superfluous 32.

supplement, * *n.* supplying or adding something wanting 415.

suppleyd, 3 pers.sg.pret. supplicated 49. *prp. suppleyng* 1472.

supportacioun, n. used formulaically with *under* or *with . . . of*; countenance, assistance 220.

surfullinge, ger. embroidering 803.

swarte, adj. livid through suffering 1393.

syttynge, adj. suitable, proper, in keeping 77, 149.

taberdys, n.pl. tabards; short surcoats worn by knights and heralds 395.

tappettis, n.pl. figured cloths used for hangings 474; for sitting 787.

taumpynnis, n.pl. plugs for stopping apertures, hence "disk-shaped or cylindrical pieces of wood made to fit the bore of a muzzle-loading gun, rammed home between the charge and the missile to act as a wad" (*OED*) 642.

tavellis, n.pl. bobbin on which silk is wound for use in the shuttle 791.

tayle, n. female privy part 1197.

thonk, n. thanks (*sg.* form and spelling, 13–15C.) 822.

timorows, adj. causing fear; dreadful, terrible 260.

tirrikis, n.pl. a puzzling word, also in *Speke, Parrot*, 137. Scattergood suggests *theorics*, but it seems to mean some mechanical device imitating celestial movements 1511.

titivyllis, n.pl., sg. titivil > ML *Titivillus*, the name of a devil who collected fragments of words dropped, skipped, or mumbled in Divine Service (*OED*); hence a gossip or any kind of mischief-maker 642.

to-jaggid. pp. pierced through 629.

towchid, * *pp.* drawn, depicted 592, 1155.

towchis, n.pl. sly tricks 764.

tumblar, n. an acrobat; fig., a morally agile person 634. *pl.* 608.

turkis, n.pl. > OF *turkeis* > ML *lapis turchesius*, the Turkish stone. turquoises, sky-blue, apple-green gems 466.

turnnynge, ger. term in embroidery, "twisting" (Hammond) 802.

twynklyng, prp. echoic: used of a harper's playing. cf. *tinkle* 687.

tyne, n. always preceded by *little*: a short space of time or place; a little bit 505.

umblis, n.pl. umbles; the liver, kidneys and entrails of a deer, of which a part, sometimes the whole, was considered the right of the huntsman; eaten as *umble pie* 1234.

unrememberd, pp. unrecorded 1219.

vawte, n. vaulted inner roof 476.

verduris, n.pl. ? shades of green (*OED*), ? leaf and plant designs 776.

volvell, n. "an old device consisting of one or more movable circles surrounded by other graduated or figured circles, serving to ascertain the rising and setting of the sun and moon, the state of the tides, etc." (*OED*) 1511.

Walshemannys. Welshman's 1233.

wetewolddis, n.pl. formed by analogy with *cokewold*. a wittoll; a complacent cuckold 187.

whirllid, v.pret. to drive a wheeled vehicle swiftly (*OED*) 1465.

whyst, adj. still, silent 267.

worshyp, n. honor 1168.

wotithe, 3 pers.sg.pres. wot, to know 1425.

wrenchis, n.pl. tricks; used of horses, a sudden, sideways movement 1201.

wynkkith, 3 pers.sg.pres. wynk, to shut the eyes 1424.

wynshid, 3 pers.sg.pret. wynshe or wynce; used of horses, to kick restlessly 1195.

yerne, v. a term in hunting: to cry or bark together, used of hounds in the chase 1403.

Works Cited

Editions of Skelton's Writings

The Bibliotheca Historica of Diodorus Siculus Translated by John Skelton. Edited by F. M. Salter and H. L. R. Edwards. 2 vols. London: Oxford University Press for The Early English Text Society, 1956, 1957.

Complete Poems. Edited by Philip Henderson. London: Dent, 1931. Reprint. 1948.

Complete Poems. Edited by John Scattergood. London: Penguin Books, and New Haven: Yale University Press, 1983.

The Garland of Laurell. Edited by Eleanor Prescott Hammond. In *English Verse Between Chaucer and Surrey.* Durham, N.C.: Duke University Press, 1927.

Magnyfycence: A Moral Play. Edited by Robert Lee Ramsay. London: Oxford University Press for the Early English Text Society, 1908.

Pithy, Pleasaunt, and Profitable Workes. Edited by John Stow. London: Thomas Marsh, 1568. Reprint. London: Scolar Press, 1970.

Poetical Works. Edited by Alexander Dyce. 2 vols. London: Thomas Rodd, 1843.

Poems. Selected and edited by Robert S. Kinsman. Oxford: Clarendon Press, 1969.

Speculum Principis. Edited by F. M. Salter. *Speculum* 9 (1934): 25–37.

Secondary Works

Adair, John Eric. *The Pilgrim's Way.* London: Thames & Hudson, 1978.

Albohazen Haly Filii Abenragel (Ibn Abi Al-Rijal, Abu Al-Hasan 'Ali). *Libri de iudiciis astrorum.* Basel, 1551.

Albumasar (Abu Ma 'Sar). *De magnis coniunctionibus annorum revolutionibus.* Venice, 1489.

The Anglican Missal. Mount Sinai, N.Y.: Frank Gavin Liturgical Foundation, 1961.

Aubrey, John. *Remaines of Gentilisme and Judaisme.* In *Three Prose Works*, edited by John Buchanan Brown. Fontewell, Sussex: Centaur Press, 1972.

Backhouse, Janet. *The Lindisfarne Gospels.* Oxford: Phaidon Press, 1981.

Benham, Hugh. *Latin Church Music in England, 1460–1575.* London: Barrie and Jenkins, 1977.

Berners, Dame Juliana. *The Boke of St. Albans.* Edited by W. Blades. London: Eliot Stock, n.d.

Boccaccio, Giovanni. *Concerning Famous Women.* Translated by Guido Guarino. New Brunswick, N.J.: Rutgers University Press, 1963.

251

————. *Genealogie deorum gentilium libri*. 2 vols. Bari: Laterza, 1951.

Bradley, Henry. "Two Puzzles in Skelton." *Academy*, 1 August 1896.

Brie, Friedrich. "Skelton Studien." *Englische Studien* 37 (1906): 1–87.

Brown, Carleton, ed. *Religious Lyrics of the XVth Century*. Oxford: Clarendon Press, 1939.

Brownlow, F. W. "The Boke . . . called Speake Parrot." *ELR* 1 (1971): 3–26.

————. "The Date of *The Bowge of Courte* and Skelton's Authorship of 'A Lamentable of Kyng Edward IIII.' " *ELN* 22 (1984): 12–20.

————. "*Speke, Parrot*: Skelton's Allegorical Denunciation of Cardinal Wolsey." *SP* 65 (1968): 124–39.

Burns, Robert. *Songs and Poems*. Edited by James Kinsley. 3 vols. Oxford: Clarendon Press, 1968.

Butler's Lives of the Saints. Edited by Herbert Thurston and Donald Attwater. 4 vols. New York: P. J. Kenedy, 1956.

Carpenter, Nan Cooke. *John Skelton*. New York: Twayne Publishers. 1967.

————. "Skelton's Music: A Gloss on *Hippates*." *ELN* 8 (1970): 93–97.

Caxton, William. *Prologues and Epilogues of William Caxton*. Edited by W. J. B. Crotch. London: Oxford University Press for the Early English Text Society, 1928.

Child, Francis James. *The English and Scottish Popular Ballads*. 5 vols. Boston: Houghton, Mifflin Co., 1884–98. Reprint. New York: Dover, 1965.

Cokaine, Sir Thomas. *A Short Treatise of Hunting*. Edited by W. R. Halliday. Oxford: Oxford University Press, 1932.

Curry, Walter Clyde. *Chaucer and the Mediaeval Sciences*. 2d. ed. New York: Barnes & Noble, 1960.

Curtius, E. R. *European Literature and the Latin Middle Ages*. New York: Pantheon Books, 1953. Reprint. New York: Harper, 1963.

De Lincy, Le Roux. *Le livre des proverbes français*. 2 vols. Paris, 1842.

Dobson, E. J. *English Pronunciation, 1500–1700*. 2 vols. Oxford: Clarendon Press, 1957.

Eade, J. C. *The Forgotten Sky: A Guide to Astrology in English Literature*. Oxford: Clarendon Press, 1984.

Eckhardt, Caroline D., ed. *Essays in the Numerical Criticism of Medieval Literature*. Lewisburg, Pa.: Bucknell University Press, 1980.

Edward, Duke of York. *The Master of Game*. Edited by William A. and F. Baillie-Grohman. London: Chatto & Windus, 1909.

Edwards, Anthony S. G., ed. *Skelton: The Critical Heritage*. London: Routledge & Kegan Paul, 1981.

Edwards, H. L. R. *Skelton: The Life and Times of a Tudor Poet*. London: Jonathan Cape, 1949.

Faral, Edmond. *Les arts poétiques du XIIe et du XIIIe siècle*. Paris: Champion, 1924.

Fish, Stanley Eugene. *John Skelton's Poetry*. New Haven: Yale University Press, 1965.

Fowler, Alastair. *Silent Poetry: Essays in Numerological Analysis*. London: Routledge & Kegan Paul, 1970.

————. *Triumphal Forms*. Cambridge: Cambridge University Press, 1970.

Garin, Eugenio. *Astrology in the Renaissance*. London: Routledge & Kegan Paul, 1983.

Gingerich, Owen, and Melvin J. Tucker. "The Astronomical Dating of Skelton's *Garland of Laurel*." *HLQ* 32 (1968–69): 207–20.

Goldstine, Herman H. *New and Full Moons, 1001 B.C. to A.D. 1651*. Philadelphia: American Philosophical Society, 1973.

Gordon, I. A. *John Skelton*. Melbourne: Melbourne University Press, 1943.

Le Grand Kalendrier des Bergiers. Lyons, 1510.

Graves, Robert. *The Crowning Privilege*. London: Cassell, 1955.

———. *Goodbye to All That*. Rev. ed. New York: Anchor Books, 1957.

———. *Oxford Addresses on Poetry*. London: Cassell, 1962.

Greene, R. L. *The Early English Carols*. 2d ed. Oxford: Clarendon Press, 1977.

Harrison, Frank Ll., ed. *The Eton Choirbook*. 2 vols. London: Stainer & Bell, 1956–62.

Heiserman, A. R. *Skelton and Satire*. Chicago: University of Chicago Press, 1961.

Heninger, S. K., Jr. *Touches of Sweet Harmony: Pythagorean Cosmology and Renaissance Poetics*. San Marino, Calif.: Huntington Library, 1974.

Hieatt, A. Kent. *Short Time's Endless Monument*. New York: Columbia University Press, 1960.

Hodnett, Edward. *English Woodcuts, 1480–1535*. London: Bibliographical Society, 1935.

Hollander, John. *The Untuning of the Sky*. Princeton: Princeton University Press, 1961. Reprint. New York: Norton, 1970.

Honigmann, E. A. J. *The Stability of Shakespeare's Text*. Lincoln: University of Nebraska Press, 1965.

Housman, A. E., ed. *D. Iunii Iuvenalis saturae*. London: Grant Richards, 1905.

Johnson, Francis R. *Astronomical Thought in Renaissance England*. Baltimore: Johns Hopkins University Press, 1937.

Kinsman, Robert S. "The 'Buck' and the 'Fox' in Skelton' *Why Come Ye Not to Courte?*" *PQ* 29 (1950): 61–64.

———. "Eleanora Rediviva: Fragments of an Edition of Skelton's *Elynour Rummyng*, ca. 1521." *HLQ* 18 (1954–55): 315–27.

———. "The Printer and Date of Publication of Skelton's *Agaynste a Comely Coystrowne* and *Dyuers Balettys*." *HLQ* 16 (1952–53): 203–10.

Kinsman, Robert S., and Theodore Yonge. *John Skelton: Canon and Census*. Renaissance Society of America: Monographic Press, 1967.

Kuhn, Thomas S. *The Copernican Revolution*. Cambridge: Harvard University Press, 1957.

Landes, David S. *Revolution in Time: Clocks and the Making of the Modern World*. Cambridge: Harvard University Press, Belknap Press, 1983.

Leland, John. *The Itinerary of John Leland*. Edited by Lucy Toulmin Smith. 6 vols. London: Bell, 1907.

Leo, Alan [W. F. Allan]. *Astrology for All*. 4th ed. London, 1910. Reprint. New York: Astrologer's Library, 1978.

———. *Casting the Horoscope*. 3d ed. London, 1912. Reprint. New York: Astrologer's Library, 1978.

———. *How to Judge a Nativity*. 3d ed. London, 1912. Reprint. New York: Astrologer's Library, 1983.

Lewis, C. S. *English Literature in the Sixteenth Century*. Oxford: Clarendon Press, 1954.

Lilly, William. *Christian Astrology Modestly Treated Of in Three Books*. London, 1647.

Loewenstein, David A. "Skelton's Triumph: *The Garland of Laurel* and Literary Fame." *Neophilologus* 68 (1984): 611–22.

Lydgate, John. *Falls of Princes*. Edited by Henry Bergen. 4 vols. London: Oxford University Press for The Early English Text Society, 1924–27.

———. *Minor Poems*. Edited by H. N. MacCracken. 2 vols. London: Oxford University Press for The Early English Text Society, 1911, 1934.

McKerrow, Ronald B. *Printers' and Publishers' Devices in England and Scotland, 1485–1640*. London: Bibliographical Society, 1913.

MacQueen, John. *Numerology: Theory and Outline History of a Literary Mode*. Edinburgh: Edinburgh University Press, 1985.

Malory, Sir Thomas. *Works*. Edited by Eugène Vinaver. Oxford: Clarendon Press, 1947.

Meale, Carol M. "The Compiler at Work: John Colyns and BL MS Harley 2252." In *Manuscripts and Readers in Fifteenth-Century England*, ed. Derek Pearsall. Cambridge: D. S. Brewer, 1983.

Michelson, Neil F. *The American Book of Tables*. 4th ed. San Diego: Astro Computing Services, 1982.

More, Sir Thomas. *A Dialogue of Comfort*. Edited by Louis L. Martz and Frank Manley. New Haven: Yale University Press, 1976.

Müller, Johann, of Königsberg (Regiomontanus). *Ephemerides*. Augsburg, 1488.

Murphy, James D. *Three Medieval Rhetorical Arts*. Berkeley: University of California Press, 1971.

Nelson, William. *John Skelton, Laureate*. New York: Columbia University Press, 1939.

———. "Skelton's Quarrel with Wolsey." *PMLA* 51 (1936): 383–96.

Nelson, William, and H. L. R. Edwards. "The Dating of Skelton's Later Poems." *PMLA* 53 (1938): 601–22.

Ó Crohan, Tomás. *The Islandman*. Translated by Robin Flower. Reprint. Oxford: Clarendon Press, 1951.

Parr, Johnstone. "Astronomical Dating for Some of Lydgate's Poems." *PMLA* 67 (1952): 251–58.

———. "The Horoscope of Edippus in Lydgate's *Siege of Thebes*." In *Essays in Honor of Walter Clyde Curry*. Nashville: Vanderbilt University Press, 1954.

———. *Tamburlaine's Malady, and Other Essays On Astrology in Elizabethan Drama*. Reprint. Westport, Conn.: Greenwood Press, 1971.

Patch, Howard. *The Goddess Fortuna*. Cambridge: Havard University Press, 1927.

Plomer, H. R. *English Printers' Ornaments*. London: Bibliographical Society, 1924.

Pollard, A. W., and G. R. Redgrave. *A Short-Title Catalogue of Books Printed in England, Scotland, and Ireland . . . 1475–1640*. London: Bibliographical Society, 1926. 2d ed., rev., 2 vols., 1976, 1986.

Pollet, Maurice, *John Skelton*. Lewisburg, Pa.: Bucknell University Press, 1971.

Ptolemaeus, Claudius. *Tetrabiblos*. Edited and translated by F. E. Robbins. Cambridge: Harvard University Press, 1948.

Reese, Gustave. *Music in the Middle Ages*. New York: Norton, 1940.

Reuchlin, Johann. *Vocabularius Breviloquus*. Basel, 1480.

Ringler, William. "John Stow's Editions of Skelton's *Workes* and of *Certaine Wor-thye Manuscript Poems*." *Studies in Bibliography* 8 (1956): 215-16.

Root, Robert K., and Henry Norris Russell. "A Planetary Date for Chaucer's *Troi-lus*." *PMLA* 39 (1924): 48-63.

Sale, Helen Stearns. "The Date of the *Garlande of Laurell*." *MLN* 5 (1928): 314-16.

Scot, Reginald. *The Discoverie of Witchcraft*. Edited by Montague Summers. Reprint. New York: Dover, 1972.

Seymour-Smith, Martin. *Robert Graves: His Life and Work*. New York: Holt, Rine-hart and Winston, 1982.

Seznec, Jean. *The Survival of the Pagan Gods*. Reprint. New York: Harper, 1961.

Shumaker, Wayne, and J. L. Heilbron. *John Dee on Astronomy*. Berkeley: Univer-sity of California Press, 1978.

Spearing, A. C. *Medieval Dream Poetry*. Cambridge: Cambridge University Press, 1976.

Stevens, John. *Music and Poetry in the Tudor Court*. Lincoln: University of Nebraska Press, 1961.

———. "Rounds and Canons from an Early Tudor Song-Book." *Music and Letters* 32 (1951): 29-37.

Stewart, H. F., ed. *Boethius: The Consolation of Philosophy*. Cambridge: Harvard University Press, 1962.

Stoefler, Johann. *Ephemeridum Opus Ioannis Stoefleri*. Tübingen, 1531.

Tabulae Astronomicae. Venice, 1483.

Taylor, Gary. *Three Studies in the Text of "Henry V."* Oxford: Clarendon Press, 1979.

Thomas, Keith. *Religion and the Decline of Magic*. London: Weidenfeld & Nicolson, 1971.

Tilley, Morris Palmer. *A Dictionary of Proverbs in the Sixteenth and Seventeenth Cen-turies*. Ann Arbor: University of Michigan Press, 1950.

Trowell, Brian. "Proportion in the Music of Dunstable." *Proceedings of the Royal Musical Association* 105 (1978-79): 100-141.

Tucker, Melvin J. *The Life of Thomas Howard, Earl of Surrey and Second Duke of Norfolk, 1443-1524*. The Hague: Mouton, 1964.

———. "The Ladies in Skelton's 'Garland of Laurel.' " *RQ* 22 (1969): 333-45.

———. "Setting in Skelton's *Bowge of Courte*: A Speculation." *ELN* 7 (1970): 168-75.

———. "Skelton and Sheriff Hutton." *ELN* 4 (1967): 254-59.

Tuckerman, Bryant. *Planetary, Lunar, and Solar Positions, A.D. 2 to A.D. 1649 at Five-Day and Ten-Day Intervals*. Philadelphia: American Philosophical Society, 1964.

Tuve, Rosamund. *Seasons and Months: Studies in a Tradition of Mediaeval English Poetry*. Paris: Librairie Universitaire, 1933.

Warton, Thomas. *History of English Poetry*. 4 vols. London, 1824.

Weaver, Helen, ed. *The Larousse Encyclopedia of Astrology*. New York: New Ameri-can Library, 1980.

White, T. H., trans. *The Bestiary*. New York: Putnams, 1960.

Whiting, Bartlett Jere. *Proverbs, Sentences, and Proverbial Phrases*. Cambridge: Harvard University Press, 1968.

Winn, James Anderson. *Unsuspected Eloquence: A History of the Relation between Poetry and Music*. New Haven: Yale University Press, 1981.

Winser, Leigh. " 'The Garlande of Laurell': Masque Spectacular." *Criticism* 19 (1977): 51–69.

Wormald, F., and C. E. Wright, eds. *The English Library before 1700*. London: London University Press, 1958.

Index to Introduction and Commentary